WITHDRAWN

CONTROLLER'S GUIDE

ROLES AND RESPONSIBILITIES FOR THE FIRST YEARS

CONTROLLER'S GUIDE

ROLES AND RESPONSIBILITIES FOR THE FIRST YEARS

STEVEN M. BRAGG

WILEY

JOHN WILEY & SONS, INC.

The chapters in this book first appeared in *Controllership: The Work of the Managerial Accountant, 7ᵗʰ edition,* Janice M. Roehl-Anderson and Steven M. Bragg, John Wiley & Sons, 2004.

Library of Congress Cataloging-in-Publication Data:

Bragg, Steven M.
 Controller's guide : roles and responsibilities for the first years / Steven M. Bragg.
  p. cm.
 Includes index.
 ISBN 0-471-71393-7 (cloth)
  1. Controllership. 2. Chief financial officers. 3. Corporations--Accounting. 4.
Corporations--Finance. I. Title.

HG4026.B662 2005
658.15'1--dc22

                 2004059593

PREFACE

The title of *Controller's Guide: Roles and Responsibilities for the First Years* clearly specifies its purpose; a person newly hired into the controller position needs this book in order to understand the demands of the position and to succeed in the role.

The book describes the role of both the controller and chief financial officer within the corporation, as well as how these roles vary between companies of different sizes. These issues are addressed in Chapters 1 through 3. Chapter 4 describes the various sources of generally accepted accounting principles (GAAP) as well as where the original source material can be located by the new controller. Chapter 5 continues the discussion of accounting rules, but now turns to internal accounting, also known as cost accounting; it takes the new controller through traditional costing concepts, such as job and process costing, as well as the most recent costing systems, such as throughput, target, and activity-based costing.

Chapter 6 shows the new controller how to analyze information through the use of ratio and trend analysis, which is also a good way to pinpoint the control problems that can be resolved through the control systems changes noted in Chapter 7. The new controller may work with an internal audit department; Chapter 8 describes the composition and role of the audit committee, as well as the general functions of the internal audit group.

The book then moves on to more general management topics. Chapter 9 covers the globalization of business with discussions of international trade and its impact on the U.S. economy, as well as how to successfully implement global business strategies. Chapter 10 turns to the accounting department staffing—how to recruit, hire, promote, and motivate employees. Chapter 11 delves into the new controller's role in dealing with company investors—the information needs of the various investor groups, various methods of communication with them, and the use of a standard disclosure policy. The book concludes with an analysis of tax strategy in Chapter 12, where the impact of a number of key issues on a company's tax liability—the cash method of accounting, inventory valuation, acquisitions, net operating loss carryforwards, transfer pricing, and so on—are covered.

In sum, the book is designed to give the new controller a firm foundation in the concepts of managing the accounting department, locating GAAP information, analyzing and knowing what to do with key accounting information, and setting up control systems that reduce a company's risk of loss. A knowledge of these core issues is central to the new controller's success in the position.

Steven M. Bragg
Centennial, Colorado
January 2005

CONTENTS

1

ACCOUNTING IN THE CORPORATION

IMPORTANCE OF THIS CHAPTER

Though this chapter is relatively short, the new controller should read it carefully and ponder the key topics of discussion. This chapter points out that the accounting function has become much more complex, both in terms of tasks and global reach as well as in its impact on other parts of the business. In many respects, the controller position has the greatest corporate-wide impact of any management position, so the new controller must spend time considering how he or she will fit into the complex gearing of the modern corporation in order to achieve the greatest positive impact.

Before a controller can delve into the specifics of the controller job description, it is first necessary to determine how the accounting function fits into the rest of the organization. This used to be a simple issue; the accounting staff processed transactions to support business operations—period. This required a large clerical staff managed by a small cadre of people trained in the underlying techniques for processing those transactions. In this environment, the stereotypical image of an introverted controller pounding away at a calculator was largely accurate.

The role has undergone a vast change in the last few decades, as technological improvements, the level of competition, and a shifting view of management theory have resulted in a startlingly different accounting function. This section describes how the accounting function now incorporates many additional tasks, and can even include the internal auditing and computer services functions in smaller organizations. It then goes on to describe how this functional area fits into and serves the needs of the rest of the company, and how the controller

1

fits into the accounting function. Finally, there is a discussion of how ethics drives the behavior of accounting employees, and how this shapes the way the accounting staff and controller see their roles within the organization.

In short, this chapter covers the high-level issues of how the accounting function and its controller fit into the modern company, not only to process its transactions, which was its traditional role, but also to provide additional services.

TASKS OF THE ACCOUNTING FUNCTION

The accounting function has had sole responsibility for processing the bulk of a company's transactions for many years. Chief among these transactions have been the processing of customer billings and supplier invoices. Though these two areas comprise the bulk of the transactions, there has also been a long history of delegating asset tracking to the accounting function. This involves all transactions related to the movement of cash, inventory, and fixed assets. Finally, the accounting staff has been responsible for tracking debt, which can involve a continuous tracking of debt levels by debt instrument, as well as the payments made to reduce them. These have been the transaction-based activities of the accounting staff.

A multitude of changes in the business environment have altered the role of the accounting function. One change has been the appearance of the computer services function. In a larger company, this function is managed within its own department and does not fall under the responsibility of the controller. However, it is common for the computer services group to fall under the management umbrella of the controller in a smaller company. Likewise, the internal auditing function frequently falls under the controller's area as well. This function has expanded in importance over the last few decades as companies realize the benefits of having an internal watchdog over key controls. Though it should report directly to the board of directors, it is common for a small internal auditing staff to report instead to the controller. It is becoming more common for the computer services and internal auditing functions to be integrated into the role of the accounting staff, especially in smaller companies.

Besides adding new functional areas, the accounting staff has other new responsibilities that have arisen due to the increased level of competition. With worldwide barriers to competition crumbling, every company feels the pinch of lower competitive prices and now asks the accounting staff to provide analysis work in addition to the traditional transaction processing. These tasks include margin analysis on existing or projected product lines, geographic sales regions, or individual products.

TARGETED FINANCIAL ANALYSIS

One of the controller's key tasks is proactively analyzing company issues and recommending changes. In one case, a new controller solved a company's low-profitability problems by preparing a one-page grid showing the sales volume and profitability of every customer. The president promptly dropped most of the customers having low volume and low margins, resulting in the company deliberately losing 1/3 of its customers—and raising its profitability.

In addition, the accounting staff may even be asked to serve on new product design teams, so that they can determine the projected cost of new products, especially in relation to target costs. Further, the accounting staff must continuously review and report on nonproduct costs, which can range from advertising to utilities. This level of cost review and reporting calls for a different kind of accounting staff than the traditional kind that did nothing but process large volumes of transaction-related paperwork. It now requires highly trained cost accountants and financial analysts, almost always with college degrees and professional certifications, to conduct the work.

In addition, technology has drastically altered the skill levels required of the accounting staff. For example, employees must now know how to implement and operate accounting software, electronic data interchange systems, paperless systems using digitized documents, and electronic cash. Because most of these elements of technology directly impact the transaction processing staff, it is necessary to raise the standard of knowledge for these people. Consequently, the education level of even the lowest people in the accounting hierarchy must be improved to deal with changing circumstances.

The world of business has become more international. Many companies are doing an increasing volume of business with companies based in other countries. This greatly increases the complexity of accounting, for a company must now determine gains and losses on sales to other countries. There may even be bartering transactions with organizations that do not have ready access to currency. In addition, if there is no separate finance function, the accounting staff may be called on to handle letters of credit and hedging transactions that are designed to reduce the level of risk that goes with foreign dealings. All of these issues call for a level of skill that was not required in the days of simple transaction processing.

In the face of more intensive competition, many companies are also merging or acquiring subsidiaries. This adds a great deal of complexity to the accounting staff's work, for it must now coordinate a multitude of additional tasks in other locations. This includes setting up standard procedures for the processing of receipts, shipments, and cash. Also, closing the financial books at the end of each reporting period becomes much more complex, as the accounting staff must now coordinate the assembly and consolidation of information from multiple subsidiaries. Even if a company decides to consolidate all of its accounting facilities into one central processing location to avoid all this trouble, it still requires the management expertise to bring together the disparate accounting systems into a smoothly operating facility. This is not an easy task. The environment of mergers and acquisitions greatly increases the skill needed by the accounting staff.

The tasks of the accounting function are itemized below. The tasks that belong elsewhere—but are commonly given to the accounting staff in a small company—are noted under a separate heading.

- *Traditional accounting tasks*
    - Accounts payable transaction processing
    - Accounts receivable transaction processing
    - Asset transaction processing
    - Debt transaction processing

- *New accounting tasks*
    - Bartering transactions
    - Coordination and consolidation of accounting at subsidiaries
    - Currency translations
    - Margin analysis
    - Nonproduct cost analysis
    - Selection, implementation, and operation of accounting software and related systems
    - Target costing

- *New tasks assigned to the accounting function of smaller companies*
  - Computer services systems installation and maintenance
  - Hedging and letter of credit transactions
  - Internal auditing programs

Given today's highly volatile and ever-changing business environment, the only safe statement to make about the new activities presented in this section is that they will only become more complex, requiring even greater skill by the accounting staff to be accomplished in a manner that is both efficient and effective.

ROLE OF THE ACCOUNTING FUNCTION

Having noted the expanded number of tasks now undertaken by the modern accounting function, it is important to also note how the role of the accounting staff has changed in relation to the rest of the company.

When the number of accounting tasks was more closely defined around transaction processing, it was common for the accounting staff to be housed in an out-of-the-way corner of a business, where it would work without being impeded by other functions. Now, with a much greater number of tasks, the accounting staff finds itself involved in most major decisions. For example, the cost accountant is expected to serve on product design teams and to let other team members know if new designs will have costs that will meet targeted cost goals. An accounting analyst may be asked by the sales manager to evaluate the profitability of a lease deal being extended to a customer. The controller is frequently asked to sit in on executive committee meetings to give opinions on the cash flow issues for acquisitions or purchases. The accounts receivable clerk may work closely with the sales staff to collect overdue invoices from customers. For these reasons and others, the accounting function now finds itself performing a variety of tasks that make it an integral part of the organization.

A particularly important area in which the role of the accountant has changed is related to processes. When another area of the company changes its operations, which is increasingly common, the accounting staff must devise alterations to the existing systems for processing transactions that will accommodate those changes. For example, if the manufacturing function switches to just-in-time production or computer-integrated manufacturing, this has a profound impact on the way in which the accounting staff pays its bills, invoices customers, monitors job costs, and creates internal reports. Also, if the materials management staff decides to use material requirements planning or integrated distribution management, these new systems will issue information that is of great use to the accounting staff; it should connect its systems to those of the materials management staff to access that information. To alter its processes, the accounting staff must first be aware of these changes, requiring the accounting staff to engage in more interaction with other parts of the company to find out what is going on.

The most historically important role that the accounting staff must change is that of being a brake on other activities. Because most accountants are trained in implementing controls to ensure that assets are not lost, the accounting staff tends to shoot down changes proposed by other departments—the changes will interfere with the controls. The accounting personnel must realize that changes put forward by other functions are not intended to disrupt controls, but to improve the company's position in the marketplace or to increase its efficiency. This means that some controls must be modified, replaced, or eliminated. It is very helpful for the accounting personnel to have an open mind about altering systems, even when the new systems interfere with the accounting staff's system of controls.

In today's increasingly competitive environment, it is very important for companies to develop strong relationships with their key suppliers and customers. These business partners will demand extra services, some of which must be fulfilled by the accounting staff. These changes may include using electronic data interchange transactions, providing special billing formats to customers, or paying suppliers by electronic transfer. If these steps are needed to retain key business partners, then the accounting staff must be willing to do its share of the work. Too frequently, the accounting staff resists these sorts of changes, on the grounds that all transactions must be performed in exactly the same manner. The accounting department must realize that altering its way of doing business is sometimes necessary to support ongoing business relationships.

Altering the focus of the accounting staff from an introverted group that processes paper to one that works with other parts of a company and is willing to alter its systems to accommodate the needs of other departments is required in today's business environment. This is in great contrast to the accounting department of the past, which had a minimal role in other company activities, and which was its conservative anchor.

ROLE OF THE CONTROLLER

The controller has traditionally been the one who manages a few key transaction cycles, monitors assets, and delivers financial statements. Though the details of the position are covered in Chapter 2 suffice it to say here that the position has expanded to a great extent. As noted earlier in this chapter, the accounting function as a whole is now required to take on additional tasks, to work with other departments more closely, to continuously offer advice to senior management, and to alter systems to match the changing needs of other areas of the company. All of these changes have had a massive impact on the role of the controller within the organization.

The key factor is that, due to the vastly increased interaction with other departments, the controller must be highly skilled in interdepartmental dealings. This involves constant interactions with fellow department heads, attendance at a swarm of meetings, and the issuance of opinions on a variety of topics regarding the running of functions with which the controller previously had no connection. Because of this changed role, the controller must now have top-notch interpersonal and management skills—the former to deal with other departments and the latter to oversee the changes needed by the other departments.

FORMING ALLIANCES

The controller position impacts nearly every part of the company. If the new controller is to succeed in the position, it is extremely important to build strong relationships with the managers of other departments. For example, if there is a large inventory investment, be sure to form a strong bond with the warehouse or materials manager. Also, do not ignore informal lines of communication; in many instances, a very senior person in an innocuous job may have considerable informal control over key functions. In one instance, the author found that the person in charge of developing quotes had the best overall knowledge of company operations!

In addition, the controller must govern a group of employees that is much more educated than was previously the case. This requires constant attention to the professional progress of each person in the department, which requires goal setting, mutual discussion of training requirements, and continuous feedback regarding employee performance. This clearly calls for management skills of an order far higher than formerly required of a controller that presided over a clerical function.

Also, the wider range of functions managed by the controller now requires a wider range of knowledge. Besides the traditional training in accounting, a controller now needs at least a passing knowledge of computer systems, internal auditing, and administrative functions (because this area frequently falls under the controller's area of responsibility). In addition, traditional accounting functions have now become more complex; a controller must know about outsourcing accounting functions and managing in a high-speed growth environment, as well as the increasing complexities of tax laws, Securities and Exchange Commission (SEC) filings, and generally accepted accounting principles. It would take a perpetual student to have an in-depth knowledge of all these areas, so it is more common for the controller to manage a cluster of highly trained subordinates who are more knowledgeable in specific areas, and who can advise the controller as problems arise.

In short, the role of the controller has expanded beyond that of a pure accountant to someone with broad management and interpersonal skills who can interact with other departments, as well as manage the activities of an increasingly well-educated group of subordinates, while also working with them to further their professional careers. This is a much more difficult role for the modern controller, requiring someone with at least as much management experience as accounting knowledge.

IMPACT OF ETHICS ON THE ACCOUNTING ROLE

With the globalization of business, competition has become more intense. It is possible that the ethical foundations to which a company adheres have deteriorated in the face of this pressure. There have been innumerable examples in the press of falsified earnings reports, bribery, kickbacks, and employee thefts. There are vastly more instances of ethical failings that many would perceive to be more minimal, such as employee use of company property for personal use, "smoothing" of financial results to keep them in line with investor expectations, or excessively robust sales or earnings forecasts. The controller and the accounting staff in general play a very large role in a company's ethical orientation, for they control or have some influence over the primary issues that are most subject to ethical problems—reported earnings, cash usage, and control over assets. This section discusses how the accounting function can modify a company's ethical behavior—for good or bad.

The accounting function can have a serious negative impact on a company's ethical standards through nothing more than indifference or lack of caring. For example, if the controller continually acquiesces to management demands to slightly modify the financial statements, this may eventually lead to larger and larger alterations. Once the controller has set a standard for allowing changes to reported earnings, how can the controller define where to draw the line? Another example is when the accounting staff does not enforce control over assets; if it conducts a fixed-asset audit and finds that a television has been appropriated by an employee for several months, it can indirectly encourage continuing behavior of this kind simply by taking no action. Other employees will see that there is no penalty for removing assets and will then do the same thing. Yet another example is when the accounting staff does not closely review employee expense reports for inappropriate expenditures. Once again, if employees see that the expense report rules are not being enforced, they will gradually include more expenses in their reports that should not be included. The accounting staff has a significant negative influence over a company's ethical standards simply by not enforcing the rules.

The previous argument can be turned around for an active accounting department. If the controller and the rest of the accounting staff rigidly enforce company policies and procedures and acquire a reputation for no deviations from these standards, the rest of the corporation will be dragged into line. It is especially important that the controller adhere closely to the highest standards, for the rest of the accounting staff will follow the controller's lead. Conversely, if the controller does not maintain a high ethical standard, the rest of the accounting staff will have no ethical leader, and will quickly lapse into apathy. Accordingly, the controller is a company's chief ethics officer, for the position has such a strong influence over ethics. It is a rare week that passes without some kind of ethical quandary finding its way to the controller for resolution.

DRAWING THE LINE

The new controller may have been specifically hired due to lack of experience, with the management team hoping they can steamroll ethically-suspect business practices past the new hire. Thus it is useful to promptly inquire into the reason for the last controller's departure, and to also call the external auditors to discuss their views of how far the company has stretched accounting rules in the past.

It is not sufficient to merely say that the accounting staff must uphold high ethical standards, if the standards are not defined. To avoid this problem, the controller should create and enforce a code of ethics. This document may not originate with the controller—many chief executive officers (CEOs) prefer to take on this task. However, the controller can certainly push for an ethical code to be developed higher in the organization. Some illustrative topics to include in a code of ethics are:

- Bidding, negotiating, and performing under government contracts
- Compliance with antitrust laws
- Compliance with securities laws and regulations
- Conflicts of interest
- Cost consciousness
- Employee discrimination on any grounds
- Gifts and payments of money
- Hazardous waste disposal
- International boycotts
- Leave for military or other federal service
- Meals and entertainment
- Political contributions
- Preservation of assets
- Restrictive trade practices
- Standards of conduct
- Use of company assets
- Workplace and product safety

The wide range of ethical topics, some going well beyond the financial arena, make it obvious that the CEO really is the best source of this document, rather than the controller, though the controller can certainly contribute to those portions relating to financial issues.

Once the code of ethics has been created, it must be communicated to all employees. Once again, this is the CEO's job, but the controller should constantly reinforce it with his or her staff. It is especially helpful if the controller visibly refers to the ethical code whenever an ethical issue arises, so that the accounting staff knows that the controller is decisively adhering to the code.

A code of ethics becomes the starting point in the series of judgments a controller must follow when confronted with an ethical issue. The logical series of steps to work through are:

- *Consult the code of ethics.* Having a corporate code of ethics is a great boon to the controller, for he or she can use it as the basis for any ethics-related decision. A senior company officer would have difficulty forcing the controller to adopt a different course of action than what is prescribed by the code of ethics, since this would go against a directive of the Board of Directors. If the controller feels it is necessary to take a course of action contrary to what is stated in the code, then the reasons for doing so should be thoroughly documented. If there is no code, then proceed to the next step.

- *Discuss with immediate supervisor.* The controller's immediate supervisor is probably either the Chief Financial Officer (CFO), Chief Operating Officer (COO), or CEO. These are the most senior positions in the company, occupied by people whose behavior should be at an ethically high standard. Consulting with them for advice is a reasonable second step in the absence of a code of ethics. However, if the supervisor is the one causing the ethical problem, then skip this step and proceed to the next one.

- *Discuss with a trusted peer.* There is usually someone within the company in whom the controller places a great deal of trust. If so, consult with this person in regard to the proper course of action. Be more circumspect in doing so with a person outside the company, since this runs the risk of spreading information elsewhere, with possible deleterious consequences. If there is no one with whom to discuss the issue, then proceed to the next step.

- *Discuss with the company's ethics committee.* If there is an ethics committee, this is a good forum for discussion. Unfortunately, many companies do not have such a committee, or it meets so infrequently that the immediate needs of the controller may not be met through this approach. In either case, proceed to the next step.

- *Discuss with the Board's audit committee.* Many boards have an audit committee, which should be comprised entirely of independent directors. If so, the controller should take his or her concerns to this group. Keep in mind that this is a serious step, since the controller is now going around the corporate reporting structure, which may have unenviable consequences later on if the controller chose not to tell senior management of this action.

- *Consider leaving the company.* If all these avenues are untenable or result in inadequate advice, the controller should seriously consider leaving the company in the

DECIDING WHEN TO QUIT

It is exceptionally damaging for a new controller to be involved in any situation that has even the slightest taint of accounting scandal, since it is nearly impossible to be hired into a succeeding job where this problem is known. Unfortunately, it is frequently better for the new controller to leave a new position where ethical concerns are rampant, rather than to stay on the job and attempt to fix the underlying issues. To assist in making the difficult stay-or-quit decision, consider finding a senior-level mentor who can offer unbiased advice on the correct course of action.

near future. Reaching this final step probably means that the ethical issue is caused by senior management, and also that there are no outside checks on their ethical behavior, such as an audit committee of the Board of Directors.

It is extremely important that the controller issue consistent rulings on ethical issues, so that employees know they are being treated fairly. Though it may seem like a vast increase in paperwork, it may be useful for the controller to record all ethical rulings in a single document, so that there is a good reference source in the event of future ethical problems. This allows the controller to go back and see what judgment was given in previous cases, thereby giving the controller adequate grounds for treating new issues in a similar manner.

In summary, the accounting staff has a large role in enforcing ethical standards throughout a company, since it has such strong influence over several key areas that require ethical judgments, such as the quality of reported earnings, control over assets, and the uses of cash. Accordingly, it is very much in the controller's interests to have a code of ethics that the accounting staff can adhere to in enforcing the appropriate ethical standards.

EVOLVING ROLE OF ACCOUNTING

Though there are many variables that can impact the direction of the accounting function and the controller's role in the future, there are a few broad trends that are likely to continue, and from which one can predict the evolving role of accounting.

The accounting function is in the midst of a fundamental change from being a clerical group without significant training to a cadre of very experienced technicians and managers. Though there will always be a need for clerical help (indeed, this group will continue to comprise the majority of the department), there will be an increasing focus on bringing in more experienced personnel. This prediction is based on the technological trend that brings continued levels of automation to the accounting function, thereby reducing the need for clerks. Also, the same trend toward more technology means that a greater proportion of the accounting employees must have better training in how to use the new hardware and software. These trends will force the accounting department of the future to stock up on highly trained personnel with good management skills.

The accounting department is likely to become a more common route to top management positions. The accounting area has always been a fertile one for training people in the nuts and bolts of transactions, and how they must function. This is useful for a lower-level manager, but now that the department also handles a multitude of additional tasks, such as cost analysis, target costing, and advanced finance functions, it becomes a much better training area for higher-level managers. The company of the future will not only see large numbers of well-trained people advancing out of accounting, but they will also see a large proportion of new recruits clamoring to get into it, so that they too can receive the necessary training and experience.

This section discussed some evolutionary changes to expect in the role of the accounting function and the controller. It is likely that there will be a decrease in the proportion of purely clerical positions in the accounting area, in favor of more senior personnel with extra technical and management skills. Also, because of the greater breadth of responsibility to be obtained in this area, it will become more common for senior management personnel to come out of this area.

2

CONTROLLER'S RESPONSIBILITIES

IMPORTANCE OF THIS CHAPTER

This chapter contains a detailed job description for the new controller, and so is worthy of considerable review if only due to the presence of that information. The number of tasks may at first seem overwhelming, since they cover so many subject areas. The best way to handle the situation is to first address crucial short-term issues like cash forecasting and meeting debt requirements, and then delegate tasks to the more capable staff. This will gradually leave enough time to carefully plan how best to address the remaining responsibilities.

A controller's job can vary dramatically based on a company's size and whether it has other managers in place who handle related functions. If a company is small and there are few other managers, the controller may end up with a formidable list of tasks on the job description. However, as a company grows in size, the role becomes more precisely and narrowly defined. This chapter covers the full range of the activities that may be assigned to a controller, beginning with the classical management areas of planning, controlling, reporting, and maintaining key accounting processes, and expanding into ancillary functions that may become part of the controller's job, depending on the circumstances. In addition, the chapter touches on variations in the controller's title, and why the term *controller,* though most commonly used, is perhaps not the best description for the job. The chapter concludes with a review of the relations between the controller and chief financial officer (CFO), the future job description of the controller, and how to manage in an explosive growth environment. This wide-ranging discussion gives the reader a comprehensive view of the controller's job.

VARIATIONS ON THE TITLE

Numerous titles can be applied to the position of the chief accounting officer; however, the most common title used is controller. The duties are sometimes assumed by a chief accountant, office manager, comptroller, treasurer, assistant treasurer, or secretary. However, with the increased emphasis on accounting control, increased management duties, and for additional statistical and financial decision-making information, the duties of the position are more frequently being segregated into the role of a separate manager called the controller. This is especially true in larger organizations, where there is much more specialization. The term controller is an unfortunate one, for it seems to emphasize the control function only; as the reader will find after reading this chapter, there are a number of other basic functions this person performs, such as planning, reporting, and management, that are just as important as the control function. The chief accounting officer (CAO) title is a more complete description of the position; however, due to common usage, the term *controller* will have the same meaning as *CAO* in this book.

PLANNING FUNCTION

The establishment and maintenance of an integrated plan of operation is a major function of the controller. The business objective is profit, and planning is necessary to fulfill it, for profits do not "just happen." Visualize, then, the role of the modern controller in business planning.

First, there is a responsibility to see that a plan exists and that it is supported by all levels of management. The implication of an integrated plan is that all parts will link together to support the business objective. For this reason, all members of management must participate willingly and contribute to the information in the plan. It must be the company's plan and not the controller's plan. The controller's primary task is to act as the coordinator who assembles and maintains the plan, which results in a statement of forecasted income and expense, as well as a set of supporting schedules and assumptions. In more detail, the following points describe the controller's key tasks related to the plan:

- Verify that the sales plan or forecast supports known corporate policies and objectives, such as geographic areas to enter and types of products to sell.

- Verify that the sales plan appears to have realistic assumptions, such as an expected sales amount per salesperson that is valid based on past history.

- Verify that the production plan supports the sales schedule. This involves comparing the amount projected to be sold to the amount to be produced, while factoring in the amount of finished goods inventory already on hand.

- Verify that the production plan is within facility capabilities. This involves comparing projected production volumes to the company's history of production rates, also factoring in the addition of extra shifts.

- Verify that expense levels are in proportion to other activities. For example, the utilities expense must go up if the company is adding a facility, while the travel expense must increase if there will be a larger sales staff.

- Verify that there is sufficient funding for the projected activity. If there is not a sufficient amount of debt or equity funding, the plan must be recast on a smaller scale.

Once the plan has been completed, the controller should test or appraise its adequacy and report to the CFO or chief executive officer (CEO) on the results of this analysis. It must be judged based on the following concerns:

- In light of past experience, is it realistic?
- Does it reflect economic conditions that are expected to prevail in the period of the plan?
- Have the related expenses for product lines designated to be discontinued, such as production equipment or inventory disposal, been considered?
- Does it meet the company's requirements for return on investment and such other ratio or other tests as may be applicable?

Some of the testing and analysis will be accomplished as preliminary plans are formulated, and the rest will await the total picture. However and whenever it is done, the controller is the counselor and coordinator, extending advice and suggestions to all who need it during the plan preparation. Final responsibility for the plan rests with the CEO, and responsibility for each operating function must be that of the manager in charge of each function. Nonetheless, though responsibility for the plan lies elsewhere, the controller should be deeply immersed in the underlying mechanics and assumptions of the plan; the company relies on the controller to perform this function.

CONTROL FUNCTION

The management function of control is the measurement and correction of performance so that business objectives and plans are accomplished. Management control seeks to compel performance to a plan or standard. The controller assists in this function by providing information to the managers of each function, so that they can enforce control-related issues. The controller cannot enforce control issues in other departments, since there is no managerial oversight of those areas, but the controller does correct control-related problems within the accounting function.

Activities in the control function absorb a large portion of the accounting staff's time. Some control information is provided to management by the accounting staff every day; other data are prepared less frequently, as circumstances require. For example, larger companies that are labor intensive may find that hourly or daily information on labor performance may be helpful, or weekly manufacturing expense figures may be needed.

However, the controller's involvement does not end with the mere feedback of reporting information to various parts of a company. Instead, the controller must devote a great deal of time to flowcharting existing systems, examining the results for control issues, and implementing process changes that will eliminate the control problems. Only after all this activity will a controller be able to issue reports on the results of controls.

A manager cannot control the past. Instead, one can study past action to determine the place and cause of deviation. Here, as in planning, the best kind of control is forward looking. The controller must keep this orientation in mind while participating in the control function, giving constant thought to steps that might be taken before the operating action to ensure the desired performance level. This is preventive or anticipatory control.

A controller must become heavily involved in all stages of the control function, which extends from system analysis through problem identification and change implementation, ending in control reports that note the results of the control alterations. This is one of the most crucial tasks for the controller.

REPORTING FUNCTION

Insofar as it concerns internal management, the reporting function is closely related to both the planning and control functions. Reporting is essential to make planning and control effective. Yet the reporting function is not merely one of presentation of tabulations and is not wholly routine, although some phases can be automated. Moreover, the management that makes decisions often cannot be kept adequately informed solely from periodic statements regardless of how well designed they may be. The reporting function encompasses the *interpretation* of the figures, and the controller's duty is not discharged until management actually understands what is being presented.

Ensuring that management understands what it reads calls for an entirely separate set of skills than those given a controller in business school. This requires constant informal meetings with all recipients of accounting reports, not only to go over excessively large variances, but also simply to ensure that they understand what they are reading. A good supplemental method is to construct a formal training program that describes the nature and significance of the information being issued, and to constantly update and again present this training to management. Even a quarterly reiteration of the training is not always sufficient.

In addition, the controller may be required to report to outside entities, which usually calls for some reformatting of the internal reports. Typical recipients of reports are shareholders, creditors, the general public, customers, the Securities and Exchange Commission (SEC), and the Internal Revenue Service (IRS).

The controller is not only responsible for assembling data on a large number of topics into easily readable reports for consumption both inside and outside the company, but also for ensuring that the recipients understand what they are given.

USING REPORTS TO MEET FELLOW MANAGERS

In many companies, the only product the rest of the management team sees from the controller is periodic reports. Knowing this, the new controller should use a discussion of the delivery, format, and content of reports as an excuse to meet the management team. Review their reporting needs with them, and make sure they promptly receive the revised information. There is no better way to make a good first impression.

ACCOUNTING FUNCTION

The systematic recording of financial transactions is often regarded as the principal function of the controller. The controller is expected to apply sound accounting principles and practices within the company, as well as to stay current on the latest technological advances, so that this can be done in the most effective and efficient manner possible. The last few decades have revealed further advances in management theory that a controller is now expected to implement in the accounting function, including:

- *Benchmarking key practices.* A controller should regularly compare the performance of the accounting department for various tasks against the results of other accounting functions at other companies, not necessarily in the same industry, to see if anyone else is doing it better, and, if so, to copy their practices into the accounting department. This results in a major improvement in the department's operating effectiveness.

- *Converting to electronic transactions.* Many of the larger companies now send transactions to each other with electronic data interchange, rather than with paper-based transactions. This is a boon to the accounting department, because the transactions can be automatically entered into the accounting computer system (since it is already in electronic format) without any error-prone manual rekeying of information.

- *Reducing cycle time.* The controller should actively engage in cycle time reduction, so that the time required to complete the primary transactions are greatly reduced. This allows a company to act more quickly, as well as to generate information about the results of its actions, both of which allow it to compete at a higher level.

- *Outsourcing accounting functions.* The controller should look into handing some or all accounting functions over to suppliers who are better equipped to handle key transactions. For example, many companies now outsource their payroll processing to suppliers that calculate taxes, make tax deposits, and pay employees by direct deposit. The controller should review this option for other accounting functions, too.

- *Reengineering key functions.* Some accounting functions may require so much effort to complete that it is best to scrap the system and start with a new approach that vastly reduces the effort, error rate, and cost of the old function.

All of these new methodologies ensure that today's controller will be armed with enough tools to greatly improve the operational effectiveness of the accounting function.

ADDITIONAL CONTROLLER FUNCTIONS IN SMALLER COMPANIES

The controller of a smaller company will find that the position includes a number of additional tasks besides those already enumerated in the last section. This is because a small company cannot afford to also hire a CFO, an office manager, a computer services manager, and a human resources director. Consequently, all of these functions may fall on the controller. When applying for a controller position with a small company, it is useful to see if these other positions are filled—if not, the controller will have a much wider range of job activities. The main activities in each of those areas will probably fall under the controller's managerial umbrella.

The most common additional functions that a controller will take on are those in the finance area. These tasks are normally handled by the CFO, which is a position that many small companies dispense with if they have minimal funding needs or are not publicly held. The primary tasks of the finance function are:

- Acquiring insurance coverage
- Conducting public offerings
- Dealing with investors
- Dealing with lenders
- Determining customer credit levels
- Investing pension funds
- Investing surplus funds

Of the tasks normally handled by a CFO, the controller usually has little trouble in managing insurance, credit, and investment decisions. However, conducting a public offering is usually well outside the experience of most controllers, and so it would behoove a controller to recognize this inadequacy and bring in qualified help if a company decides in favor of a public offering.

A small company, usually one with less than 100 employees, frequently does not have a human resources manager. This means that the function, once again, must be managed by the beleaguered controller. Many of these new functions are administrative and procedural in nature—tasks for which most controllers are amply qualified. However, others, such as career planning and recruiting, are not. These later tasks are sometimes shifted elsewhere in the organization, depending on who is most qualified to handle them. The most typical human resources functions are:

- Administering changes to the pension plan
- Administering new-employee paperwork
- Conducting employee safety training
- Conducting recruiting for all positions
- Devising a career plan for key managers
- Maintaining employee files
- Processing medical claims
- Processing workers' compensation claims
- Updating the employee manual

Given the large proportion of clerical tasks in the human resources function, which are similar to the clerical functions of the accounting area, most controllers are fairly comfortable in administering this department. Some tasks, such as safety training and administering the pension plan, require some extra knowledge to handle. The most uncommon tasks for a traditional controller are creating staffing plans and recruiting. These tasks are so different that the CEO sometimes hands them off to someone else in the organization.

Taking Additional Tasks to an Extreme

In one of the author's first positions as a controller, there was no janitorial staff—everyone cleaned up after themselves. One day, a toilet overflowed in the bathroom next to the author's office. While mopping up the water, the phone rang—a venture capitalist was calling to inquire about investing funds. The author took the call with a mop in one hand.

The most common additional function for the controller to manage is administration. This includes the secretarial pool (if any), the reception function, all office equipment, and the telephone system. Because this area impacts all functions, it is common to have a disproportionate volume of complaints about it that take up an excessive amount of a controller's time. Accordingly, it is frequently handed off to an assistant controller. In addition, it is wise to outsource the repair and maintenance of all office equipment and the telephone system to a qualified supplier. This reduces the controller's day-to-day management to contacting suppliers and ensuring that the administrative staff is supplemented by a sufficient number of temporary help to complete short-term projects, such as special mailings, that pass through this area. The most common administrative functions are:

- Answering incoming calls
- Ensuring that all copiers and fax machines are operational

- Ensuring that the telephone system is operational
- Managing administrative staff
- Planning for the timely replacement of aging office equipment
- Sorting and delivering incoming mail
- Stamping outgoing mail
- Working with temporary help agencies to bring in personnel for special projects

Finally, the controller sometimes manages the computer services function. Most small companies maintain only the minimum number of computer applications, and these are usually packaged software, which allows them to avoid a full-time department to handle this function. Instead of a separate department, the controller is in charge of backing up the computer system, ensuring that it is repaired promptly, that the system is expanded as the situation requires, and that new software is implemented in an efficient manner. Due to the highly technical nature of this work, a controller is well advised to outsource as much of this work as possible rather than dealing with it internally; not only does this approach reduce the controller's workload, but it also brings in much more qualified personnel than most small companies can afford to keep in-house. The main computer services functions are:

- Backing up the computer system
- Enforcing computer security standards
- Expanding the systems as needed
- Installing new hardware and software as needed
- Maintaining all hardware and software
- Maintaining and repairing the computer network
- Providing system training to employees

The controller must be especially careful to make provisions for system crashes. This means that there must not only be daily backups of the software, but also off-site storage of the backups to ensure that they are not damaged if the main facility is destroyed. This should also include power backup systems to ensure that the computers remain operational even if the main power source goes down. The controller should also consider a disaster recovery plan that details how to make the system operational again as soon as possible in the event of a major problem. Though other parts of the computer services function can be outsourced, this one must be handled internally, and correctly—if the controller does not prevent a serious computer crash that renders key systems inoperable, this may have a major, and negative, impact on senior management's view of how the controller is performing.

There are additional areas that the controller of a smaller company may find him- or herself supervising. The most likely areas are human resources, administration, computer services, and finance. The controller is well advised to outsource as much of this extra work as possible in order to put it in the hands of experts from suppliers, while also handing off selected tasks to other members of the organization who may be more qualified to perform them. The remaining tasks must be managed by the controller or a subordinate. Because these are areas in which most controllers are only partially trained, this can involve a very rapid and intensive learning experience.

CONTROLLER'S JOB DESCRIPTION

Though the previous sections briefly discussed a number of the main aspects of the controller's job, they do not show a complete view of the position's responsibilities. This section answers that need by showing a complete controller job description. If a controller needs a job description for a company procedures or human resources manual, the description noted here is in sufficient detail to be "lifted" out of this book for immediate use, with some modification based on each controller's circumstances. The description is summarized into subheadings, so that tasks are noted under such categories as finance, human resources, or computer services, which allows the reader to ignore those broad functional areas that do not apply to him or her. The tasks are noted in the order in which they are most likely to be the controller's responsibility, starting with accounting, finance, and administration, and then progressing through the computer services and human resources functions. Also, the description assumes that there is a staff handling all transactions, so it does not refer to actually handling specific transactions, only ensuring that they are correct. The description is as follows:

- *Position Title:* Controller
- *Reports To:* Chief Financial Officer
- *Supervises:* All accounting, finance, administration, computer services, and human resources personnel (varies by size of company and presence of other managers).
- *Tasks:*
  - *Accounting*
    Assist in the annual audit as required.
    Ensure that accounts payable are not paid earlier than required.
    Ensure that accounts receivable are collected promptly.
    Ensure that all reasonable discounts are taken on accounts payable.
    Ensure that customer billings are issued promptly.
    Ensure that job costs are calculated.
    Ensure that the monthly bank reconciliation is completed.
    Issue interim management reports as needed.
    Issue timely financial statements.
    Maintain an orderly accounting filing system.
    Maintain the chart of accounts.
    Manage outsourced functions.
    Manage the accounting staff.
    Manage the production of the annual plan (budget).
    Process payroll in a timely manner.
    Provide financial analyses as needed.
    Review systems for control weaknesses.
  - *Finance*
    Arrange for banking services.
    Arrange for debt financing.
    Conduct public offerings.
    Invest excess cash.
    Invest pension funds.
    Issue credit to customers.
    Maintain insurance coverage.
    Maintain lender relations.

Manage the finance staff.

Monitor cash balances.

○ *Administration*

Bring in temporary personnel for special projects.

Ensure that incoming mail is properly distributed.

Ensure that office equipment is operational.

Ensure that outgoing mail is sent in a timely manner.

Manage outsourced maintenance work.

Manage the secretarial staff.

Upgrade office equipment as needed.

○ *Computer Services*

Back up the computer system.

Implement hardware and software.

Maintain a current disaster recovery plan.

Maintain computer security systems.

Manage the computer services staff.

Manage outsourced functions.

Provide system training.

Select hardware and software.

○ *Human Resources*

Administer safety training.

Administer the pension plan.

Maintain employee benefits paperwork.

Maintain employee files.

Maintain employee manual.

Manage career planning.

Manage the human resources staff.

Process medical claims.

Process workers' compensation claims.

Recruit employees.

This generic and very wide-ranging controller job description can be used as the basis for a more customized description that is tailored to individual circumstances.

RELATIONSHIP OF THE CONTROLLER TO THE CHIEF FINANCIAL OFFICER

In a larger company, there is a clear division of tasks between the controller and the CFO. However, there is no clear delineation of these roles in a smaller company, because there is usually no CFO. As a company grows, it acquires a CFO, who must then wrestle away some of the controller's tasks that traditionally belong under the direct responsibility of the CFO. This transition can cause some conflict between the controller and CFO, which is discussed in this section. In addition, the historical promotion path for the controller has traditionally been through the CFO position; when that position is already occupied, and is likely to stay that way, there can be some difficulty with the controller. This section also discusses that issue.

In a small company, the controller usually handles all financial functions, such as setting up and maintaining lines of credit, cash management, determining credit limits for customers, dealing with investors, handling pension plan investments, and maintaining insurance policies. These are the traditional tasks of the CFO, and when a company grows to the point of needing one, the CFO will want to take them over from the controller. This can turn into a power struggle, though a short-lived one, because the controller always reports to the CFO and will not last long if there is no cooperation. Nonetheless, this is a difficult situation, for the controller has essentially taken a step down in the organizational structure upon the arrival of the CFO. For example, the CFO replaces the controller on the executive committee. If the controller is an ambitious one, this will probably lead to that person's departure in the near term. If the controller is a good one, this is a severe loss, for someone with a detailed knowledge of a company's processes and operating structure is extremely difficult to replace.

The controller should take a job elsewhere if he or she perceives that the person newly filling the CFO position is a roadblock to further advancement. However, this does not have to be a dead-end position. The controller should talk to the CFO about career prospects within the company and suggest that there may be other responsibilities that can replace those being switched to the CFO. For example, a small minority of controllers manage the materials management department; this will become increasingly common as controllers realize that much of the paperwork they depend on originates in that area and that they can acquire better control over their processes by gaining experience in this area. There may also be possibilities in the areas of administration, human resources, and computer services, which are sometimes run by controllers. The fact that there is a new CFO does not mean that a controller should immediately quit; there may be other opportunities involving related tasks that can shift the controller's career in other directions.

FINDING A NEW ROLE UNDER A CFO

One of the reasons why a CFO is hired is to acquire other companies. If so, the new controller not only does not have to worry about being in a dead-end job, but even has a large number of new positions to choose from, since the acquiring company has the right to staff the accounting management positions of all acquired companies in any manner it chooses. At worst, the acquired accounting departments may be centralized, leaving the controller with the massive chore of creating a single large accounting function for the entire conglomerate.

The CFO position is one with an extreme emphasis on money management, involving such tasks as determining the proper investment vehicles for excess cash, dealing with lenders regarding various kinds of debt, making presentations to financial analysts, and talking to investors. None of these tasks are ones that the controller is trained to perform. Instead, the traditional controller training involves handling transactions, creating financial statements, and examining processes. The requirements for the CFO position and the training for the controller position are so different that it seems strange for the controller to be expected to advance to the CFO position, and yet that is a common expectation among accountants. As noted in the next section, the controller may not want to assume that the CFO position is an obvious next step, and that perhaps the controller position may now lead into other management areas.

There can be some difficulty between the controller and the CFO, especially when a CFO is brought in for the first time. This commonly results in the departure of the controller if that person perceives that the next promotion step is the CFO position. This problem can be ameliorated by looking for opportunities to shift the controller into other functional areas. These opportunities are noted in the next section.

FUTURE CHANGES IN THE CONTROLLER'S ORIGINS AND RESPONSIBILITIES

The accounting function has changed drastically over the last half-century, and the controller has changed along with it. Where the position used to require someone with a tight focus on processing transactions and financial statements, the job now requires much more managerial skill, as well as a general idea of such diverse bodies of knowledge as taxation, business process improvement, outsourcing, and computer systems. This calls for a controller with a much more diverse background than was previously the case. It also points toward a different career direction for the controller of the future.

The controller of the future will come from a different educational and experience background. Most companies currently call on the "Big Four" auditing firms for their controllers, and many auditors enter the Big Four on the assumption that they will eventually be hired by their clients into that role. However, auditors are trained in the areas of generally accepted accounting principles, verifying the accuracy of financial statements, and reviewing underlying accounting processes to ensure that they function correctly. Though these tasks are still part of the controller's job description, and will remain so for the foreseeable future, an increasing proportion of the controller's job now includes tasks for which an auditor is not prepared. These new tasks include computer systems selection, implementation, and management, as well as outsourcing, cycle time reduction, benchmarking, and process reengineering. Because of these new tasks, company management will find that it can fill the position with more thoroughly qualified personnel from other sources. One source will be the certified management accountant (CMA) program, which emphasizes a greater body of knowledge than the certified public accountant (CPA) exam. The better companies will also look to consulting firms for people with a detailed knowledge of process improvement and systems management. Finally, top management will eventually realize that controllers do not have to be CPAs; on the contrary, it will be more important to have good management skills and be surrounded by a team of highly qualified accounting professionals who can advise on the more technical accounting issues. In short, controllers will come from other sources than auditing firms, because that source no longer provides people with a complete set of skills.

The future direction of the controller position is probably toward something with much more responsibility. Companies are competing more and more on such issues as rapid cycle times and low costs, and the controller is an integral part of the work required to improve them. As management realizes that the controller has an enormous impact on these most critical competitive areas, it will place the controller in charge of them. This means that the controller of the future will become more of a chief process officer (CPO), with general authority to alter processes. This function will cross department lines as much as the processes that the controller is fixing, so the position must have added authority to make changes. This added authority will raise the controller in the management hierarchy to a point above those of other department heads. We may also find that the controller will be more likely to manage new areas that are heavily driven and influenced by processes, especially materials management. The controller of the future will occupy a more influential position, due to his or her influence over company-wide processes.

As the controller position adds company-wide processes to its area of authority, the controller will find that, due to this extra responsibility, promotional opportunities will veer away from the CFO position and toward the chief operating officer (COO) position. This does not mean that there will be a wholesale abandonment of the CFO position, since that remains the goal of most controllers, but controllers will have such an in-depth knowledge of all of a company's operations that they will become the first choice for promotion to be COO, or at least be one of the heavy favorites for the position.

There are changes already underway that are preventing many controllers from reaching the coveted CFO position, and which may provide further impetus in the direction of promotions to the COO position. The trouble with the CFO position is that its job requirements are significantly different from those of a controller, and few controllers are trained to take over the job. It involves lender and investor relations, as well as making the proper investments of spare cash. The job requirements for the CFO position really call for someone with experience in the treasury side of the business, or perhaps from Wall Street, to take it over.

If we do see CFOs being promoted from directions other than the controller position, this also calls into question the traditional reporting relationship that has the controller reporting to the CFO. If the CFO does not have a background that yields any knowledge of the accounting field, then it does not make much sense to have that person control the function. Instead, it may become more appropriate to have the controller report straight to the CEO, alongside the CFO. Due to the new sources of CFO hiring, there are ample reasons for shifting the controller out from under the management of the CFO.

The controller of the future may come from many sources, rather than straight from an auditing firm, and that the promotion path of the position will include the COO position, rather than the usual CFO position. This path will open up because the controller will become more involved in company-wide positions, as well as because CFOs will increasingly be drawn from the ranks of Wall Street.

MANAGING EXPLOSIVE GROWTH

A controller sometimes finds him- or herself in a situation in which a company has just released a "hot" product, it embarks on a massive expansion of sales territories or it goes on an acquisition binge, either of which result in a phenomenal rate of growth. This frequently results in a difficult situation for the controller, because there are never enough resources to handle the flood of transactions swamping the department. This section discusses how to prioritize tasks in such an environment. It also notes the same issues for the finance, computer services, and human resources functions, in case the controller is in charge of those areas as well.

In an explosive growth environment, the key focus of the accounting staff is on the conservation of cash. This is because a growing company is constantly investing cash in working capital and facilities, leaving little cash available for further growth or as a reserve in case of a sudden downturn in company fortunes. The controller plays a major part in cash conservation. The following points note the most important areas in which the controller can affect cash flow:

- *Send invoices promptly.* It is difficult to collect cash from customers if they have not yet been billed. To avoid this problem, the controller must pay strict attention to the billing process, especially the speed with which invoices are created and sent. This may also involve a switch to electronic invoicing, an alteration in payment terms to encourage faster payment, or delivery of the invoice with the shipment. Any of these system modifications will result in a faster cash flow.

- *Collect accounts receivable promptly.* Increasing the speed of collections also improves the cash flow. The controller can do this by adding more staff to the collections effort, concentrating the bulk of the collection effort on the largest overdue invoices, working closely with the sales staff to obtain payments, concentrating on issuing accurate invoices that customers cannot complain about, and tightening the terms of credit being offered; all of these actions will slowly improve the speed of collection.

- *Minimize mistakes.* Customers do not pay their bills on time if they are protesting inaccuracies on the bills. To avoid this payment delay, the controller can focus on ensuring that mistakes are eliminated. This can be done by using constant feedback from the collections staff to fix recurring problems in the customer billing database (e.g., mailings to the wrong address or target person). Another approach is to have the accounting software flag any invoices that are missing critical information, especially a customer purchase order number. In addition, there can be a mandatory proofreading of all very large invoices prior to issuance, so that there will be no problems with any invoices that can seriously impact cash flow.

ELIMINATE ERRORS TO CONSERVE CASH

A major cause of delayed cash flow is billing errors. If an invoice is perfectly constructed and delivered to the correct customer contact, it will probably be paid approximately within terms. However, if anything goes wrong, the payment interval will likely double the standard terms. To avoid delays, double-check invoices before they go out, verify contact information with the sales staff, and have a second person proofread invoices prior to mailing. Be especially careful when the invoices are for very large amounts.

- *Conduct cost accounting promptly.* A growing company must know immediately if it is selling a product that is not returning enough of a profit; otherwise, it will not spin off enough cash flow to sustain a high rate of growth. The controller can push for a very rapid costing review of new products, both before they are issued as well as after they have been produced for a short time, to see if there are significant variances from expected margins. The results of these costing studies should be immediately communicated to upper management, so that steps can be taken to revise the product costs or prices to yield better profits.

These accounting functions all have the most immediate bearing on cash flow. If there is a question of having to allocate resources away from other accounting activities in order to emphasize these cash flow areas, the controller should consider some outsourcing, which will leave more staff time available for these tasks. For example, the payroll function is normally handled by clerical personnel who are equally capable of becoming involved in billings or cash collections.

If the controller also manages the finance function, there are several additional issues to consider in a high-growth environment. The main one is predicting future cash flows. This is because an accurate cash forecast tells management how much extra cash it will need from outside sources, as well as the timing of that need. This becomes the foundation for efforts to acquire additional debt or equity funding. In addition, the controller should keep a close watch over the risk and return of any investments, in order to maximize the company's investments while maintaining as low a risk profile as possible. Finally, the controller must devise an orderly system for clearing incoming payments through a system of lockboxes, funneling these payments into a central account, and then disbursing the money back out for accounts payable through outlying banks that take extra time to clear payments. This system of lockboxes and controlled disbursements maximizes the amount of a company's cash on hand, as well as the time period during which it can be used. These are the key finance-related tasks for a controller to manage in an explosive growth environment.

If the controller also manages the computer services function, the key factor is not to let problems with the computer systems bog down other company operations that are relying on it. The main reason for this factor is that computer services is a support function that is the linchpin of nearly all transaction processing, and if it is not operational, the company cannot function. This principle requires the controller to take several actions. One is to back up the system regularly, as well as to make provision for rapidly bringing the system back on line if it goes down (usually through redundant systems or rapid on-site servicing). Also, if there is a conversion to new hardware or software, the controller must ensure that some sort of system is still supporting company operations at all times—it may be the old system or the one replacing it, but a growing company must be assured of having some sort of computer system up and running at all times. Thus, the controller's role in the computer services area is a conservative one: Just make sure that the systems do not fail.

A controller may also be responsible for the human resources function in a high-growth situation. If so, the primary focus is on where to find qualified candidates for positions throughout the company. Without enough staff, no company has a chance of continuing its growth, so this is absolutely crucial. There are a variety of techniques available for finding new staff, such as the Internet, recruiting firms, newspaper advertising, paying bonuses to in-house staff to bring in acquaintances, and using targeted publications that are distributed to specific trade disciplines. Also, since the human resources staff is usually overwhelmed by its recruiting work, the controller can ease the work burden by outsourcing other tasks. For example, benefits and pension administration can go to a supplier. In short, the controller must focus on recruiting when in charge of the human resources function of an explosive growth company.

This section summarized the controller's management functions in an explosive growth situation. The management goals change drastically in this environment. For example, the accounting and finance areas must focus on cash management. Computer services to key functional areas must not be interrupted. The human resources staff must focus on recruiting new employees, to the exclusion of any other activities. These are the key controller tasks in an explosive growth environment.

3

CHIEF FINANCIAL OFFICER: FROM CONTROLLER TO FACILITATOR OF CHANGE

IMPORTANCE OF THIS CHAPTER

The new controller needs to know all about the chief financial officer (CFO), not only because she reports to this position, but also because becoming a CFO is the next logical step in the controller's career track. This chapter gives insights into the motivations and responsibilities of the position.

Years ago, chief executive officers (CEOs) were satisfied with finance chiefs who could manage the analysts on Wall Street, implement financial controls, manage initial public offerings (IPOs), and communicate with the board—in other words, possess strong financial skills. However, in today's business climate in which competitors appear out of thin air, where e-commerce is changing entire industries, the ability to change quickly has become a necessity for growth, if not for survival. Chief executive officers are no longer satisfied with financial acumen. They are demanding more from their finance chiefs. They are looking for individuals who can fill a multitude of roles: business partner, strategic visionary, communicator, confidant, navigator, and creator of value. Bottom-line CEOs want someone who will drive improvement quickly—a facilitator of change. This chapter focuses on how to drive change in an organization. It is not about running a meeting or facilitating groups, but about implementing critical management practices that will help chief financial officers (CFOs) implement major business changes.

UNDERSTANDING WHAT CHIEF EXECUTIVE OFFICERS WANT

Facilitating change sounds simple until one is in the trenches trying to make significant improvement in how a business operates. Chief executive officers want creators of value, but often do not see that redefining the role of finance from controlling to driving operational improvements requires changing how the senior team operates and interacts with finance and following a systematic approach. In some organizations, line managers see finance as a necessary but unpopular support function that always changes budget numbers. In other organizations, norms have developed within the senior management group where there is an unwritten rule: "You don't ask too many tough questions about my area and I won't ask you too many questions about your area." In one particular case, a relatively new CFO saw large opportunities for improvement. These opportunities just happened to be in the operational areas and the president of those businesses did not need "the new guy" telling him what to do. Even though the new CFO had a good relationship with the CEO, any immediate improvement efforts became mired in political turmoil. Moving from controller to facilitator of change is not an easy transition. However, it can be done if CFOs focus on several key concepts.

TASK OF THE CFO

In today's business climate, the quote "There are the quick and then there are the dead" is quite true. How does a CFO drive change quickly? Creating value and becoming the business partner so many CEOs demand means facilitating change that not only affects finance but also directly impacts the operating units. To accomplish this end, CFOs must become skilled in several key management practices. The CFO must:

- Develop and communicate a compelling finance agenda.
- Build a commitment to change within finance.
- Change executive management practices.
- Enlist the support of the CEO.
- Mobilize the organization.
- Institutionalize continuous improvement.

By applying these concepts, CFOs can begin to accelerate the implementation of major organizational changes, as seen in Exhibit 3.1.

DEVELOP AND COMMUNICATE A COMPELLING FINANCE AGENDA

Chief executive officers say they want finance chiefs who can bring their organization to another level of performance. They want CFOs who are strategic thinkers and aggressive implementers, who can execute successfully. Because the finance agenda may affect the operating groups, an important skill is creating commitment around what is to be accomplished. One of the key reasons that change often fails is a decrease in organizational commitment. This often occurs when senior executives continuously change priorities, do not focus, or do not show their personal commitment to an effort by spending time on managing the effort. To implement and then institutionalize change, senior executives need a constancy of purpose—some stability in a normally chaotic world. The question becomes how do you create stability and yet stay flexible and dynamic to address market changes.

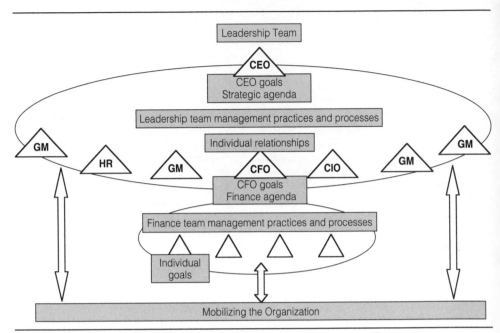

EXHIBIT 3.1 BECOMING A FACILITATOR OF CHANGE

The first step in creating a constancy of purpose and building commitment is developing a clear finance agenda. The finance agenda describes the five to seven key outcomes to be accomplished in the next 12 months, stated in crisp, definitive language where there will be no doubt when they have been accomplished. Essentially, the finance agenda is an organization's objectives for the year. It is a set of objectives that the CFO has memorized and can describe within two minutes at any moment and in any location. For example, a strategic agenda may look as follows:

- A fully functional shared services group for finance in the Americas
- A simplified and focused rolling budget process
- Books closed within three days
- A simple value-based scorecard and a value-based measurement system for each business
- Return-on-investment (ROI) calculations for any software implementation and process for measuring the ROI on subsequent module installations
- Accurate monthly financial summaries for each of the business units

---

SOURCES OF THE AGENDA

The CFO cannot run the risk of trying to lead the organization through the achievement of a set of goals that they do not care about, since this carries a high risk of failure. Instead, talk to the various company constituencies—managers, staff, creditors, investors, and so on—and determine what key problems are of major concern to them. By sprinkling these topics throughout the agenda, there will be much more commitment to accomplishing the total list.

Interestingly enough, creating this agenda sounds simple, and many executives say they already have clear objectives. But the key questions are: Are you fluent in your ability to describe them from memory? Is your organization clear? When asked specifically, "What are the five to seven key outcomes that you need to accomplish this year?", less than 60 percent of the executives can explain what they need to accomplish from memory in specific, crisp language in only a few minutes. Some need to go to their desk drawer to pull out their objectives. If I ask, "How many of the people reporting to you could articulate the key outcomes that you need to accomplish (i.e., those for the organization)?", the number drops to less than 50 percent. And if asked, "How well do your peers on the executive staff know your specific objectives?" or "How well does the entire finance organization know your overall objectives?", the number is well below 50 percent. Imagine less than 50 percent of the people or peers knowing what a senior executive (in other words, what their organization) needs to accomplish.

Chief financial officers may be thinking that they already have clear goals and wondering why this is so different. On the surface it looks similar to any standard goal-setting process, but in reality it is fundamentally different. The difference is in how fluent one is in describing the objectives, how focused they are, and whether they are "top of mind" or stored in a desk drawer. How does this affect organizational behavior? Competing priorities is a reality in today's organizations, yet it is an executive's job to help focus the energy of the organization on what is important and build commitment around those objectives. The first question people ask is whether the executive is personally committed. They draw their conclusions by observing his or her behavior.

Communicating a clear set of objectives is critical in telling the organization what is important. However, in today's information-overload work environment, a few presentations will not suffice. Communication experts say that senior executives often need to use every opportunity to repeat their messages to the point where they are literally "sick of repeating themselves." Only then do people begin to remember the message. Furthermore, this begins to reinforce the executive's personal commitment to the objectives. Bob Galvin at Motorola constantly spoke about Six Sigma quality. By communicating this message every opportunity he had, the organization began to believe that he was serious in his personal commitment to the change. This was then followed by actions that continued to reinforce the organization's belief that Six Sigma was important.

Forcing oneself to memorize strategic agenda and carrying it around in his or her head allows one to communicate continuously. Imagine a CFO is standing in the elevator and a new business analyst asks him a question about the finance department. Or the CFO is in the cafeteria and a manager wonders whether what he is doing is adding value. If within two minutes he can clearly, simply, and specifically cite what finance is trying to accomplish, the analyst in the elevator knows the focus. That person can then communicate the focus to peers with little translation error. Furthermore, a manager can immediately determine if what he or she is doing contributes to the overall direction of the finance organization, because the manager knows exactly what the CFO is trying to accomplish. This type of clarity, constancy of purpose, and reinforcement helps individuals commit to a direction.

Another benefit is that by keeping the agenda focused, specific integration among functions is much easier. For example, if a key objective for finance is implementing a balanced scorecard in the businesses, it is easy to determine whether the line executives also have that on their strategic agenda. If not, there is a disconnection, and it can be surfaced immediately. If a CFO is having lunch with one of the business unit presidents, who asks if the organization could design a new supply-chain reporting mechanism, the CFO can immediately mentally scroll through his or her strategic agenda and understand the implications of this request. If this is not part of the agenda, the CFO can tell the unit president that this will not be possible for another several months or begin negotiating. Because many decisions happen in informal dialogue by the CFO and the organization, by knowing exactly what it needs to accomplish, people can determine trade-offs on an ongoing basis. They can determine the value of activities immediately since if something does not contribute to the overall finance agenda, it may not be worth doing. Eventually, the organization becomes fast and flexible.

Several years ago, a general manager strongly believed in this model. He knew exactly what he needed to accomplish and could state his objectives anywhere, anytime. He would use any and every opportunity with people in his organization and his peers to reinforce his message. Over time, everyone knew exactly what the business needed to accomplish. People began to realize how committed he was to accomplishing those objectives. They knew exactly what he wanted to achieve, and could make a personal decision on whether they wanted to be on board. The majority decided to stay and help him meet those objectives; some who did not like where the organization was headed decided to leave. However, no one questioned the direction or his commitment to change. Also, because he was fluent about his objectives and his focus, any time another general manager or the senior vice president asked for help or additional work, he immediately knew how this would affect his goals. Because everyone knew what he was trying to accomplish, any time his organization was asked to do other work, he could use the strategic agenda to negotiate, because there would always be trade-offs. By observing his behavior, the organization began to mobilize around the required changes. There was no question about leadership spending enough time, no question about leadership driving change, and no question about what was important to the business. This organization consistently surpassed its financial, customer satisfaction, and employee satisfaction targets.

BUILD A COMMITMENT TO CHANGE WITHIN FINANCE

Once some thought has been given to the strategic agenda, it is time to build commitment around what the CFO wants to accomplish. If the CFO has developed a compelling finance agenda, the most important step toward commitment has already been taken, clearly describing what the CFO and the function need to accomplish. It is amazing how often this type of clarity is neglected, either because of not understanding how powerful this can be, political maneuvering to keep accountabilities hazy, or just little time to be specific. Yet when people are asked to commit to something, the more they can understand the specific implications, the easier it is for them to make a decision about commitment.

Also, a common misunderstanding is that people will only commit to something in which they have been involved in every step. This is not necessarily true. People want to be able to influence the direction (what needs to be done) and the approach (how things will be done) and have an open authentic dialogue around the realism of the objectives. They do not always need to be involved in every step. Some executives exhibit reluctance in communicating their agenda and providing direction because they want it to "evolve from the team." This often leads to several consequences. First, people often become frustrated by the lack of direction and then make comments like "He's not managing this department" or "She's getting the executive salary, but we always have to figure out what needs to get done." Second, people believe that most executives must be goal-driven, and therefore managers know what they want to accomplish; by not stating it explicitly, people begin to wonder. They wonder if the manager has a hidden agenda, if it is a test, or they begin to doubt the manager's leadership skills. It is much more effective to know what one wants to accomplish, use a straw model to begin the discussion, and openly listen to the staff and allow them to influence the agenda.

Another attempt to build commitment is often labeled "team building." Managers often believe that if they conduct a series of team-building exercises or off-sites, their team will suddenly be committed to driving change. Unfortunately, in most cases, people engage in the team-building exercises, but under the day-to-day pressures the new behaviors are most likely forgotten and rarely reinforced—especially if the senior executive only talks change, but does not reinforce the message with his own behavior. There is a mountain of evidence in the learning and training literature about how little learning transfers from external or simulated learning events back to on-the-job behaviors. Team building can be much more effective if it is integrated into day-to-day work. For example, several years ago, an executive requested team building to increase commitment for his staff. The conversation went like this:

> **Consultant:** "I'm sure we could help, but before talking about team building, let's talk about what are you seeing that suggests team building is the answer? What do you want them to commit to?"
>
> **Executive:** "Our meetings are totally unproductive—all we do is talk and talk with no decisions; no one is on the same page, and we can never wrap up."
>
> **Consultant:** "What has been the impact of this?"
>
> **Executive:** "We keep revisiting decisions, never coming to closure. Last time, we talked about whether we were going to assemble parts in Taiwan for almost two hours with no decision."
>
> **Consultant:** "It sounds like there is a lot going on and not something we're going to address with one team-building session. It sounds like we need to begin addressing how the executive team works together. I have found that most managers hate dealing with all this touchy-feely stuff. They see no value in it. However, if we begin to address some of these issues as part of trying to accomplish an objective, people tend to be more open about the process. What's pressing right now that you need to accomplish in the short term?"
>
> **Executive:** "We do need to finalize our strategic marketing plan."
>
> **Consultant:** "Now there is something people can probably sink their teeth into. We can address some of these behavior issues that you've cited as part of developing the strategic plan. We can include some team-building activities. Of course, to begin implementing some of these changes, you will need to play an active role and be open to some of my coaching. Are you okay with that?"
>
> **Executive:** "Sure. Why don't we set aside some time on Friday to think through the agenda and the process."

Focusing on a clear business objective that is tied to the overall strategic agenda and clarifying that behavior change does not occur overnight; integrating team-building activities into operational issues can help build commitment.

A prerequisite to many of these activities is the CFO's ability to explain what he wants to accomplish and why. The CFO must understand his personal motivations and convictions. He should spend a few minutes reflecting. The CFO needs to understand his personal motivations for why he wants to achieve certain goals. What drives him? Why is he passionate about these goals? If he is not passionate about a certain goal, why is he pursuing it? What will he do to ensure success? After he has had time to develop his agenda and the reasons why it is important, the CFO should think about and practice how he will tell his staff.

There are a variety of ways that this can be done. The most critical factor is that the CFO engage in genuine dialogue with the staff, listening to their views and allowing them to influence his opinions. The CFO's finance agenda literally becomes the finance team's goals. Because the CFO is the head of the function, the agenda that he creates with his direct reports becomes the agenda for finance. Some executives conduct an off-site in which they discuss the strategic agenda; others embed the discussions in their regular staff meetings. Having an open dialogue with the staff is critical. It is amazing how many teams have never had this type of open, honest dialogue, or the dialogue is complex, discussing a litany of actions and no one understands the "big picture." Following is an adaptation from a director of finance's (George's) off-site.

> *"As you see on the agenda today, we are going to spend most of our meeting talking about the agenda for finance and specific goals. I've had some time reflecting on what I think we need to accomplish this year and have captured this on my list of goals. Realize that this strategic agenda is what finance needs to accomplish this year. I'd like to spend the next few minutes describing each goal and why I think it's important. After that I'd like us to have an open discussion on whether these items make sense since your individual and department goals will be tied to this agenda." The director goes on to explain each of his seven goals. The dialogue around one particular goal is worth highlighting. "One of the items I've listed is to create tighter financial controls." One of the other directors challenges the goal. "George, is that really something we want to focus on. We just spent months decentralizing some of the processes because we were constantly getting complaints that we're like the audit police, always saying what the business could and could not do." George replies, "Bill, I understand your reluctance. I struggled with this one myself. But look at our numbers, almost everywhere you look we're struggling. Look at our new product development, over 50 percent of our new products produce little to no profit. Our travel expenses and miscellaneous expenses are totally out of sync with industry standards. I truly believe that successful businesses have fiscal discipline and rigorous controls. The challenge will be in how we help our operating managers take more accountability for the numbers. We can't remain in the cop role. That's why this objective is tied to my second goal, which is the reconfiguration of finance so that we have our best analysts dedicated to different business units providing analytic support. I also intend to raise the issue of ownership of the numbers and finance's role with the CEO and my peers at an upcoming executive meeting." Bill responds, "I still don't like it, but I can understand your point. We'll see how this plays in front of the executive committee." "Absolutely," says George, "we need to think of this as version one, and that's why I wanted your input. We will probably have to revisit this after my discussions at the executive meeting. We will also have to set more specific targets so that we can tell when we've been successful."*

TIME TO BUILD SUPPORT

The director of strategic planning at one Fortune 500 company claims that she spends 25 percent of her time determining the appropriate strategy, and 75 percent convincing the rest of the company to follow it. The CFO is in a similar position—be prepared to budget a very large amount of time for communicating with the company about strategic issues. This is the single largest difference between the CFO and controller positions.

This type of dialogue is important in building commitment. The key factor is how well the CFO maintains the balance between setting a definitive direction and letting the staff have input. The CFO should also help his staff understand that this is not a linear process. After his discussion with them, the finance agenda still needs to be discussed at the executive meeting, where the focus might change. However, it is important to solicit their input prior to that meeting.

A key element in obtaining commitment is the CFO's own behavior. Everyone has heard the cliche, "It's not what you say, but what you do." Too often, we forget. In one project, a senior vice president told his team that he would dedicate at least 50 percent of his time to the effort. One week after the effort started, he was spending at most two hours per week on the project. People started to question his leadership and his commitment. His reaction was, "They should know I'm committed. I authorized the effort and I am providing the budget." Unfortunately, that is not enough. In many organizations, commitment is measured by how much time people spend on what they say is important. Time has become our most precious resource. Needless to say, in this case, people interpreted the executive's behavior as a lack of leadership, they never fully committed themselves, and the effort stumbled.

A CFO is a role model whether he or she wants to be or not. CFOs must remember to demonstrate the outcomes and behaviors that they want, and then clearly set an expectation that their staff will continue the process, for example, clarifying that they are soliciting input prior to the meeting, telling them that once the finance objectives are finalized they expect them to communicate with their staffs. The CFO should clearly state that he or she expects their direct reports to have a similar session with their managers. They should first think about the key goals in their areas, why they want to focus on those goals, and how those goals link to the overall strategic agenda, and then conduct similar meetings where their staff has input. This approach allows the CFO to begin changing the basic operating style of the department.

CHANGE EXECUTIVE MANAGEMENT PRACTICES

Changing the finance organization is often hard work, but because the CFO has direct responsibility for that function, it is often easier than driving change across the operating units. Yet in many cases, change also needs to occur in those units. To begin this process, the executive team must develop a set of management practices that allows the CFO to implement his or her finance agenda and begin to function as an advisor and consultant to not only the CEO but also the operating units. Unfortunately, many executive teams develop management practices that are often counterproductive to implementing change quickly. Following is an example of several executive meetings that highlight how patterns often develop:

- *Team 1.* The group rarely gets together to discuss operations. When they do get together, there is an unwritten rule that no one points out a deficiency in someone else's area. The prevailing climate is "don't mess with mine and I won't mess with yours." Executive meetings are characterized by a lot of dialogue, but little or no action. Rarely are action items or decisions documented. Individuals rarely challenge each other and almost never challenge the CEO.

- *Team 2.* This team does get together to discuss operations. However, everyone needs to fully agree with a recommendation before it is acted on. The constant drive to consensus often takes so long that participants turn off and agree just to move on. Rarely is substantive conflict present. The meeting is characterized as nice and cordial. Meeting minutes may be taken, but they are lengthy and difficult to understand.

- *Team 3.* This team also meets, but many one-on-one meetings have taken place before or outside of the meeting either between the CEO and other executives or between executives. There is no common database of knowledge; no one is on the same page. The CEO or senior executive drives the meeting, pushing forward through the agenda. Others participate when their area is up for discussion and spend the time reading e-mail or finishing administrative tasks. Minutes might be taken.

- *Team 4.* These meetings are brawls. Managers get together and fight. Conflict rules the session; people challenge each other and debate each other. Debates are often subjective interpretations of data or opinions. There are no clear processes on how to work through information and come to resolution.

Although these are sample meetings, many meetings are similar to one or more of these profiles.

For a CFO, the focus is on ways in which to help the management team understand his or her new role, what he or she wants to accomplish, and how they need to contribute to those objectives. Therefore, understanding the management practices of the executive team is important. Changing these practices and the dynamics of the executive team is the first challenge in moving into a change agent role. Executive teams that are able to drive change through the organization, who operate work toward a common agenda, and are able to work through many organizational challenges have the following characteristics (practices):

- *Regular meetings.* The executive team meets regularly to discuss operations. Research and practice have shown that if management teams do not meet on a regular basis to discuss work, the group slowly begins to splinter. Individuals may still be able to run their areas effectively, but cross-boundary issues become harder to resolve.

- *Constructive confrontation.* Because all individual executives are accountable to meet the business or function goals and are accountable as a team to meet the overall business goals, there is a clear expectation to question and challenge each others' operations.

- *Listening.* All executives actively listen to and are able to stimulate substantive and honest dialogue about issues and potential solutions.

- *Shared agenda.* The executive group reviews and challenges each others' strategic agenda to ensure consistency and integration across organizations. All of their goals directly and clearly reinforce the CEO's goals.

- *Clear feedback.* Managers have clear review processes in which they review operations, make course corrections, provide feedback, and ensure accountability.

- *Decisive, fast-paced meetings.* Meetings are held regularly to discuss operations in which it is expected that each participant provides input and advice to other areas and solicits input for his or her area. The pace is fast, yet the meeting is comprehensive. Decisions are made; actions are determined, documented, and communicated in a comprehensive manner.

PREVENTING COMFORTABLE MEETINGS

The primary reason for a meeting is to reach a decision, which may require very little time. A long meeting is possibly a sign of a small amount of productive decision making surrounded by a thick blanket of unnecessary chatting time. Managers use a variety of techniques to keep meetings short, such as removing chairs from the room, scheduling meetings in five-minute increments, and locking the doors as soon as a meeting has begun (thereby encouraging promptness).

- *Consensus with qualification decision making.* Participants debate and look at all angles of a recommendation or impending decision. If consensus cannot be achieved after listening to all the options, the most senior individual will make the decision and everyone will be committed to its outcome. Decision is data driven and made quickly.

- *Data driven.* Decision making is driven by data, and clear procedures and templates for the type of data needed are developed for decision-making purposes.

- *Role of support functions.* Support functions act as consultants to the operating units, challenging and working with them to improve performance.

- *Role models.* Executive leadership role models desired behavior.

- *Continuous improvement.* The executive team periodically steps back and looks at its own management processes to assess effectiveness. Based on these assessments, continuous improvement actions will be taken.

If an executive team does not operate in this manner, if finance is not given the liberty to challenge the operations, or if finance is not seen as a strategic partner, changes in how the executive team operates may be in order. To begin this change, it is important to remember that this is the boss's team. The CFO is one among many peers, and in some cases, depending on the relationships, the power may be unequally distributed. The CFO might be able to influence some of the behaviors, but few major changes will take place unless the CEO is aware of the improvement potential and willing to play a role. So how does the CFO begin the process of changing the practices of the management team?

ENLIST THE SUPPORT OF THE CHIEF EXECUTIVE OFFICER

An important step in change is creating the awareness that change is necessary. One of the most difficult areas to change is management process. Most successful executives have honed their managerial skills over many decades and have strong opinions of what works and what does not. Therein lies the opportunity. Today's business environment is quite different than that of just a few years ago. Often, the management team has new players, or the challenges confronting the organization are more intense. Those organizations that are able to change their management practices are those that have a greater likelihood of success. And those practices start at the top. Consequently, enlisting the support of the CEO in reshaping the management practices of the executive team will be critical. To begin this process, the CFO must find a way to create awareness about required changes. One way to do this is:

Step 1. Lay out the agenda for finance.

Step 2. Determine what will be required to implement the strategic agenda.

Step 3. Determine how the executive team will need to change and what is required from them to manage the implementation of the finance agenda.

Step 4. Develop an action plan on helping the CEO see the team's current dynamics, how they may need to change, and his role in that change effort.

Step 5. Meet with the CEO to discuss the strategic agenda and what will be needed from the executive team and from the CEO.

Step 6. Jointly develop a way to raise any issues with the executive team.

One approach to help create awareness is to look at best practices or use white papers, articles, or other print material as a way to help educate the CEO on what could be. Begin creating an awareness on how to improve the senior team dynamics. Discussing an article or summary can be a powerful way to begin the dialogue around change. In some cases, it may be effective to bring in an outsider to counsel the group on how it can be even more effective. Once the CFO understands the CEO's reaction to reshaping the executive team's management practices, he or she can jointly develop an action plan on how to introduce these changes. An approach that can be used is to spend a few minutes during the next meeting having people read a brief overview of the new practices and then have a short discussion. Following is an example of how one finance executive addressed the issue. The CFO met several times with his boss to discuss his observations and used an article as a neutral way to begin questioning some of the management practices. After several discussions, the senior vice president understood and agreed that there were improvement opportunities. Given the formal authority of the senior vice president and his ownership of the meeting, they decided that he would introduce the topic and lead the discussion at the next staff meeting.

Andre, the senior vice president starts the meeting.

> *Our agenda is quite full today, so why don't we get started. You'll notice one of the first items is about our management practices. Several weeks ago, Cathy came to me with an article that she saw in a recent CFO magazine. Based on her reading, she thought that this would be of value to all of us. After a few discussions and after looking at the article myself, I think she's right. There are some interesting concepts in here. I don't necessarily agree with all of them, but I think it is something we should discuss implementing. There are some ideas I definitely want to put in place. So, I'd like each of you to spend five minutes reading this article and then we'll spend another 15 minutes talking about what elements we will implement.*

After everyone finishes reading, he talks about the management practices he wants to put in place and solicits people's input and opinions. The executive group decides to bring in an outside advisor to talk to individual executives, assess the team's management practices by observing several key meetings, and then facilitate a workshop in which they will decide on some of the recommendations.

MOBILIZE THE ORGANIZATION

Results can be achieved quickly when a large part of the organization is mobilized. Mobilization goes beyond communication, which is often characterized as a two-way exchange of information, to enlisting the active involvement of individuals. Communication is necessary, but not sufficient, in driving major organization changes quickly. Unfortunately, in many change efforts, this concept is misused in several ways:

- A project team spends weeks or in some cases months preparing a business case, a new design (new processes, new systems, new structure), and an implementation plan. These are then communicated to the organization through an elaborate communication plan that often involves challenge sessions or other activities to "involve" the organization. The assumption is that the organization is then mobilized and committed to the effort. Unfortunately, this is rarely so. In many cases, the executive team has never had the opportunity to clearly debate the plan in detail, they have not come up the learning curve together, and the most senior executive does not clearly demand that operating executives take accountability for the implementation. Consequently, it is often unclear whether the executive team is fully committed and this message filters throughout the organization, causing a hesitancy to proceed and a lack of commitment. The organization is not mobilized.

- In other large change efforts, organizations spend weeks preparing elaborate communication plans incorporating the most advanced delivery mechanisms. In some cases, senior executives will give one or two presentations to show their commitment to the project. Yet the strategic agenda and how the project fits into the agenda is not clear. Maybe the executive team went through several executive education sessions, but few executives have integrated the project into their objectives. Even fewer regularly talk about the project in their regular operations reviews. In some cases, the implementation is managed by a separate steering committee, further separating operating executives from the accountability for project results. The project may or may not be discussed at the executive meetings. The organization intuitively senses these disconnects and mobilization becomes much harder.

- In some change efforts, communication is often seen as a separate activity. There is a separate communication team with their own charter and work plan. The logic is that if this is not done, communication does not occur. There is some truth to this, and therefore having people focus on communication is important. However, more important is the fact that managers are responsible for communication. Communicating to the organization is one of the primary responsibilities of management, and if managers neglect this task the organization cannot be mobilized.

Mobilization occurs around a specific purpose and specific individuals. People do not mobilize around a communications team. The communications team supports, with the exchange of information, an executive's efforts around mobilizing his or her people around a strategic agenda. People also become mobilized if they see the executive team devoting their attention to these objectives.

The CFO has already completed the first steps in mobilizing an organization by clarifying the strategic agenda, using every opportunity to communicate his or her objectives, and working with the executive team to create shared understanding and common management practices. As mentioned before, a primary mode of learning in an organization is by observing behaviors, determining what works and what does not, and then modeling those behaviors.

Once the organization understands what the CFO is trying to accomplish and is mobilized, he or she will need to sustain that momentum. This is usually accomplished by ensuring operating executive accountability and involvement, determining specific measures, having clear operations review processes in which the projects are discussed, providing feedback, and communicating as a normal course of action. As mentioned earlier, communication is often seen as a separate activity. To maintain momentum, communication must be seen as an integral part of the managerial process. Communication should not be seen as separate from managing the daily operations, and a key success factor is how well the CFO integrates communications.

Several years ago, the general manager of a small $100 million business firmly believed in integrating communications into daily operations. Although she did have a communications manager, she set a clear expectation that communications was the responsibility of each director. This organization had one of the best communications efforts around—measurement-driven, clear expectations around communication, regular senior management involvement, communication events, communications integrated in performance reviews for supervisors and managers, and so on. Because this organization was measurement-driven, they could tell how well they were doing. Communication, however, left some room for improvement. After a brief analysis was conducted, it was determined that the issue was the way in which information received was actually communicated. There was a breakdown in communications after executive team meetings. People wanted to know what was decided. How often are decisions captured from executive team meetings in a way that people can immediately understand what was decided? The decision was made that during the executive meeting all major decisions would be documented, and then prior to the end of the meeting the decisions would be reviewed and the group would decide what could be posted. In some cases, because of the highly confidential nature of discussions or because of the timing of decisions, not everything could be posted. This information was then posted on the intranet, and directors would review these decisions in their staff meetings. By integrating communications as a part of normal operations and making it a managerial responsibility, this organization dramatically improved its communication effectiveness.

INSTITUTIONALIZE CONTINUOUS IMPROVEMENT

Facilitating change is an ongoing process—the more effective a CFO is at instituting a continuous improvement mentality and process, the easier it will be to keep driving change. A continuous improvement mentality suggests that we are constantly reviewing and questioning how we are doing and using a systematic measurement-driven approach to improving performance. Many organizations have implemented processes such as total quality management, Six Sigma, and continuous improvement to help sustain changes. The most common methodology is characterized by the following approach: define, measure, analyze, improve, and control. This approach was developed by the manufacturing industry to improve efficiencies given ever-shrinking margins, but it is now expanding into other industries. The philosophy of continuous improvement is:

- Define a problem to solve; it should be realistic and doable.
- Measure current performance to set a baseline and determine measures.
- Analyze what is causing the gap.

- Determine a realistic target and then implement the improvements.
- Implement control mechanisms to ensure that the new activities become institutionalized.

The most effective teams also use this process to continuously improve their management practices. One group of executives periodically reviewed their management practices in an effort to improve how they managed the business. They reviewed how well they made decisions, how well they held each other accountable, how open they were to other opinions, whether their meetings included substantive dialogue, how well they communicated expectations to presenters, and so forth.

DRIVING CHANGE THROUGH PERFORMANCE REVIEWS

Companies have a tendency to focus on a few performance improvements, complete them, and then return to complacency with no further change efforts. To prevent this, give the human resources staff a mandate to incorporate process improvement into the primary performance review criteria for every employee. By doing so, the message is clearly sent—"Continue to improve or your pay level will not increase."

By institutionalizing a process by which management openly and honestly questions not only what they are doing, but also how they are managing, implementing changes quickly and effectively becomes a core competency.

4*

ACCOUNTING PRINCIPLES AND STANDARDS

IMPORTANCE OF THIS CHAPTER

The new controller must produce financial statements that follow generally accepted accounting principles (GAAP). This chapter reveals the sources of GAAP, the nature of the organizations that develop it, and where to locate GAAP rules. This information is crucial for the controller.

Who creates the basic rules of accounting that guide the accounting practices of so many accountants? There are several entities that contribute to these basic rules, as will be discussed in this chapter. We also summarize many of the accounting pronouncements that have been issued by these organizations, and describe where to go to obtain more detailed information about them.

COMMITTEE ON ACCOUNTING PROCEDURE

The Committee on Accounting Procedure (CAP) was created in 1939 by the American Institute of Accountants (now known as the American Institute of Public Accountants, or AICPA). It issued a total of 51 *Accounting Research Bulletins* that responded to specific accounting problems as they arose; this tight focus led to an increasing number of complaints against the CAP over time, because it did not attempt to create an overall accounting framework to which specific accounting pronouncements could then be attached in an

---

* Reprinted with permission from Chapters 4–5 of Steven M. Bragg, *Accounting Reference Desktop* (Hoboken: Wiley, 2002).

orderly manner. Another problem was that it was accused of not conducting a sufficient volume of detailed research to back up the reasoning behind its pronouncements. Yet another issue was the perception that it acted in the interests of the American Institute of Accountants, which was considered a conflict of interest. Furthermore, its pronouncements were not binding on any organizations that issued financial reports. On the plus side, it developed a uniform accounting terminology that was widely used thereafter. Because of the preceding problems, the CAP was eliminated in 1959 in favor of the Accounting Principles Board.

ACCOUNTING PRINCIPLES BOARD

The Accounting Principles Board (APB) was formed in 1958 by the AICPA. Its 18- to 21-member Board and supporting staff was active in conducting research on accounting issues and promulgating standards. Even though it was phased out in 1973, its APB bulletin numbers 43, 45, 46, and 51, as well as 19 opinions still form a part of GAAP. The APB gained more regulatory force than its predecessor, because the AICPA required its member CPAs to identify and justify any departures from the APB's opinions and statements, while it also gained support from the Securities and Exchange Commission. Nonetheless, it foundered due to its direct support by the AICPA—a more independent organization was needed, which resulted in the Financial Accounting Foundation.

FINANCIAL ACCOUNTING FOUNDATION

The Financial Accounting Foundation (FAF) was founded in 1972. Its 16-member Board of Trustees is expressly independent from the AICPA, since they come from a number of sponsoring organizations, such as the AICPA, the Financial Executives Institute, the Institute of Management Accountants, the Securities Industry Association, and others. It also has a number of at-large trustees who are not tied to any sponsoring organizations. The FAF does not directly promulgate any accounting standards—rather, it raises funds for the operation of the Financial Accounting Standards Board (FASB) and Government Accounting Standards Board (GASB) that conduct this work, as noted in the following sections. Its fundraising function is enhanced by its being a 501(c)(3) taxable entity, so that contributions to it are tax-deductible. It also exercises general oversight of the FASB and GASB by appointing Board members to them, as well as two advisory councils to those entities. It also approves their annual budgets. The FAF, FASB, and GASB are all located in Norwalk, Connecticut.

FINANCIAL ACCOUNTING STANDARDS BOARD

The successor to the Accounting Principles Board is the Financial Accounting Standards Board (FASB) created in 1973. It has a Board of seven members, each of whom have a five-year term, and who can be reelected once. It has a staff of about 40 personnel. The organization is funded through the FAF. Its mission is to "establish and improve standards of financial accounting and reporting for the guidance and education of the public, including issuers, auditors, and users of financial information." It maintains a web site at *www.rutgers.edu/accounting/raw/fasb/welcome.htm.*

The FASB's authority to issue statements on and interpretations of accounting standards comes from several sources. One is the Securities and Exchange Commission, which designated it as the source of accounting principles to be used as the basis for financial statements filed with it. The FASB received similar support from the AICPA through its Rule 203. However, the FASB has no enforcement powers whatsoever—it needs continuing support from the SEC, AICPA, and state boards of accountancy to ensure that its rules are followed.

The FASB works with the Financial Accounting Standards Advisory Council, which is appointed by the FAF. The council's 30 members advise the FASB about technical issues, project priorities, and the selection of task forces to deal with specific accounting issues.

There is a basic flow of work that the FASB pursues when constructing a new accounting pronouncement:

1. *Admission to agenda.* The FASB's criteria for inclusion of an accounting issue in its work schedule are that there is diverse practice in dealing with it that causes varying financial reporting results that can be misleading; there must also be a technically feasible solution and an expectation that a solution will be generally accepted.

2. *Early deliberations.* The FASB clarifies the issues and obtains opinions regarding each accounting item on its agenda. If a prospective pronouncement appears to be a major project, it will appoint an advisory task force of outside experts to review it, which tends to involve the services of about 15 people. The FASB staff will then write a discussion memorandum with the assistance of this group.

3. *Public hearing.* The FASB will announce a hearing date that is 60 days in advance. Depending on the issue, these meetings may be very well attended by interested parties.

4. *Tentative resolution.* Two-thirds of the Board votes in favor of issuing an exposure draft, which includes a proposed effective date and method of transition to the new accounting rule. This document is not the final one, being rather a draft that is made available for public discussion.

5. *Final deliberations and resolution.* Once responses from the public to the exposure draft have been made, the FASB will make minor adjustments to it and take a final vote. The finalized standard, which includes dissenting views, is then published.

6. *Follow-up interpretations.* There may be some issues related to a new standard that do not become apparent until after it has been in use for a short time. If so, the FASB may clarify or elaborate on the newly issued statement. These interpretations must also be made available for public comment for at least 30 days before being finalized and published.

LEARNING ABOUT UPCOMING GAAP CHANGES

New GAAP rulings appear all the time. The new controller should not be surprised by any of these rulings, since the Financial Accounting Standards Board issues notices about upcoming GAAP changes through several publications. As a member of the American Institute of Certified Public Accountants, you receive a monthly copy of the *Journal of Accountancy.* Toward the back of this publication is a complete list of upcoming pronouncements, as well as detailed information concerning the most recently released GAAP.

The process just noted requires a considerable amount of FASB resources, and so cannot be used to address all accounting issues. To provide more rapid resolution to more urgent or minor issues, it may choose to shift them to its Emerging Issues Task Force (EITF). The EITF is a very active group that is mostly composed of public accounting people who are aware of emerging issues before they become widespread. The chief accountant of the SEC attends its meetings. If it can reach a rapid consensus on an issue, then its findings are published at once, and become a basis for GAAP. If there is less consensus, then the issue is shifted to the FASB to be resolved through the more tortuous process just described. The EITF has been criticized because less public discussion is involved in its proceedings than under the more formalized FASB review process.

The FASB also issues technical bulletins when it addresses issues not covered by existing standards, which will not cause a major change in practice, which have a minimal perceived implementation cost, and which do not result in a unique new accounting practice—in short, technical bulletins address less controversial topics.

A potential problem over the long term is that the SEC, which is a prime sponsor of the FASB, wants it to issue standards that are oriented toward publicly held companies, over which the SEC has reporting control. However, this means that the more onerous reporting requirements intended for larger public companies are also being forced on smaller private firms that do not have the resources to comply with them. Though there would be great inefficiencies involved in setting up a double accounting standard, one for public and one for private companies, this will be an ongoing cause of tension within the FASB as it continues to churn out pronouncements.

GOVERNMENT ACCOUNTING STANDARDS BOARD

The entity that establishes accounting principles for state and local governments is the Government Accounting Standards Board (GASB), which was created in 1984. It is the successor organization to the National Council on Governmental Accounting, whose standards are still in force unless the GASB has issued specific changes or replacements to them. The GASB's methods of operation (and basic rule-making procedures) are nearly identical to those of the FASB, which is its sister organization. It has seven Board members and a staff of about ten employees. Like the FASB, it works with an advisory council, this one being called the Government Accounting Standards Advisory Council, which is appointed by the FAF. This council consults with the GASB about technical issues, project priorities, and the selection of task forces to deal with specific issues. An interesting variation from the FASB's council is that this one periodically conducts an annual membership survey to identify emerging issues.

Its funding comes from the FAF, as is the case for the FASB. The primary source of funding that goes to the FAF is from state and local governments, as well as the General Accounting Office.

The GASB's pronouncements are recognized as authoritative by the AICPA, but there is no entity like the SEC supporting it (which only deals with publicly held companies), and so it tends to have less overall influence than the FASB. Also, since its funding sources are fewer than for the FASB, it has a substantially smaller staff.

The GASB maintains a general web site at *www.rutgers.edu/accounting/raw/gasb/welcome.htm,* as well as another web site at *www.seagov.org* that is dedicated to the measurement of government performance standards.

INTERNATIONAL ACCOUNTING STANDARDS BOARD

A large number of organizations now do business in multiple countries, and so must deal with different accounting standards within each country where they have subsidiaries. Though a company's headquarters may be located in the United States, which forces the entity as a whole to report under FASB standards, it may be required to make reports, such as loan-related financial statements, at the local level that require different accounting standards. Also, companies that are based abroad but that want to issue securities within the United States must restate their financial results to comply with American accounting rules. In an attempt to standardize the accounting rules of many countries, the International Accounting Standards Board (IASB) was created in April 2001. It is the successor body to the International Accounting Standards Committee (IASC), which in turn was formed in 1973 through an agreement made by the national professional accountancy bodies of Australia, Canada, France, Germany, Japan, Mexico, the Netherlands, Ireland, the United Kingdom, and the United States. Its 14-member Board members serve five years, which can be renewed once.

The IASB is controlled by a parent organization, which is the IASC Foundation, a Delaware nonprofit corporation. Its role is quite similar to that of the FAF in relation to the FASB and GASB—that is, it provides funding and general oversight to the IASB, while also appointing its members. Meanwhile, the IASB is solely responsible for setting international accounting standards, with the support of the Standards Advisory Council and the Standing Interpretations Committee, both of which are funded and supported by the IASC Foundation.

The IASB's staff works on the development of a single set of international accounting standards, coordinating its efforts with the national standards-setting bodies, stock exchanges, and securities regulatory agencies in many countries, as well as such international groups as the United Nations and World Bank. It accounting standards are issued in the form of *International Financial Reporting Standards,* which are devised through the same process used by the GASB and FASB.

ACCOUNTING STANDARDS

Generally Accepted Accounting Principles (GAAP) come from the pronouncement of the Accounting Procedures Committee of the AICPA (which concluded its operations in 1959), the Accounting Principles Board of the AICPA (which concluded its operations in 1973), and the Financial Accounting Standards Board (FASB), which is now the primary authoritative source of GAAP. *Account Research Bulletins* (ARB) are the official pronouncements of the Accounting Procedures Committee, while the Accounting Principles Board issued numbered *Opinions.* The FASB uses a number of pronouncements, including *Interpretations, Statements, Statements of Financial Accounting Concepts,* and *Technical Bulletins.* Its Emerging Issues Task Force (EITF) also issues a voluminous number of *Abstracts.* In addition, the AICPA issues a number of *Statements of Position* (SOPs). The identifying numbers, titles, and summaries of all of these GAAP sources, with the exception of EITF abstracts and AICPA Statements of Position, are included in the following sections.

The summaries noted here are not intended to provide the full range of information needed by the accountant to fully research a particular GAAP issue. Instead, one can peruse the list to see which reference sources are most applicable to the problem at hand. At that point, one should refer to the source document to obtain the greatest possible detail. In many cases, source documents also include examples that are invaluable in determining the application of the principles under discussion to actual situations.

There are several sources of GAAP documents. One can go to the FASB web site, located at *http://raw.rutgers.edu/raw/fasb,* to find the complete text of all FASB Statements. A more complete source of nearly all GAAP documents is the excellent three-volume set of *Original Pronouncements,* published by the AICPA. It contains all FASB Statements, Accounting Research Bulletins, Opinions of the Accounting Principles Board, AICPA Interpretations, FASB Interpretations, FASB Concept Statements, and FASB Technical Bulletins. The documents show only those pronouncements that have not been superseded, and also highlight any text that has been superseded or modified by later pronouncements, thereby eliminating some potential confusion regarding which pronouncements constitute current accounting standards. It can be purchased from the AICPA web store for $99, which is located at *www.cpa2biz.com.* As of this publication date, the *Original Pronouncements* could be purchased only by AIPCA members—the membership application can be found at the AICPA web site, which is located at *www.aicpa.org.* The information contained within the *Original Pronouncements* is current up until June 1 of each year, and so the most recent year's publication is not usually available until late summer or early fall. Statements of Position can be ordered separately from the AICPA under the title of *AICPA Technical Practice Aids.* It is also available through the AICPA Web store, and can be purchased there at an AICPA member price of $80 and $100 for nonmembers. Abstracts published by the EITF are available on an annual subscription basis for $338 per year, or may be purchased individually for $44.75 each. They can be ordered by calling the FASB at 800-748-0659, or by ordering on-line by accessing *http://stores/yahoo.com/fasbpubs.*

ACCOUNTING RESEARCH BULLETINS

The Accounting Research Bulletins in Exhibit 4.1 are only those that have not been superseded by later accounting standards. Note that the first one listed, ARB No. 43, is a summary of all preceding ARBs.

Number	Title	Description
43	Restatement of Revision of Previous Bulletins	Represents a revision and summary of the first 42 Accounting Research Bulletins, covering such topics as the form of financial statements, working capital, inventory pricing, intangible assets, contingency reserves, capital accounts, depreciation, taxes, government contracts, pension plans, and pension plan annuity costs.
45	Long-Term Construction-Type Contracts	Describes the use of the percentage-of-completion method and the completed contract method to account for construction contracts.
46	Discontinuance of Dating Earned Surplus	Cancels the dating of an earned surplus following a quasi-reorganization.
51	Consolidated Financial Statements	Discusses the consolidation procedure, the treatment of minority interests, the treatment of stock dividends of subsidiaries, and the uses of both combined and parent company financial statements.

EXHIBIT 4.1 SUMMARY OF CURRENT ACCOUNTING RESEARCH BULLETINS

OPINIONS: ACCOUNTING PRINCIPLES BOARD

The Opinions listed in Exhibit 4.2 are only those that have not been superseded by later accounting standards. Several of these Opinions, such as APB Nos. 9, 14, 16, 17, 20–22, and 25, are still the primary source documents for key accounting issues.

Number	Title	Description
2	Accounting for the Investment Credit	Discusses the presentation and recognition of the investment tax credit arising from the Revenue Act of 1962.
4	Accounting for the Investment Credit	Discusses the impact of the Revenue Act of 1964 on the investment tax credit, as well as an additional allowable method for reporting the credit, net of reported federal income taxes.
6	Status of Accounting Research Bulletins	Contains revisions to those sections of ARB No. 43 relating to Treasury stock, current assets and liabilities, stock dividends and splits, and depreciation and appreciation.
9	Reporting the Results of Operations	Concludes that net income should include all profit and loss transactions, with the exception of prior-period adjustments. It also specifies the separate treatment of extraordinary items in the income statement.
10	Omnibus Opinion— 1966	Covers the allocation of income taxes among different reporting periods, offsetting securities against taxes payable, and denies the use of the installment method of accounting.
12	Omnibus Opinion— 1967	Covers the classification and disclosure of allowance accounts, depreciation disclosure, and the reporting of changes in equity, and affirms the use of the interest method when amortizing debt discounts and premiums.
14	Accounting for Convertible Debt and Debt Issued with Stock Purchase Warrants	Discusses the applicability of accounting for stock purchase warrants separately from attached debt instruments.
16	Business Combinations	Discusses the purchase and pooling methods of accounting for a business combination, and the circumstances under which each one can be used. It also covers the treatment of acquisition costs, contingent compensation, and the amortization of goodwill.
17	Intangible Assets	Specifies the types of intangibles that may be recorded as assets, how to arrive at their cost, and how they may be amortized.
18	The Equity Method of Accounting for Investments in Common Stock	Specifies the circumstances under which the equity method of accounting can be used, as well as how it should be calculated and then disclosed on the investor's financial statements.
20	Accounting Changes	Discusses the proper treatment of changes in accounting principle, estimate, and reporting entity, as well as of errors in previously issued financial statements, plus how this information is to be disclosed in the financial statements.
21	Interest on Receivables and Payables	Discusses the determination of the proper valuation of a note when it is exchanged for either cash, property, or services. It also covers the selection of an appropriate present value discount rate, as well as the disclosure of discounts or premiums from the face value of a note.

EXHIBIT 4.2 SUMMARY OF CURRENT ACCOUNTING PRINCIPLES BOARD OPINIONS

Number	Title	Description
22	Disclosure of Accounting Policies	Requires the disclosure of significant accounting policies alongside the financial statements.
23	Accounting for Income Taxes—Special Areas	Discusses the proper accounting for income taxes in relation to the undistributed earnings of subsidiaries, investments in corporate joint ventures, bad debt reserves of savings and loan institutions, and the policyholders' surplus of stock life insurance companies.
25	Accounting for Stock Issued to Employees	Specifies the rules to use when accounting for stock awards. The core principle is that the accounting is based on the intrinsic value of the award, which is the difference between the compensation value of the award, measured as the number of shares multiplied by the fair market value per share, and employee value, measured as the employee price per share multiplied by the number of shares.
26	Early Extinguishment of Debt	Requires that gains or losses from the early extinguishment of debt be recognized in the current period.
28	Interim Financial Reporting	Describes the information that should be contained within interim financial reports, including changes in accounting principles and the disclosure of summarized interim financial data by publicly traded companies.
29	Accounting for Nonmonetary Transactions	Verifies that nonmonetary transactions should be valued based on their fair values, except in a limited number of cases where nonmonetary exchanges are not considered to be the culmination of an earnings process.
30	Reporting the Results of Operations	Discusses the proper disclosure of discontinued operations, as well as the reporting of gains or losses from business disposals. It also defines those transactions that should be categorized as extraordinary items.

EXHIBIT 4.2 SUMMARY OF CURRENT ACCOUNTING PRINCIPLES BOARD OPINIONS *(CONTINUED)*

INTERPRETATIONS: FASB

The Interpretations listed in Exhibit 4.3 are intended to clarify or expand on any accounting pronouncements that have previously been issued, usually addressing very specific topics.

Number	Title	Description
1	Accounting Changes Related to the Cost of Inventory	If there is a change in the costs included in inventory, this is considered an accounting change that must be justified based on some improvement in the level of financial reporting, and not just on favorable income tax results.
4	Applicability of FASB Statement No. 2 to Purchase Business Combinations	When using the purchase method to account for a business combination, costs should be allocated to assets both resulting from and to be used in research and development activities of the acquired entity. However, assigned R&D costs must then be expensed at the time of the combination if the related assets have no identifiable future use.

EXHIBIT 4.3 SUMMARY OF CURRENT FASB INTERPRETATIONS

Number	Title	Description
6	Applicability of FASB Statement No. 2 to Computer Software	Specifies that the purchase or development of a process for internal sales or administrative purposes is not classified as research and development costs. The cost associated with the purchase or lease of computer software for use in R&D activities should be charged to expense unless it has an alternative future use. Software development costs through the preproduction phase are considered R&D costs, while programming and testing costs incurred for the improvement of a production model are not considered R&D expenses.
7	Applying FASB Statement No. 7 in Statements of Established Enterprises	Describes the situations under which a consolidating entity should report the effect of a development stage subsidiary's change in accounting principle, based on the requirements of FASB Statement No. 7.
8	Classification of a Short-Term Obligation Repaid Prior to Being Replaced by a Long-Term Security	Requires the reporting of a short-debt repayment as a current liability if the repayment occurs prior to the incurrence of long-term debt that was intended to pay for the short-term debt repayment.
9	Applying APB Opinions Nos. 16 and 17 When a Savings and Loan or Similar Institution Is Acquired in a Purchase Business Combination	Disallows the use of the "net spread" method for assigning costs to the assets of an acquired company; it also provides guidelines for assigning costs to accounts receivable and payable, as well as intangible assets and savings deposits due on demand.
14	Reasonable Estimation of the Amount of a Loss	Specifies the conditions under which losses can be accrued.
18	Accounting for Income Taxes in Interim Periods	Describes the computation of interim-period income taxes and related disclosures, applies the computation to specific situations, and describes special computations that are applicable to multiple jurisdictions.
19	Lessee Guarantee of the Residual Value of Leased Property	Describes the specific situations under which a lease provision can be construed as being a lessee's guarantee of the residual value of leased property, as well as the maximum limitations on the amount of such a guarantee.
20	Reporting Accounting Changes Under AICPA Statements of Position	Notes that any change made to a company's financial statements under an AICPA Statement of Position (SOP) shall do so in accordance with the requirements of the specific SOP.
21	Accounting for Leases in a Business Combination	Notes that a lease's classification as noted in FASB Statement No. 13 shall not be changed because of a business combination, unless the lease's provisions have been specifically modified.
23	Leases of Certain Property Owned by a Governmental Unit or Authority	Narrows the range of leases of government property to be categorized as operating leases, based on the presence of four criteria.
24	Leases Involving Only Part of a Building	Notes that one can reasonably determine the fair value of a partial building lease based on other types of information, if comparable sale data are not available.

Exhibit 4.3   Summary of Current FASB Interpretations *(continued)*

Number	Title	Description
26	Accounting for Purchase of a Leased Asset by the Lessee During the Term of the Lease	Specifies that an asset purchase under the terms of a capital lease, and the corresponding lease termination, are covered by a single accounting transaction that may call for an adjustment in the carrying amount of the lease obligation.
27	Accounting for Loss on a Sublease	Allows the recognition of a loss on the difference between a lease and a sublease, and also specifies that this loss is to be included in the overall gain or loss reported on the disposition of a business segment.
28	Accounting for Stock Appreciation Rights and Other Variable Stock Option or Award Plans	Specifies that a company must record a compensation expense at the end of each reporting period for the amount by which the market price of its stock exceeds the option price for any stock appreciation rights or similar plans.
30	Accounting for Involuntary Conversions of Nonmonetary Assets to Monetary Assets	Requires that a gain or loss be recognized when corporate assets are involuntarily converted to cash, even in cases where the cash is subsequently reinvested in replacement assets.
33	Applying FASB Statement No. 34 to Oil- and Gas-Producing Operations	Specifies the conditions under which an oil- and gas-producing operation whose assets are accounted for under the full cost method may capitalize interest costs.
34	Disclosure of Indirect Guarantees of Indebtedness of Others	Specifies that the disclosure requirements noted in FASB Statement No. 5 for guarantees of indebtedness must also be used for indirect guarantees.
35	Criteria for Applying the Equity Method of Accounting for Investments in Common Stock	Describes the conditions under which the equity method of accounting should be used to account for an investor's stake in an investee's voting stock of 50 percent or less.
36	Accounting for Exploratory Wells in Progress at the End of a Period	Notes that the costs incurred through the end of a reporting period for an exploratory well that is discovered to be a dry hole prior to the date of statement issuance shall be charged to expense within the period.
37	Accounting for Translation Adjustment Upon Sale of Part of an Investment in a Foreign Entity	Holds that an accumulated foreign currency translation adjustment be recognized upon the sale of part of an investment in a foreign entity in proportion to the amount of the investment being disposed of.
38	Determining the Measurement Date for Stock Option, Purchase, and Award Plans Involving Junior Stock	Specifies that the measurement date for award plans involving junior stock is the date when it is known the exact amount of the common stock for which the junior stock can be exchanged.
39	Offsetting of Amounts Related to Certain Contracts	Defines the right of setoff under which an accountant may net assets and liabilities on the balance sheet, as well as its applicability to conditional or exchange contracts.
40	Applicability of Generally Accepted Accounting Principles to Mutual Life Insurance and Other Enterprises	Requires that mutual life insurance and other enterprises cannot state that they have prepared financial statements in accordance with GAAP in cases where they have actually diverted from GAAP in order to comply with other regulatory accounting practices.

Exhibit 4.3 Summary of Current FASB Interpretations *(continued)*

Number	Title	Description
41	Offsetting of Amounts Related to Certain Repurchase and Reverse Repurchase Agreements	Modifies FASB Interpretation No. 39, regarding setoffs of assets and liabilities, to allow this practice in the statement of financial position for receivables and payables that are related to repurchase agreements and reverse repurchase agreements.
43	Real Estate Sales	States that sales of real estate with property improvements or integral equipment that cannot be removed and used separately from the real estate without incurring significant costs should be accounted for under FASB Statement No. 66, "Accounting for Sales of Real Estate."
44	Accounting for Certain Transactions Involving Stock Compensation	Narrows the use of APB No. 25 to just employees, and clarifies the rules for the grant of stock awards to employees of affiliates of the issuer.

EXHIBIT 4.3 SUMMARY OF CURRENT FASB INTERPRETATIONS *(CONTINUED)*

STATEMENTS OF FINANCIAL ACCOUNTING STANDARDS: FASB

The Statements listed in Exhibit 4.4 are considered to be the primary source of GAAP to the extent that they supersede any previous pronouncements, either by the FASB or any predecessor organization.

Number	Title	Description
2	Accounting for Research and Development Costs	Requires one to charge research and development costs to expense when they are incurred, and describes the disclosure of R&D information in the financial statements.
3	Reporting Accounting Changes in Interim Financial Statements	Describes the reporting requirements in interim financial statements in relation to changes to LIFO inventory costing, and to cumulative-effect types of accounting changes.
4	Reporting Gains and Losses from Extinguishment of Debt	Requires that gains and losses caused by a debt extinguishment shall be reported as an extraordinary item, if material. It also describes the disclosure requirements for such transactions.
5	Accounting for Contingencies	Describes how to account for loss contingencies, including the accrual of a loss contingency if there is a probability of loss and its amount can be reasonably estimated. Alternatively, gain contingencies can be recognized only when they have been realized.
6	Classification of Short-Term Obligations Expected to Be Refinanced	Allows an entity to reclassify its short-term debt as long-term debt, but only if it both intends to complete the required refinancing and has the ability to do so.
7	Accounting and Reporting by Development Stage Enterprises	Describes the types of entities that are considered to be in the development stage, and requires them to use the same accounting methods as those of established companies.

EXHIBIT 4.4 SUMMARY OF CURRENT STATEMENTS OF FINANCIAL ACCOUNTING STANDARDS

Number	Title	Description
10	Extension of "Grandfather" Provisions for Business Reporting	Extends the grandfather provisions of APB Opinion No. 16 that create an exemption from some criteria used to determine the applicability of the pooling of interests method of accounting for a business combination.
11	Accounting for Contingencies —Transition Method	Requires a company to restate its financial statements for preceding periods in order to comply with FASB Statement No. 5.
13	Accounting for Leases	Describes the proper accounting by both parties to a lease, including the determination and treatment of operating and capital leases by lessees, and the determination and treatment of sales type, direct financing, and leveraged leases by lessors.
15	Accounting by Debtors and Creditors for Troubled Debt Restructurings	Describes the proper accounting by both parties to a troubled debt restructuring, including modifications to the yield of a loan, and the circumstances under which gains or losses can be recognized.
16	Prior Period Adjustments	Allows prior-period adjustments only if there are material errors or if there are some income tax benefits associated with preacquisition loss carryforwards of a purchased entity.
18	Financial Reporting for Segments of a Business Enterprise—Interim Financial Statements	Stops the FASB Statement No. 14 requirement to report segment information for interim periods.
19	Financial Accounting and Reporting by Oil and Gas Producing Companies	Requires oil- and gas-producing companies to use the successful efforts method to account for the costs of producing mineral resources, as well as such issues as cost capitalization and amortization, property conveyances, income taxes, and financial statement disclosures.
21	Suspension of the Reporting of Earnings per Share and Segment Information by Nonpublic Enterprises	Suspends the requirement in APB Opinion No. 15 and FASB Statement No. 14 to report segment information, but only for nonpublic entities.
22	Changes in the Provisions of Lease Agreements	Requires the current recognition of a gain or loss when new debt proceeds are used to retire existing debt, under certain provisions.
23	Inception of the Lease	Alters the lease inception date to the date of lease agreement or any earlier commitment in cases where the property to be covered by a lease has not yet been purchased or constructed.
24	Reporting Segment Information in Financial Statements that Are Presented in Another Enterprise's Financial Report	Eliminates the requirement to present segment information in some instances where additional entity financial statements are presented alongside consolidated statements.
25	Suspension of Certain Accounting Requirements for Oil and Gas Producing Companies	Suspends the use of some provisions of FASB Statement No. 19 due to some variations between that statement and SEC reporting requirements.
27	Classification of Renewals or Extensions of Existing Sales-Type or Direct Financing Leases	Requires a lessor to classify a lease as a sales-type lease if it is an extension of an existing sales-type or direct-financing lease.

EXHIBIT 4.4   SUMMARY OF CURRENT STATEMENTS OF FINANCIAL ACCOUNTING STANDARDS *(CONTINUED)*

Number	Title	Description
28	Accounting for Sales with Leasebacks	Modifies FASB Statement No. 13 to allow the recognition of some profit or loss on sale and leaseback transactions if the seller has minimal usage of the property after the transaction, or if the sale profit exceeds the present value of minimum lease payments due.
29	Determining Contingent Rentals	Defines contingent rentals, as well as what payments should be included in the reporting of minimum lease payments due for this type of rental.
30	Disclosure of Information about Major Customers	Requires that an entity report the amount of sales made to a government entity if those sales are at least 10 percent of its total revenues.
34	Capitalization of Interest	Describes the rules for capitalizing interest costs in some situations where assets are being acquired, built, or modified, and how the rules will vary if the amount of interest to be capitalized is considered material or not.
35	Accounting and Reporting by Defined Benefit Pension Plans	Describes the rules for the annual financial statements associated with a defined-benefit pension plan, requiring the inclusion of such information as net assets available for benefits, changes in these benefits, and the present value of plan benefits.
42	Determining Materiality for Capitalization of Interest Cost	Deletes language from FASB Statement No. 34 that might be construed as allowing one to avoid interest capitalization, and also points out that the same statement does not contain new materiality tests.
43	Accounting for Compensated Absences	Specifies that a liability be accrued for the future absences of employees under certain circumstances.
44	Accounting for Intangible Assets of Motor Carriers	States that the unamortized intangible costs associated with a motor carrier's right to transport goods across state lines should be charged against income.
45	Accounting for Franchise Fee Revenue	Describes the primary accounting concepts for franchisors, including the proper treatment of franchise fee costs and revenues, commingled revenue, agency sales, repossessed franchises, and continuing product sales.
47	Disclosure of Long-Term Obligations	Describes the financial disclosures needed in cases where there are unconditional purchase obligations and future payments on long-term borrowings and redeemable stock.
48	Revenue Recognition When Right of Return Exists	Allows revenue recognition for transactions involving a right of return only if a set of minimum conditions are met.
49	Accounting for Product Financing Arrangements	Defines a product-financing arrangement, and requires that it be accounted for as a borrowing transaction, instead of a sale.
50	Financial Reporting in the Record and Music Industry	Describes the accounting practices for both licensors and licensees in the music and recording industry, including revenue recognition for licensing fees, minimum license guarantees, artist compensation, and other costs.
51	Financial Reporting by Cable Television Companies	Describes how to account for the revenues and expenses related to cable television systems, both while under construction, in the prematurity period, and when in operation.

EXHIBIT 4.4   SUMMARY OF CURRENT STATEMENTS OF FINANCIAL ACCOUNTING STANDARDS *(CONTINUED)*

Number	Title	Description
52	Foreign Currency Translation	Describes the treatment of foreign currency translation adjustments in accordance with the operating status of a foreign subsidiary, as well as the treatment of foreign currency transactions with other entities.
54	Financial Reporting and Changing Prices: Investment Companies	Avoids the previous requirements in FASB Statement No. 33 which requires investment companies to make disclosures regarding the effects of changing prices.
57	Related-Party Disclosures	Describes the rules to follow when reporting on related-party transactions.
58	Capitalization of Interest Cost in Financial Statements that Include Investments Accounted for by the Equity Method	Limits the capitalization of interest costs on an investor's financial statements in a limited number of situations involving the use of the equity method of accounting for an investment in another business entity.
60	Accounting and Reporting by Insurance Companies	Describes the reporting to be used for insurance entities in relation to the treatment of contracts, premiums, claims, and investments.
61	Accounting for Title Plant	Requires that costs incurred to build a title plant be capitalized until activated, and also specifies the treatment of maintenance expenses that are incurred thereafter.
62	Capitalization of Interest Costs in Situations Involving Certain Tax-Exempt Borrowings and Certain Gifts and Grants	Specifies situations in which interest costs are to be capitalized, as well as situations where the capitalization of interest costs is *not* allowed.
63	Financial Reporting by Broadcasters	Describes the reporting requirements for broadcasters, including treatment of exhibition rights, license agreements, barter transactions, and network affiliation agreements.
64	Extinguishment of Debt Made to Satisfy Sinking Fund Requirements	Specifies that the classification of gains or losses that result from the extinguishment of debt that is required by a sinking fund need not be reported as extraordinary items.
65	Accounting for Certain Mortgage Bank Activities	Specifies that mortgage loans and similar loans be reported at the lower of cost or market. It also notes the treatment of loan origination and commitment fees, loan placement fees, and premiums paid to service loans.
66	Accounting for Sales on Real Estate	Describes the rules for recognizing the profitability of real estate sales. Different standards apply to land sales than to other types of sales, to which the percentage of completion or installment methods may be applied.
67	Accounting for Costs and Initial Rental Operations of Real Estate Projects	Sets forth the rules regarding the types of costs that may be capitalized in relation to real estate projects, as well as the point after which costs may no longer be capitalized.
68	Research and Development Arrangements	Describes the accounting for research and development activities that are performed by a company for other entities. If there is a repayment obligation, its amount must be recorded as a liability.
69	Disclosures about Oil- and Gas- Producing Activities	Describes the disclosures required by oil- and gas-producing entities, and reduces or eliminates many of the disclosures by those entities that are not publicly held.

EXHIBIT 4.4 SUMMARY OF CURRENT STATEMENTS OF FINANCIAL ACCOUNTING STANDARDS *(CONTINUED)*

Number	Title	Description
71	Accounting for the Effects of Certain Types of Regulation	Describes the accounting by most types of public utilities for regulation of the variety that allows utilities to set prices that will recover the cost of and capital cost of services provided.
72	Accounting for Certain Acquisitions of Banking or Thrift Institutions	Requires that the fair value of liabilities assumed in the acquisition of a bank or thrift entity over the fair value of acquired assets be amortized by the interest method. Also, any financial assistance obtained from a regulatory agency as part of the combination shall be recorded as an asset if the amount of the receipt can be determined and is likely to be received.
73	Reporting a Change in Accounting for Railroad Track Structures	Requires that railroads change their reporting of depreciation for railroad track structures, including a restatement of this information in prior reporting years.
78	Classification of Obligations that Are Callable by the Creditor	Requires that long-term liabilities callable by creditors be classified as current liabilities on the balance sheet, subject to some qualifications.
79	Elimination of Certain Disclosures for Business Combinations by Nonpublic Enterprises	Eliminates APB Opinion No. 16's requirement for nonpublic entities to report *pro forma* results of combinations under the purchase method.
84	Induced Conversions of Convertible Debt	Requires that the debtor recognize an expense equal to the fair value of any extra consideration given to creditors in order to persuade them to convert their convertible debt holdings to equity.
85	Yield Test for Determining Whether a Convertible Security Is a Common Stock Equivalent	Replaces the cash yield test as previously specified in APB Opinion No. 15 with the effective yield test to determine if convertible securities shall be designated common stock equivalents for the purpose of computing primary earnings per share.
86	Accounting for the Costs of Computer Software to Be Sold, Leased, or Otherwise Marketed	States that software development costs shall be expensed as research and development costs prior to the point when technological feasibility has been proven, after which they may be capitalized and then amortized over the remaining estimated life of the product.
87	Employers' Accounting for Pensions	Establishes new standards for the treatment of pension accounting, superseding previous releases. The primary change is the accounting for a single-employer defined-benefit pension plan.
88	Employers' Accounting for Settlements and Curtailments of Defined Pension Benefit Plans and for Termination Benefits	Describes the accounting for the settlement of obligations under a defined-benefit pension plan, termination benefits, and the curtailment of such a plan. It also defines settlement and curtailment.
89	Financial Reporting and Changing Prices	Replaces FASB Statement No. 33 and its later amendments. It also specifies that the disclosure of current cost and constant purchasing power information is voluntary.

EXHIBIT 4.4 SUMMARY OF CURRENT STATEMENTS OF FINANCIAL ACCOUNTING STANDARDS *(CONTINUED)*

Number	Title	Description
90	Regulated Enterprises— Accounting for Abandonments and Disallowances of Plant Costs	Describes the accounting for abandonments of utility plants, as well as the disallowance of plant costs by regulators for the calculation of rate changes. Abandoned assets that are to be included in rate-making calculations should be included at their present value, while disallowed costs should be recognized as a loss.
91	Accounting for Nonrefundable Fees and Costs Associated with Originating or Acquiring Loans	Describes how to account for the costs related to lending, or buying a loan, as well as costs related to leasing activities.
92	Regulated Enterprises— Accounting for Phase-In Plans	Modifies FASB Statement No. 71 to account for phase-in plans, which are intended to reduce the impact of utility rate increases that are tied to the implementation of expensive new power-generation facilities.
93	Recognition of Depreciation by Not-for-Profit Organizations	Requires that not-for-profit organizations disclose depreciation information, though not for some types of art or historical treasures.
94	Consolidation of All Majority-Owned Subsidiaries	Requires that majority-owned subsidiaries be included in the corporate parent's financial statements on a consolidated basis unless there is no control or control is temporary.
95	Statement of Cash Flows	Describes a new format for cash flow reporting that replaces the statement of changes in financial position and which is to be a key part of all financial statements. It categorizes cash flows by operating, investing, and financing activities.
97	Accounting and Reporting by Insurance Enterprises for Certain Long-Duration Contracts and for Realized Gains and Losses from the Sale of Investments	Describes the accounting for universal life–type contracts, as well as for limited-payment long-duration insurance contracts and investment contracts. It also revises the reporting for realized gains and losses that was originally itemized in FASB Statement No. 60.
98	Accounting for Leases: Sale-Leaseback Transactions Involving Real Estate, Sales-Type Leases of Real Estate, Definition of the Lease Term, and Initial Direct Costs of Direct Financing Leases	Itemizes the types of accounting required by the parties to a sale-leaseback transaction, while also modifying a number of issues originally set forth in FASB Statement No. 13.
99	Deferral of Effective Date of Recognition of Depreciation by Not-for-Profit Organizations	Changes the effective date of FASB Statement No. 93 to fiscal years beginning on or after January 1, 1990.
101	Regulated Enterprises— Accounting for Discontinuation of Application of FASB Statement No. 71	Specifies how a company should report in its financial statements that it is no longer subject to certain types of regulation, including the elimination of any actions by regulators that had been itemized as assets or liabilities in previous financial reports. The profit impact of any such changes should be recorded in the current period as extraordinary items.

Exhibit 4.4 Summary of Current Statements of Financial Accounting Standards *(continued)*

Number	Title	Description
102	Statement of Cash Flows— Exemption of Certain Enterprises and Classification of Cash Flows from Certain Securities Acquired for Resale	Exempts some employee benefit plans and certain types of investment companies from following the dictates of FASB Statement No. 95, regarding the presentation of a statement of cash flows.
104	Statement of Cash Flows—Net Reporting of Certain Cash Receipts and Cash Payments and Classification of Cash Flows from Hedging Transactions	Allows banks and similar entities to report in a statement of cash flows some cash flows related to deposits and loans.
106	Employers' Accounting for Postretirement Benefits Other than Pensions	Requires that postretirement health care benefits be accounted for by accruing the expected cost of future benefits at the time when employees are still working for the company.
107	Disclosures about Fair Value of Financial Instruments	Requires all organizations to itemize the fair value of all financial instruments in the statement of financial position, if this information can be determined.
109	Accounting for Income Taxes	Outlines the bases and resulting rules upon which one should account for income taxes, focusing on an asset and liability approach to the presentation of income tax information.
110	Reporting by Defined-Benefit Pension Plans of Investment Contracts	Mandates that an investment contract held by a defined-benefit pension plan be stated at its fair value, while only contracts including mortality risk can be recorded at their contract value.
111	Rescission of FASB Statement No. 32 and Technical Corrections	Rescinds FASB Statement No. 32, and also makes technical corrections to several other documents.
112	Employers' Accounting for Postemployment Benefits	Requires that the liability associated with postemployment benefits be recognized if several requirements are met, as well as that the amount of the liability can be reasonably estimated and it is probable that a liability has been incurred.
113	Accounting and Reporting for Reinsurance of Short-Duration and Long-Duration Contracts	Describes how insurance entities should account for the reinsuring of insurance contracts, requiring reinsurance receivables and prepaid reinsurance premiums to be reported as assets.
114	Accounting by Creditors for Impairment of a Loan	Describes the proper accounting for the impairment of some types of loans by creditors, requiring that these loans be recorded at their discounted present values.
115	Accounting for Certain Investments in Debt and Equity Securities	Describes the different types of reporting for debt and equity securities. Debt that is intended to be held to maturity is reported at amortized cost, while both debt and equity securities to be sold in the near term are reported at fair value, with unrealized gains or losses included in current earnings. Finally, debt and equity that falls into neither category is reported at fair value, with any unrealized gains or losses reported in shareholders' equity.

EXHIBIT 4.4 SUMMARY OF CURRENT STATEMENTS OF FINANCIAL ACCOUNTING STANDARDS *(CONTINUED)*

Number	Title	Description
116	Accounting for Contributions Received and Contributions Made	Describes the standards to be used when making or receiving contributions. Essentially, contributions are made and received at their fair value, while conditional contributions are recognized only when all associated conditions have essentially been met.
117	Financial Statements of Not-for-Profit Organizations	Describes the reporting format to be used by not-for-profit organizations.
118	Accounting by Creditors for Impairment of a Loan—Income Recogniztion and Disclosures	Modifies FASB Statement No. 114 to allow creditors to use existing methods for recognizing interest income on an impaired loan.
120	Accounting and Reporting by Mutual Life Insurance Enterprises asnd by Insurance Enterprises for Certain Long-Duration Participating Contracts	Increases the coverage of FASB Statements Nos. 60, 97, and 113 to assessment enterprises, fraternal benefit societies, and mutual life insurance organizations.s
121	Accounting for the Impairment of Long-Lived Assets and for Long-Lived Assets to be Disposed of	Describes how to account for the impairment or disposition of long-lived assets, some identifiable intangibles, and goodwill related to those assets. The basic requirement is to periodically review these assets for impairment by comparing expected future cash flows to their carrying value.
123	Accounting for Stock Compensation	Describes the required reporting for employee compensation plans that include the use of company stock, such as stock appreciation rights, stock options, stock purchase plans, and restricted stock.
124	Accounting for Certain Investments Held by Not-for-Profit Organizations	Describes how not-for-profit organizations must use fair value when reporting on equity securities whose fair values can be determined, as well as all investments in debt securities.
125	Transfers of Financial Assets and Extinguishment of Liabilities	Describes the reporting requirements related to the transfer of financial assets and the extinguishment of liabilities through the recognition of those financial assets under a business's control and derecognizing both those over which control no longer exists and those liabilities that have been extinguished.
126	Exemption from Certain Required Disclosures about Financial Instruments for Certain Nonpublic Entities	Modifies FASB Statement No. 107 to make the reporting requirements in that document optional if the business is nonpublic, its total assets are less than $100 million, and the business has not been involved with any derivative-related transactions during the reporting period.
127	Deferral of the Effective Date of Certain Provisions of FASB Statement No. 125	Adds new criteria to those listed in FASB Statement No. 125 for determining whether a sale or a pledge of collateral for debt has occurred when a transfer of assets arises. It also describes how to account for pledged collateral.

EXHIBIT 4.4 SUMMARY OF CURRENT STATEMENTS OF FINANCIAL ACCOUNTING STANDARDS *(CONTINUED)*

Number	Title	Description
128	Earnings per Share	Describes how to compute and report on earnings per share information, replacing the use of primary earnings per share with basic earnings per share. Requires the use of a dual presentation of basic and diluted earnings per share if a business has a complex capital structure.
129	Disclosures of Information about Capital Structure	Itemizes the standards for reporting a business's capital structure, and spreads this requirement to nonpublic businesses.
130	Reporting Comprehensive Income	Describes how to report comprehensive income, as well as related revenues and expenses in the financial statements.
131	Disclosures about Segments of Enterprise and Related Information	Replaces FASB Statement No. 14; describes reporting requirements about operating segments, products and services, geographic area, and major customers, both in annual and interim financial statements. This is not applicable to not-for-profit and nonpublic businesses.
132	Employers' Disclosures about Pensions and Other Postretirement Benefits	Describes the types of disclosures required for employers' pension and related retirement plans, which include information about changes in benefit obligations, as well as the fair values of plan assets. It also allows nonpublic companies to have reduced reporting requirements.
133	Accounting for Derivative Instruments and Hedging Activities	Requires that a business entity recognize all derivatives within the statement of financial position, and that they be measured at their fair value. This Statement encompasses the use of derivatives that are embedded in other types of contracts.
134	Accounting for Mortgage-Backed Securities Retained After the Securitization of Mortgage Loans Held for Sale by a Mortgage Banking Enterprise	Modifies paragraphs 4 and 6 of Statement No. 65 (Accounting for Certain Mortgage Bank Activities) and paragraph 12(a) of Statement No. 115 (Accounting for Certain Investments in Debt and Equity Securities).
135	Rescission of FASB Statement No. 75 and Technical Corrections	Rescinds Statement No. 75 (Deferral of the Effective Date of Certain Accounting Requirements for Pension Plans of State and Local Governmental Entities) in favor of GASB Statement No. 25. It also excludes benefit pension plans sponsored by government entities from the scope of Statement No. 35.
136	Transfers of Assets to a Not-for-Profit Organization or Charitable Trust that Raises or Holds Contributions for Others	Describes the proper accounting for transactions where a donor contributes assets to a not-for-profit entity that then shifts the assets to a donor-specified third beneficiary.
137	Accounting for Derivative Instruments and Hedging Activities—Deferral of the Effective Date of FASB Statement No. 133	Amends paragraphs 48 and 50 of Statement No. 133.

EXHIBIT 4.4 SUMMARY OF CURRENT STATEMENTS OF FINANCIAL ACCOUNTING STANDARDS *(CONTINUED)*

Number	Title	Description
138	Accounting for Certain Derivative Instruments and Certain Hedging Activities—An Amendment of FASB Statement No. 133	As noted in the title. It is effective for all fiscal quarters and years beginning after June 15, 2000.
139	Rescission of FASB Statement No. 53 and Amendments to FASB Statements Nos. 63, 89, and 121	Substitutes Statement of Position No. 00-2 (Accounting by Producers or Distributors of Films) for FASB Statement No. 53. It also revises earlier FASB statements related to accounting by broadcasters, changing prices, and the impairment or disposition of long-lived assets. It should be applied to all fiscal years beginning after December 15, 2000.
140	Accounting for Transfers and Servicing of Financial Assets and Extinguishments of Liabilities	Describes the accounting standards to be used for transactions related to the transfer and servicing of financial assets, as well as the extinguishment of liabilities. It retains most of Statement No. 125's pronouncements, but revises the rules for accounting for securitizations and related transfers of financial assets.
141	Business Combinations	Describes the use of the purchase method of accounting to account for business combinations; it eliminates the use of the pooling of interests method of accounting.
142	Goodwill and Other Intangible Assets	Describes how to report intangible assets in the financial statements, though not intangible assets acquired through a business combination. It also notes how intangible assets should be accounted for on an ongoing basis.

EXHIBIT 4.4   SUMMARY OF CURRENT STATEMENTS OF FINANCIAL ACCOUNTING STANDARDS *(CONTINUED)*

STATEMENTS OF FINANCIAL ACCOUNTING CONCEPTS: FASB

The seven Concepts standards that have been listed in Exhibit 4.5 issued by the FASB (of which No. 3 has been superseded) are designed to provide the accountant with a background for the understanding of accounting standards.

Number	Title	Description
1	Objectives of Financial Reporting by Business Enterprises	Specifies that financial reporting is designed to allow one to predict cash flows, entity resources and how they are used, and information that the reader can use to make economic decisions.
2	Qualitative Characteristics of Accounting Information	Specifies that accounting information should be comparable and consistent between periods, as well as understandable, reliable, and relevant.

EXHIBIT 4.5   SUMMARY OF CURRENT STATEMENTS OF FINANCIAL ACCOUNTING CONCEPTS

Number	Title	Description
4	Objectives of Financial Reporting by Non-business Organizations	Establishes the objectives of financial reporting by nonbusiness organizations, which are similar to those for business organizations. It defines nonbusiness organizations, identifies transactions common to them that are uncommon for business organizations, and notes that financial reports for these entities should provide additional information about the level of services provided and the quality of stewardship by managers.
5	Recognition and Measurement in Financial Statements of Business Enterprises	Specifies the types of information to include in financial statements, and the timing of its presentation.
6	Elements of Financial Statements	Defines the core elements to be found in financial statements, which are comprehensive income, revenue, expenses, gains, losses, owner investments, owner distributions, assets, liabilities, and equity.
7	Using Cash Flow Information and Present Value in Accounting Measurements	Describes why and when present value, fair value, and the interest rate method for amortization are used to provide valuations, and how future cash flows can be used to determine this information.

EXHIBIT 4.5   SUMMARY OF CURRENT STATEMENTS OF FINANCIAL ACCOUNTING CONCEPTS *(CONTINUED)*

TECHNICAL BULLETINS: FASB

Technical Bulletins, summarized in Exhibit 4.6, are intended to clarify or elaborate on underlying accounting standards. They typically address narrow subject areas that are not directly addressed by existing accounting standards; part of the resulting discussion may lead to some variations from GAAP that are targeted only at the tightly defined areas that are directly addressed by the Technical Bulletins. Any such changes are not expected to create major variations from current GAAP, nor should they be costly to implement.

Number	Title	Description
79-1	Purpose and Scope of FASB Technical Bulletins and Procedures for Issuance	Notes that technical bulletins are intended to provide guidance in applying the opinions, statements, and interpretations previously issued by both the FASB and its predecessors, as well as to address issues not directly covered by those GAAP standards.
79-3	Subjective Acceleration Clauses in Long-Term Debt Agreements	Does not authorize the restatement of long-term debt as short-term debt in situations where there are subjective acceleration clauses in debt agreements, and where there is little likelihood of acceleration.
79-4	Segment Reporting of Puerto Rican Operations	Specifies that a domestic corporation's Puerto Rican operations should be considered part of its domestic operations, and not a foreign entity.

EXHIBIT 4.6   SUMMARY OF CURRENT FASB TECHNICAL BULLETINS

Number	Title	Description
79-5	Meaning of the Term "Customer" as it Applies to Health Care Facilities Under FASB Statement No. 14	Specifies that an insuring entity is not a customer of a health care facility, for the purposes of reporting on customers who represent at least 10 percent of an entity's business.
79-9	Accounting in Interim Periods for Changes in Income Tax Rates	Specifies the method for determining the reduction in the corporate tax rate resulting from the Revenue Act of 1978 for those entities not using a calendar year as their fiscal year.
79-10	Fiscal Funding Clauses in Lease Agreements	Specifies that the presence of a fiscal funding clause will not result in a lease being considered cancelable if the probability of the clause being invoked is remote.
79-12	Interest Rate Used in Calculating the Present Value of Minimum Lease Payments	Allows a business to use its secured borrowing rate when determining the present value of minimum lease payments, as long as that rate is reasonable and would be representative of the type of financing used for the lease.
79-13	Applicability of FASB Statement No. 13 to Current Value Financial Statements	Requires that the provisions of FASB Statement No. 13 be applied to financial statements that have been prepared on a current value basis.
79-14	Upward Adjustment of Guaranteed Residual Values	Prohibits the use of upward adjustments of estimated residual values resulting from renegotiations of the guaranteed portions of residual values.
79-15	Accounting for Loss on a Sublease Not Involving the Disposal of a Segment	Describes a loss on a sublease, and specifies that it be recognized as soon as it is expected to be incurred.
79-16	Effect of a Change in Income Tax Rate on the Accounting for Leveraged Leases	Requires that the income effect of a change in the statutory tax rate be recognized in the period immediately after the change becomes law.
79-17	Reporting Cumulative Effect Adjustment from Retroactive Application of FASB No. 13	States that the cumulative effect of modifying financial statements to comply with the provisions of FASB Statement No. 13 should not be included in the net income of any presented year unless the year prior to the earliest year presented could not be restated.
79-18	Transition Requirements of Certain FASB Amendments and Interpretations of FASB Statement No. 13	Describes the financial reporting and disclosure requirements associated with the changes required by FASB Statement No. 13.
80-1	Early Extinguishment of Debt Through Exchange for Common or Preferred Stock	Notes that the provisions of APB Opinion No. 26 do apply to the extinguishment of debt through the issuance of common or preferred stock, and also describes its presentation in the financial statements.
80-2	Classification of Debt Restructurings by Debtors and Creditors	Allows different accounting interpretations of the presence of a troubled debt restructuring by debtors and creditors.

EXHIBIT 4.6 SUMMARY OF CURRENT FASB TECHNICAL BULLETINS *(CONTINUED)*

Number	Title	Description
81-6	Applicability of Statement No. 15 to Debtors in Bankruptcy Situations	Specifies that FASB Statement No. 15, which describes troubled debt restructurings, does not apply to bankrupt companies that restructure their debt as part of a general restructuring of all of their liabilities, but does apply if there is not a general restatement of the debtor's liabilities.
82-1	Disclosure of the Sale or Purchase of Tax Benefits Through Tax Leases	Requires that a company engaged in the sale or purchase of tax benefits through tax leases disclose the method of accounting for them, as well as the methods used to recognize revenue and allocate income tax benefits and asset costs to both current and future periods.
84-1	Accounting for Stock Issued to Acquire the Results of a Research and Development Arrangement	Requires that stock exchanged for the results of a research and development arrangement be recorded at either its fair market value or the fair value of the consideration received.
85-1	Accounting for the Receipt of Federal Home Loan Mortgage Corporation Participating Preferred Stock	Requires that the 12 district banks of the Federal Home Loan Banking System record the receipt of participating preferred stock from the Federal Home Loan Mortgage Corporation at its fair value as of the date of receipt, with any resulting income being recorded as an extraordinary item.
85-3	Accounting for Operating Leases with Scheduled Rent Increases	Requires that scheduled rent increases be recognized on a straight-line basis over the lease term unless there is another systematic allocation system available that better represents the time pattern during which the leased property is being used.
85-4	Accounting for Purchases of Life Insurance	Specifies that life insurance be reported as an asset, with the change in cash surrender value during the period being offset against payments made in order to determine the amount of the insurance expense.
85-5	Issues Relating to Accounting for Business Combinations	Specifies that the costs incurred to close duplicate facilities as a result of a business combination shall be charged to expense, and shall not be included in the accounting for the business combination.
85-6	Accounting for a Purchase of Treasury Shares at a Price Significantly in Excess of the Current Market Price of the Shares and the Income Statement Classification of Costs Incurred in Defending Against a Takeover Attempt	Specifies that if Treasury stock is acquired at a price significantly higher than its market price, the difference should be accounted for as being consideration for other services provided by the company, unless no other consideration can be identified. Also notes that corporate payments to a shareholder for a standstill agreement be charged to current expense. Also, any costs incurred to defend against a takeover attempt should be charged to operating expenses, not extraordinary expenses.
86-2	Accounting for an Interest in the Residual Value of a Leased Asset	Requires that an unconditional right to own a leased asset at the end of the lease term requires the lessee to account for it as an asset. It also discusses the valuation of the residual value of leased assets for lessees, lessors, and lease brokers.
87-2	Computation of a Loss on a Abandonment	Describes the accounting for deferred income taxes associated with abandonments and the assets remaining thereafter, with separate treatment for regulated entities.

Exhibit 4.6   Summary of Current FASB Technical Bulletins *(continued)*

Number	Title	Description
87-3	Accounting for Mortgage Servicing Fees and Rights	Describes the accounting treatment for the impact of estimated future net servicing income from a refinanced loan on the amortization of capitalized costs related to the acquisition of the mortgage servicing rights for the superseded loan.
88-1	Issues Relating to Accounting for Leases	Describes the proper accounting treatment of leasing issues related to incentives in an operating lease, wrap lease transactions, money-over-money lease transactions, the time pattern of the physical use of operating lease property, and the applicability of leveraged lease accounting to a lessor's existing assets.
90-1	Accounting for Separately Priced Extended Warranty and Product Maintenance Contracts	Specifies that income from a separately priced warranty or maintenance agreement be amortized to income on a straight-line basis over the term of the agreement, except in situations where there is historical proof that some other amortization schedule would more accurately reflect the incurrence of related costs, and also describes the proper treatment of losses on such contracts.
94-1	Application of Statement No. 115 to Debt Securities in a Troubled Debt Restructuring	Specifies that any restructured loans arising from a troubled debt restructuring are subject to the provisions of FASB Statement No. 115 if it meets the definition of a "security" as defined in that Statement.
97-1	Accounting Under Statement No. 123 for Certain Employee Stock Purchase Plans with a Look-Back Option	Describes the situations in which the fair value measurement technique is used to value awards under various types of employee stock purchase plans with look-back provisions.

EXHIBIT 4.6 SUMMARY OF CURRENT FASB TECHNICAL BULLETINS *(CONTINUED)*

SUMMARIZING GAAP

The vast number of GAAP documents cited in this chapter does not even begin to include all sources of GAAP! The new controller may rightly feel overwhelmed by the mass of GAAP information to sort through, especially since some earlier documents have been fully or partially superseded. To avoid information overload, get on the subscription list for the annual release of *GAAP: Interpretation and Application* (Hoboken: John Wiley & Sons). This contains a summarization of all key aspects of GAAP, and is the single most important book a controller can own.

5*

COST ACCOUNTING AND COSTING SYSTEMS

IMPORTANCE OF THIS CHAPTER

Though the new controller will initially be judged based on the quality and timeliness of his financial statements, he can bring considerable value to the company over the long term by a thorough knowledge of the cost accounting concepts described in this chapter. By applying different costing systems to different situations, there is an excellent opportunity to focus management attention on the systematic improvement of profitability.

Cost accounting is one of the most crucial aspects of the accounting profession, for it is the primary means by which the accounting department transmits company-related performance information to the management team. A properly organized cost accounting function can give valuable feedback regarding the impact of product pricing, cost trends, the performance of cost and profit centers, and production and personnel capacity, and can even contribute to some degree in the formulation of company strategy. Despite this wide array of uses, many controllers rarely give due consideration to the multitude of uses to which cost accounting can be put. Instead, they think only of how cost accounting will feed information into the financial statements. This orientation comes from a strong tendency in business schools to train students in generally accepted accounting principles (GAAP) and how they are used to create financial statements. In this chapter, we will focus on how one can collect data, summarize it, and report it to management with the goal of helping the management team to run the business.

---

* Adapted with permission from Chapter 26 of Steven M. Bragg, *Accounting Reference Desktop* (Hoboken: Wiley, 2002).

PURPOSE OF COST ACCOUNTING INFORMATION

The cost accounting function works best without any oversight rules and regulations, because, in accordance with its stated purpose of assisting management, it tends to result in hybrid systems that are custom-designed to meet specific company needs. For example, a company may find that a major requirement is to determine the incremental cost that it incurs for each additional unit of production, so that it can make accurate decisions regarding the price of incremental units sold (possibly at prices very close to the direct cost). If it were to use accounting standards, it would be constrained to only use a costing system that allocated a portion of overhead costs to product costs—even though these are not incremental costs. Accordingly, the cost accounting system used for this specific purpose will operate in contravention of GAAP, because following GAAP would yield results that do not assist management.

Because there are many different management decisions for which the cost accounting profession can provide valuable information, it is quite common to have several costing systems in place, each of which may use different costing guidelines. To extend the previous example, the incremental costing system used for incremental pricing decisions may not be adequate for a different problem, which is creating profit centers that are used to judge the performance of individual managers. For this purpose, a second costing system must be devised that allocates costs from internal service centers to the various profit centers; in this instance, we are adding an allocation function to the incremental costing system that was already in place. Even more systems may be required for other applications, such as transfer pricing between company divisions and the costing of inventory for external financial reporting purposes (which does require attention to GAAP guidelines). Consequently, cost accounting frequently results in a multitude of costing systems, which may follow GAAP guidelines only by accident. The controller's primary concern is whether the information resulting from each system adequately meets the needs of the recipients.

Any cost accounting system is comprised of three functional areas: the collection of raw data, the processing of this data in accordance with a costing methodology, and the reporting of the resulting information to management in the most understandable format. The remainder of this chapter is split into sections that address each of these three functional areas. The area that receives the most coverage is the processing function, for there are a number of different methodologies available, each of which applies to different situations. For example, job costing is used for situations where specifically identifiable goods are produced in batches, while direct costing is most applicable in situations where management does not want to see any overhead allocation attached to the directly identifiable costs of a product. The large number of processing methodologies presented here is indicative of the broad range of options available to the controller for processing raw data into various types of reports for management use.

INPUT: DATA COLLECTION SYSTEMS

The first step in setting up a data collection system is to determine what *types* of data to gather. One can simply collect every conceivable type of data available, but this will result in immensely detailed and cumbersome collection systems that are expensive and require a great deal of employee time to collect and record. A better approach is to determine what types of outputs are required, which can then be used to ascertain the specific data items needed to create those outputs. This allows the controller to ignore many types of data, simply because no one needs them. However, the process of determining data requirements from projected outputs must be revisited on a regular basis, for changes in the business will require changes in the required cost accounting reports, and therefore changes in the types of data collected.

The process of backtracking from a required output to a set of required data elements is best illustrated with an example. If a company is manufacturing a set of products whose components and assembly are entirely outsourced, then it is logical to create management reports that focus on the prices being charged to the company by its suppliers, rather than creating an elaborate time recording system for the small number of quality inspectors who are responsible for reviewing completed goods before they are shipped out to customers. In this case, the bulk of the data used by the costing system will come out of the accounts payable and purchasing records. Another example is a software company, where the costing focus is on the labor time charged to specific development projects and the ability of project managers to meet their deadlines, rather than on the minor cost of purchasing compact disks, packaging, and training materials that are shipped to customers. In this case, most of the cost accounting data will come from the timekeeping and project-tracking databases. Thus, the nature of the business will drive the decision to collect certain types of data.

Once the controller knows what data to collect, there is still the issue of creating a data accumulation system. There are several factors that will influence this decision. One is *cost*; if there are many employees who will be recording information continuously, then the unit cost of the data collection device cannot be too expensive, or else its total cost will exceed the utility of the collected data. Another issue is *data accuracy;* if the data collected absolutely, positively must be correct, then a more elaborate solution, such as bar code scanning, which is designed to yield superaccurate results, should be the preferred solution. However, if the level of required accuracy is lower, then perhaps manual keypunch entry or handwritten data sheets would be acceptable. Another factor is the *employees* who will use the data collection systems; if they are highly trained, then they can be relied on to use complex keypunching systems, whereas a poorly trained work force that has no idea of what data it is collecting, or why it is being used, should be allowed to collect only data that will be heavily cross-checked for errors. Of additional concern is the *timeliness* of the data collected. If there is a need for up-to-the-minute transmission of data to managers, then the only solution will be some form of automated data gathering. On the other hand, only an occasional report to management may require a slower manual data gathering approach. Another factor to consider is the *existing level of automation* within the company. For example, if there is a clear production path for all products that sends every completed item down a specific conveyor belt, then the installation of a fixed bar code scanner on that conveyor is a reasonable approach for recording data about production quantities. However, this would be a poor solution if products were being hand-carried away from a multitude of production processes to the warehouse, since many of the items created would never pass by the bar code scanner. A final consideration is the *production methodology* currently in use. If it is a lean manufacturing system, such as *just-in-time,* there will be a strong orientation away from requiring employees to conduct any data entry work, since extremely focused and efficient workflows are the key to success in this environment—which is interrupted if data entry tasks are included. In these cases, one should avoid any type of manual data entry, focusing instead on more automated approaches.

Given the above parameters, it is clear that the controller must devise a wide array of data collection tools in order to collect data in the most appropriate manner. The following bullet points describe a number of the more common (and upcoming) data collection tools:

- *Punch clocks.* A data collection tool that is proving to have a great deal of longevity is the punch clock. This is used by hourly employees to record the times when they arrive for work and leave at the end of the day. The process is a simple one; take your time card from a storage rack, insert it into the top of the clock, which stamps the time on it, and return your card to the storage rack. The payroll staff then uses these cards to calculate payroll. The greatest advantage of this approach is that a time clock is very inexpensive. However, it requires conversion of the time card data by the payroll staff into another format before it can be used, which introduces the likelihood of computational errors. Also, it is difficult to use for recording time worked on specific jobs.

• *Electronic time clocks.* This clock allows employees to swipe a badge through a reader on the side or top of the clock. This results in a computer entry for the time of the scan, which is also associated with the employee code that is embedded in the card, through the use of either a bar code or a magnetic stripe. A more advanced version uses the biometric measurement of the outlines of one's hand to determine the identity of the employee (thereby eliminating the need for an employee badge, which might otherwise be lost or used to make a scan for someone who is not on the premises). This represents a significant advance over the punch clock, because there is no need for secondary calculations that might result in an error. It also yields greater control over the time-recording process, since it gives immediate feedback to supervisors regarding missed or late scans. An additional benefit is that employees can enter job numbers as part of the scanning process, so that time is charged to specific jobs. However, the electronic time clock costs up to $2,000 each, and so is usually restricted to high-volume applications where there are many employees—punch clocks are therefore only used in high-volume locations where they are more cost-effective.

QUESTION THE NEED FOR LABOR DATA COLLECTION

In many manufacturing organizations, the direct labor staff does not vary its hours any more than does the overhead staff. They are present if there is manufacturing work to do, and they are still on site if work is slow. Thus, they are a fixed cost, not variable. Also, direct labor tends to be a small proportion of total product costs. Given these issues, the new controller should question the need for installing expensive labor tracking systems.

• *Bar code scanners.* A bar code scanner is a device that reads bar code labels with either a fixed or rapidly rotating laser beam, and converts the bar code symbology into a character-based format that is then stored in the computer system. These scanners come in many shapes and sizes, ranging from a $100 fixed-beam scanner that looks like a pen (but which may require a number of scans to read a bar code) to a $10,000 fixed-position scanner that is bolted to a conveyor belt, and which emits 30 scans per second as bar-coded packages move past it. There are also portable scanners, which are heavily used in warehousing operations, that can store scanned information in local RAM memory for later uploading to a computer, or that contain direct radio frequency access to the company computer, and can therefore transmit the data immediately. The type of scanner purchased will depend on the level of automation required, and the budget available for this purpose. Bar code scanning is highly recommended for repetitive data entry situations where the *same* data is collected many times. On the other hand, it is of less use where the data collected changes constantly, or involves a large quantity of text that would require an extremely large bar code. Nonetheless, some portion of most data entry applications can involve the use of bar code scanning.

- *Terminal data entry.* An increasingly common form of data entry is to not use any new data collection devices—instead, just buy lots more computer terminals and make them available to users throughout the company. Employees can then be given direct access to the computer screens that require input from them, and can enter information directly into the computer system. This avoids the middleman data entry person, as well as the risk that the data entry staff might misinterpret the data on an employee's form and type in the wrong information. The process can be facilitated by the use of error-checking protocols within the computer software, so that users will be flagged if they make entries that are clearly outside of a narrow band of expected responses. Also, computer screens can be devised for individual users that are designed to assist them in entering only the data they have access to, and in the most efficient manner. However, it can be expensive to rig all locations in a company with computer terminals and all linking wiring, while some employees may move around so much that having them use a fixed terminal is not a viable option. Consequently, this approach may have limited applicability, depending on the situation.

- *Paper-based data entry.* Despite all of the other forms of advanced data entry noted here, the most common method for collecting data is still from a paper document. This approach is inexpensive, requires no web of interlinked electronic devices throughout a facility, and is familiar to all employees as a method of data capture. However, it does not result in a fast flow of data through an organization, since it may be days or weeks before the information contained on a form is re-keyed into the computer system. Also, it is easy to lose forms, especially when they are being used throughout a facility and there is no rigid tracking of individual forms to ensure that none are lost. Furthermore, this approach requires the services of an expensive data entry person to interpret the data on the forms (sometimes incorrectly) and type the results into the computer system. Given these problems, it is no surprise that the proportion of data gathering that uses this approach is shrinking—nonetheless, it still comprises the majority of all data gathering techniques in most organizations.

- *Electronic pen data entry.* A very new data gathering approach is the electronic pen. This is a pen that not only marks in ink on paper, but also tracks its exact position on a pad of "smart" paper (that has a built-in identifying grid that tells the pen where it is touching the paper). The pen transmits its position via the new Bluetooth data transmission protocol to any nearby receiver that is tuned to the pen's transmission frequency. This results in a digital copy of the writer's penmanship that can then be converted into text, which in turn can be stored in the company database. Though this is a nascent technology, it may become an important form of data collection in the years to come.

Thus, there are a wide range of data entry systems available. In most instances, the controller who is designing a data collection system will need to use a mix of these options to ensure that the correct mix of high data accuracy and low collection cost is achieved.

PROCESSING: DATA SUMMARIZATION SYSTEMS

Having covered the data collection portion of cost accounting, we now move to the various costing methodologies that are available for processing the raw data into a format that is most useful for management consumption. The primary advantages and disadvantages of the systems whose functions are noted in the following sections are:

- *Job costing.* This is a commonly used system that is primarily targeted at production situations where customized goods are produced for specific customers. It is very useful for tracking the exact cost of individual products, and is the only valid technique for accumulating costs for cost-plus contractual arrangements. It can also yield accurate results about the ongoing costs of a current job, which is useful for monitoring purposes. However, this system requires a large quantity of detailed data collection and data entry, which is expensive. It also runs the risk of including some inaccurate data, which requires expensive control systems to minimize. Furthermore, there may be a significant allocation of overhead costs to each job, which may be inaccurately applied.

- *Process costing.* This is also a heavily used system, and is most common in situations where large quantities of exactly the same product are created. Costs are collected in bulk for entire time periods, and then allocated out to the volume of entire production runs during that period. This results in a fair degree of accuracy when costs are averaged out and assigned to individual units. However, some degree of estimation is required when determining total production quantities completed, since some units may be only partially completed at the end of the production period. Consequently, there is some room for variation in final production costs. This method requires much less data collection than job costing, but the level of information accuracy is correspondingly less.

- *Standard costing.* This methodology has been installed in many companies as an adjunct to both the job costing and process costing systems. It is designed to set standard costs for all material and labor costs incurred by a company, against which actual results can be compared through variance analysis. This can result in excellent control over company costs, but only if the accounting staff is diligent in uncovering the reasons for variances from costing standards, and the management team is helpful in correcting the discovered problems. It is also useful for budgeting, setting prices, and closing the financial books in a rapid manner. However, it is also time-consuming to set and maintain standards; in environments where this maintenance function is not performed, standards can be so far away from actual results that variance analysis is no longer useful for management purposes. Also, a company that has adopted continuous process improvement principles will find that any standards adopted will almost immediately become obsolete, requiring constant correction. Furthermore, most standards are set at the product level, rather than at the batch level, so there is no basis of comparison when using this method for cost control over production batches. Another problem is that comparisons to actual costs tend to focus management attention on labor variances, which have historically been a large part of the cost accounting report package, even though these costs comprise only a small proportion of total production costs in most manufacturing environments. Finally, it tends to perpetuate inefficiencies, if personnel use the current standard cost as a baseline for behavior; they will have no incentive to improve costs to a point that is substantially better than the pre-set standard, resulting in languishing efficiency levels. For these reasons, standard costing is now used in a more limited role that in previous years.

- *Direct costing.* This is a favorite methodology for those managers who are constantly confronted with incremental costing and pricing decisions where the inclusion of overhead costs in a product's total cost will yield inaccurate information. Thus, direct costing is an ideal approach for determining the lowest possible price at which to sell incremental units. However, it yields inaccurate results when used for long-term pricing, since it takes no account of overhead costs that must be included in a company's standard prices if it is to assure itself of long-term profitability. It is also not allowed for inventory valuation purposes by GAAP, which requires the inclusion of allocated overhead costs.

- *Throughput accounting.* A variation on direct costing is throughput costing. This methodology holds that the only direct cost is direct materials, with even direct labor costs being thrown out when making most cost-related management decisions. The main tenet of throughput accounting is that a company must carefully manage the bottleneck operation in its production facility, so that the largest possible contribution margin is created. The main advantage of throughput accounting is that it yields the best short-term incremental profits if it is religiously followed when making production decisions. However, this can result in production mixes that seriously delay the completion of jobs for some customers, which is not good for customer relations.

- *Activity-based costing (ABC).* The ABC methodology is a much more accurate way to associate overhead costs with specific activities, which in turn can be assigned to product costs. Its main advantage is that it builds a direct correlation between the occurrence of an activity and related overhead costs, so that changes in the activity can be reliably expected to result in corresponding changes in the overhead costs. This results in valuable information for the management team, which uses it not only to gain some measure of control over its overhead costs, but also to gain an understanding of which products use more activities (and therefore overhead costs) than others. The downside of this methodology is that it requires a great deal of costing knowledge, time, and management commitment before a functioning ABC system becomes operational, and will henceforth require considerable upkeep to maintain. It also requires the construction of an ABC database that is separate from the general ledger, which can be an expensive proposition to both create and maintain. It is not really necessary in situations where there are few products, obvious process flows, and minimal machine setups, because a less complex cost accumulation system will still result in reasonably accurate product costs.

- *Target costing.* This costing methodology is the most proactive of all the methodologies, for it involves the direct intervention of the cost accounting staff in the product design process, with the express intent of creating products that meet pre-set cost and gross margin goals. This is opposed to the usual practice of accumulating costs after products have been designed and manufactured, so that managers will find out what a product costs after it is too late to make any changes to the design. This costing system is highly recommended to any company that designs its own products, since it can result in significant reductions in product costs before they are "locked in" when the design is completed. This technique usually requires a great deal of cost accounting staff time, and can lengthen the product development process, but is well worth the effort.

This brief review of the advantages and disadvantages of each costing methodology should make it clear not only that they are wildly different from each other in concept, but also that they are all designed to deal with different situations, several of which may be found within the same company. Accordingly, a controller must become accustomed to slipping in and out of a methodology when the circumstances warrant the change, and will very likely use a combination of these systems at the same time, if demanded by the circumstances.

In the following sections, we will review the workings of each of these costing methodologies.

PROCESSING: JOB COSTING

Job costing involves a series of transactions that accumulate the costs of materials, labor, and overhead (of which there are two different calculations) to a specific job. For each of these costing categories, costs are accumulated through a series of transactions before they are finally charged to a specific job. In this section, we will trace the journal entries used for all of these costs.

The basic flow of journal entries required for direct materials is noted in Exhibit 5.1, which itemizes the general format of each sequential transaction. When raw materials are purchased, they are rarely charged to a particular job upon receipt. Instead, they are stored in the warehouse, so there is a debit to the raw materials inventory and a credit to accounts payable. Once production is scheduled, the raw materials will be sent to the production floor, which triggers another transaction, to be created by the warehouse staff—a debit to the work-in-process inventory account and a credit to the raw materials inventory account.

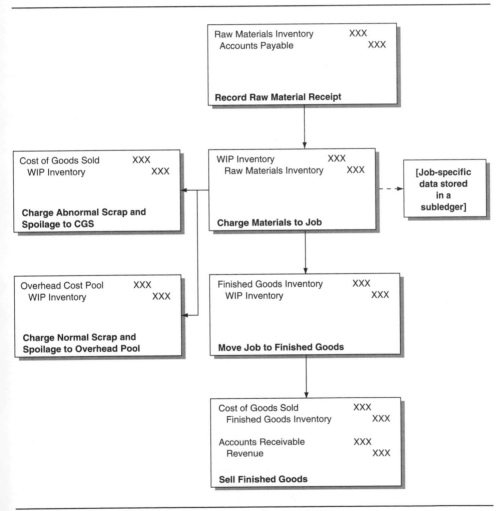

EXHIBIT 5.1   JOB COSTING TRANSACTIONS FOR DIRECT MATERIALS

Reprinted with permission: Steven M. Bragg, *Cost Accounting: A Comprehensive Guide,* Wiley, 2001, Chapter 10.

During the production process, it is quite likely that some portion of the materials will be destroyed as part of the normal production process; if so, another entry will be required that creates a debit to the overhead cost pool, and a credit to remove the cost from the work-in-process inventory account. This normal amount of scrap will then be allocated through the overhead cost pool back to product costs—we will deal with this issue shortly, when we talk about the cost flow for overhead costs. If there are excessive amounts of scrap, then these will be instead charged directly to the cost of goods sold with a debit, while the work-in-process account is reduced with a credit.

Once the production process has been completed (which may be a few moments for simple products, and months for complex ones), it is shifted back to the warehouse in the form of finished goods. To record this transaction, we use a debit to the finished goods inventory account and a credit to work-in-process inventory. Once the goods are sold from stock, a final entry relieves the finished goods inventory account with a credit, and charges the cost to the cost of goods sold with a debit.

One of the numerous benefits of a just-in-time system is that materials are in the production process for such a short period of time that there is no point in creating transactions that move their cost in and out of work-in-process inventory. Instead, a single transaction shifts raw material costs from the raw materials inventory account to cost of goods sold (though there may be an extra entry to record the cost in finished goods inventory if completed products are not immediately sold). This greatly reduces the number of potential problems that can arise with the recording of transactions.

The recording of labor costs follows a slightly different path than what is typically seen for material costs. Instead of taking a direct route into the work-in-process inventory account, labor costs either can be charged at once to the overhead cost pool or go into work-in-process inventory. The charge to an overhead cost pool is done if there is no direct relationship between the incurrence of the labor cost and the creation of a product—this results in a debit to the overhead cost pool and a credit to the wages expense account. However, if there is a direct tie between the incurrence of labor costs and the production of specific products, then the debit is instead to the work-in-process inventory (or a separate labor) account. These cost flows are shown in Exhibit 5.2.

If the wages have flowed into an overhead cost pool, these costs will be summarized at the end of the accounting period and charged to specific products based on any number of allocation methodologies. The allocation calculation will result in another transaction that shifts the overhead costs to product costs, which can occur both at the work-in-process and finished goods stages of production. Meanwhile, labor costs that have been charged directly to work-in-process inventory will then be shifted to finished goods inventory and later to the cost of goods sold in the same manner as for materials costs.

As was the case for material costs, there are a large number of labor transactions that are required to track the flow of labor costs through the production process under the job costing methodology. There is a high risk that transactional errors will arise, just because of the large number of transactions, so control systems must be created that keep errors from occurring and verify that completed transactions are correct.

The final job costing process under the job costing system is the allocation of costs to products. There are two ways to do this—either with the actual costs incurred during the production process, or else with standard costs that are later adjusted to match actual costing experience. The first of these approaches is called actual cost overhead allocation, while the later is called normal cost overhead allocation. We will address the actual cost overhead allocation first.

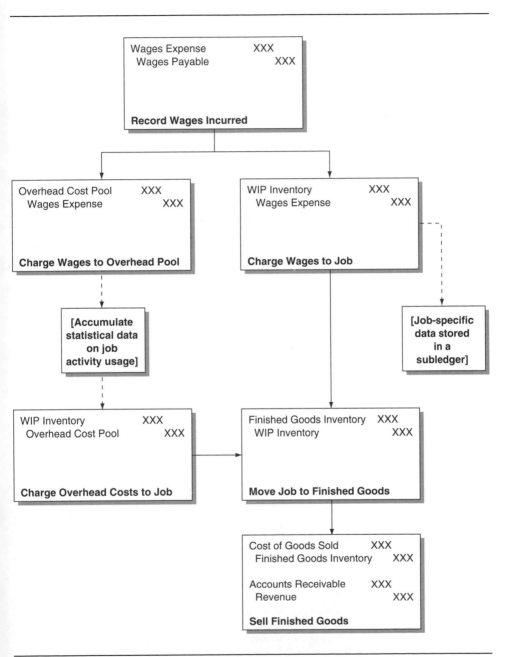

EXHIBIT 5.2 JOB COSTING TRANSACTIONS FOR LABOR

Reprinted with permission: Steven M. Bragg, *Cost Accounting: A Comprehensive Guide,* Wiley, 2001, Chapter 10.

REDUCING THE LOAD

Job costing is still the dominant form of costing used in most manufacturing organizations. The new controller may be overwhelmed by the sheer volume of transactions and likelihood of errors creeping into the process. Rather than trying to eliminate errors from the existing system, consider eliminating some of the data entry and journal entries associated with the system. For example, avoid assigning direct labor costs to jobs if this is a small proportion of total costs, and never track the locations of inventory items through work-in-process if they are being manufactured for only a few hours or days. This can eliminate a great deal of work and more than a few costing errors.

Under actual costing, there are several sources of costs that will flow into an overhead cost pool. As shown in Exhibit 5.3, all production supplies that cannot be traced to a specific product will be debited to the overhead account and credited to accounts payable (the credit may also be charged to raw materials inventory or supplies expense, if supplies were first charged to either of these accounts). As already noted, some labor costs will also be charged to the overhead account. Also, and as previously noted under the materials costing flow, normal amounts of production scrap and spoilage will be charged to overhead. Indirect wages and other indirect costs will also flow into the overhead cost pool. At the end of the accounting period, the cost pool is charged out to various products based on a variety of possible allocation calculations, which are addressed in the activity-based costing section later in this chapter. Once overhead costs have been assigned to specific products, they follow the usual pattern of being moved to the finished goods inventory while their associated completed products are held in storage, and from there to the cost of goods sold upon sale of the product.

The allocation of costs to specific jobs can be delayed for some time under the actual cost overhead allocation method, because some costs can be compiled only at the end of the month, or perhaps not until several weeks thereafter. This is a problem for those companies that want more immediate costing information. We use normal overhead cost allocations to resolve this problem. Normal costing means that a company charges out costs in the short term using a historical average for its overhead costs, rather than actual costs. This process is shown in Exhibit 5.4. This allows costs to be charged to jobs at once. To ensure that the historical average being used for allocations does not stray too far from actual results, it is periodically compared to actual costs (which must still be accumulated), and adjusted as necessary.

When actual and normal costs are compared, there should be a small variance, which can be disposed of in several ways. One approach is to charge off the entire variance to the cost of goods sold, though this can create an unusually high or low cost of goods sold. Another approach is to spread the variance among the cost of goods sold, work-in-process inventory, and finished goods inventory, based on the total balances remaining in each account at the end of the reporting period. A final approach is to retroactively charge the variance to every job. These three options require an increasing amount of work to accomplish, in the order described. For that reason, the first option is the most commonly used, while allocation to individual jobs is a rarity.

The very large number of transactions required in a job costing system makes it a very inefficient costing methodology from the perspective of the accounting department, which must verify that all of the transactions entered are correct. It can also call for the purchase of large quantities of data collection equipment, such as automated time clocks and bar code scanners, which can be quite expensive. Furthermore, this system requires some participation by production personnel in the data collection process, which detracts from their primary

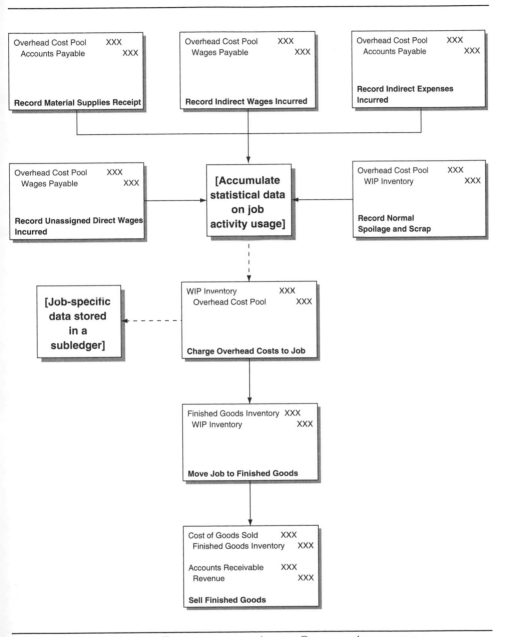

EXHIBIT 5.3 JOB COSTING TRANSACTIONS FOR ACTUAL OVERHEAD ALLOCATIONS

Reprinted with permission: Steven M. Bragg, *Cost Accounting: A Comprehensive Guide,* Wiley, 2001, Chapter 10.

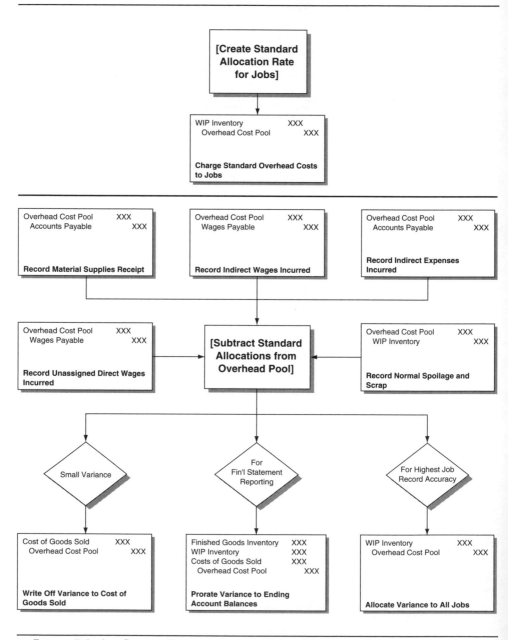

mission of manufacturing products. However, given the need for job costing information, a company may find that there is no reasonable alternative to using this system. If so, the controller should carefully review the need for each type of data that can be potentially produced by the system, and collect only those that will result in valuable information—this will create a more efficient data collection environment that focuses only on the key cost elements.

PROCESSING: PROCESS COSTING

Process costing is used in those situations when it is impossible to clearly differentiate the cost of individual units of production. For example, it is a prime candidate for use in an oil refinery, where it is impossible to track the cost of an individual gallon of diesel fuel.

The most common method for calculating process costs on a per-unit basis is to accumulate all production-related costs during the accounting period and calculate a weighted average per-unit cost based on these totals and the amount of production that was completed during the period, or which is currently still in process. An example of this calculation is shown in Exhibit 5.5.

In the exhibit, there are three blocks of calculations, each one segregated by a horizontal line. The top block contains a conversion calculation, which converts the amount of completed and work-in-process units into units to which materials and other costs can be allocated. The first column of numbers contains the calculation for the allocation of direct materials costs, while the final column of numbers calculates the allocation of all other production costs. For the purposes of this calculation, we assume that there are two types of costs—direct materials,

Units Summary	Direct Material Units	Conversion Factor	Conversion Cost Units	
Completed Units	1,000		1,000	
Ending Units in Process	350	60%	210	
Unit Totals	1,350		1,210	
Unit Cost Calculation	**Direct Materials**		**Conversion Costs**	**Totals**
Beginning Work-in-Process Cost	$20,000		$15,000	$35,000
Current Period Costs	$28,000		$21,500	$49,500
Total Costs	$48,000		$36,500	$84,500
Unit Totals (see above)	1,350		1,210	
Cost per Unit	$35.556		$30.165	
Unit Cost Allocation	**Direct Materials**		**Conversion Costs**	**Totals**
Cost of Completed Units	$35,556		$30,165	$65,721
Cost of Ending WIP Units	$12,444		$ 6,335	$18,779
Totals	$48,000		$36,500	$84,500

EXHIBIT 5.5 WEIGHTED AVERAGE COSTING CALCULATION
Reprinted with permission: Steven M. Bragg, *Cost Accounting: A Comprehensive Guide,* Wiley, 2001, Chapter 11.

which are typically added at the beginning of the production process, and all other costs, which can be added at a multitude of other points during the manufacturing sequence.

Since materials costs are assumed to occur at the earliest stage of production, the calculation of equivalent units for direct material cost allocation is quite easy—just use the number of finished goods completed (1,000) and the number of units in work-in-process inventory (350). However, for the purposes of allocating all other production costs, we must reduce the amount of work-in-process inventory by an estimate of their aggregate level of completion, which in the example is 60 percent. This results in total converted units of production of 1,210.

In the middle block of calculations, we accumulate the total cost of production and divide it by the equivalent number of units of production to determine the cost per unit. This calculation includes the costs that had been carried over in the work-in-process inventory from the preceding accounting reporting period, totaling $35,000. We add to this the current cost of production, which is $49,500, to yield a total cost of $84,500 that must be allocated to units of production. When divided by the slightly different units of production being used for direct material costs and all other production costs, we arrive at a direct material cost per unit of $35.556, and all other costs per unit of $30.165.

The lowermost block of calculations requires us to multiply the cost per unit (as determined in the middle block) by the total number of units (as determined in the top block). The calculation is identified with arrows. The result is $48,000 in direct material costs, of which $35,556 are charged to completed units and the remainder to work-in-process units. Total other production costs are $36,500, of which $30,165 are charged to completed units and the remainder to work-in-process. As a cross-check, we can see that the total allocated is $84,500, which matches the total amount of funds that were to be allocated, as noted on the far right side of the middle block.

This method is a simple one that requires very little data collection. However, some companies like to make the task even easier by avoiding the collection and interpretation of actual costs at the end of each accounting period. Instead, they prefer to use standard unit costs for their calculations, which allows them to calculate total costs more frequently and with no related data collection costs. This type of calculation is shown in Exhibit 5.6.

In the exhibit, the first block of calculations does not change—we still assume that a conversion factor must be applied to the ending work-in-process inventory for the purposes of assigning other production costs than direct materials. The difference arises in the second block, where we use only a standard cost per unit, rather than a summarization of actual costs. This cost is then carried forward into the third block of calculations, where we see that a total of $81,315 has been allocated to the ending finished goods and work-in-process inventory. However, this ending figure varies from the $84,500 that resulted from the preceding actual costing calculation in Exhibit 5.6. The difference of $3,185 was caused by a slight variance between the pre-set standard cost and the actual cost. The presence of this variance causes us to add a fourth block of calculations at the bottom of the exhibit, in which we compare the actual costs incurred during the period to the standard costs, which shows that more costs than expected were incurred in the direct materials column, while fewer costs were incurred under the other production costs column.

The main issue for the controller is what to do with this variance. If negligible, it can be charged off to the cost of goods sold. If it is so large that expensing the difference will result in an appreciable impact on reported earnings, then a more accurate approach is to apportion the variance among the cost of goods sold, work-in-process inventory, and finished goods inventory.

The data collection and calculations required for a process costing system are substantially simpler than what is required for a job costing system, and so is a favorite approach for those who wish to pare their data collection costs or who produce such large volumes of similar products that there is no point in attempting to track the costs of individual products.

Units Summary	Direct Material Units	Conversion Factor	Conversion Cost Units	
Completed Units	1,000		1,000	
Ending Units in Process	350	60%	210	
Unit Totals	1,350		1,210	
Unit Cost Calculation	**Direct Materials**		**Conversion Costs**	
Standard Unit Cost	$32,000		$31,500	
Unit Cost Allocation	**Direct Materials**		**Conversion Costs**	**Totals**
Standard Cost of Completed Units	$32,000		$31,500	$63,500
Standard Cost of Ending WIP Units	$11,200		$ 6,615	$17,815
Standard Cost Totals	$43,200		$38,115	$81,315
Period Variance				
Beginning Standard Work-in-Process Cost	$20,000		$15,000	$35,000
Current Period Actual Costs	$28,000		$21,500	$49,500
Total Period Costs	$48,000		$36,500	$84,500
Standard Cost Totals	$43,200		$38,115	$81,315
Cost Variance	$ 4,800		$(1,615)	$ 3,185

EXHIBIT 5.6 WEIGHTED AVERAGE COST ALLOCATION METHOD USING STANDARD COSTS
Reprinted with permission: Steven M. Bragg, *Cost Accounting: A Comprehensive Guide,* Wiley, 2001, Chapter 11.

PROCESSING: STANDARD COSTING

The first step in the creation of a standard costing system is to create a set of standard costs in a variety of different areas. The industrial engineering staff is assigned the task of creating direct labor standard costs, while the purchasing staff is most typically assigned the chore of creating standard costs for purchased goods, and the controller is called on to coordinate the development of a set of standard overhead costs. If there are subproducts created during the production process that may be valued at the end of each accounting reporting period, then the industrial engineering staff will calculate these standards. It is also possible to reduce the areas in which standard costs are used, with actual costs being accumulated in other areas. This mix of costing types can arise when there is some concern that reasonably accurate standard costs cannot be constructed, or if existing actual costing systems already produce reasonably accurate results.

Another issue to settle as soon in the standard cost development process as possible is the timing of changes to these standards. This can be done quite infrequently, perhaps once every few years, or as rapidly as once a month (which results in standard costs that are nearly indistinguishable from actual costs). The key determinant influencing the pace of change is the perceived pace at which actual costs are changing. If there are minimal changes to a manufacturing process, then there is certainly no reason to constantly review the process and set new standards. Conversely, a company that has installed an aggressive continuous improvement strategy will find that its standard costs are constantly falling behind changes in actual costs, which requires constant revisions to standards.

The assumptions used to create standard costs must also be addressed. For example, an industrial engineer must make some assumptions about the speed of efficiency improvements being realized by the production staff (known as the learning curve) in order to determine the future standard cost that roughly matches these expected changes in efficiency. Similarly, a standard cost must be matched to the expected production equipment configuration to be used, since this has a considerable impact on the overhead costs that can be assigned to a product. Another key assumption is the volume of production, since a large assumed production run will spread its setup cost over many units, whereas a short production run will result in higher setup costs on a per-unit basis. Yet another factor is the assumed condition of the equipment to be used in the manufacturing process, since poorly maintained or old equipment will be in operation for fewer hours than would otherwise be the case. The production system being used, such as just-in-time or manufacturing resource planning, will also have a significant impact on standard costs, since different systems result in the incurrence of different types of costs in such areas as machine setup time, equipment depreciation, materials handling costs, and inventory investment costs. An issue that is particular to direct labor is the anticipated result of union negotiations, since these directly and immediately impact hourly wage rates. A final issue to consider is the presence and quality of work instructions for the production staff; the absence of detailed and accurate instructions can have a profound and deleterious impact on costs incurred. Given the large number of issues involved in the setting of accurate standard costs, it is no surprise that this task can require the ongoing services of an experienced group of professionals, the cost of which must be considered when making the decision to use a standard costing system.

A final factor to consider when creating standard costs is the level of attainability of the costs. One option is to devise an *attainable standard,* which is a cost that does not depart very much from the existing actual cost. This results in reasonable cost targets that employees know they can probably meet. Another alternative is to use *historical costs* as the basis for a standard cost. This is generally not recommended, for the resulting costs are no different from a company's existing actual cost structure, and so gives employees no incentive to attempt to reduce costs. The diametrically opposite approach is to create a set of *theoretical standards,* which are based on costs that can only be achieved if the manufacturing process runs absolutely perfectly. Since employees cannot possibly meet these cost goals for anything but very short periods of time, it tends to result in lower employee morale. Thus, of the potential range of standard costs that can be set, the best approach is to set moderate stretch goals that are achievable.

Finally, we are ready to begin using standard costs. But for what purpose do we use them? One common usage is in budgeting. By creating detailed standard costs for all budgeting line items, company managers can be presented with financial statements that compare actual results to standard costs, so that they can see where actual results are falling behind expectations. However, this is a simple approach that requires little real attention to the setting of standards at the product level.

Another reason for using standards is to create benchmarks for inclusion in a manufacturing resources planning (MRP II) production system. This commonly used system multiplies a production forecast by a detailed set of product labor, materials, and capacity requirements to determine how many direct labor personnel and specific materials and how much machine capacity will be needed. This system requires extremely detailed and accurate standards to be successful. The standards needed by MRP II are for units of labor, materials, and capacity, rather than their costs. In other words, a direct labor standard for an MRP II system may be 12 minutes of labor, rather than its cost for those 12 minutes of $4.58.

Yet another use for standards is in product pricing. The company sales staff frequently asks the engineering staff to provide it with cost estimates for new product configurations, many of which are only slightly different from existing products. However, the engineering staff may take days or weeks to provide the sales personnel with this information—which may be too long to satisfy an impatient customer. By using standard costs, the sales staff can compile product costs very quickly with only a brief approval review from the engineering staff. Or, if the engineering staff is still in charge of creating new product cost estimates, then they can also use standard costs to more rapidly arrive at their estimates. In either case, customers will receive reliable price quotes much more rapidly than was previously the case.

A very common use for standard costs is for the valuation of inventory. Many companies do not want to be bothered with the time-consuming accumulation of actual inventory costs at the end of each accounting period, and so they create standard costs for valuation purposes, which they occasionally compare to actual costs to ensure that the inventory valuation is accurate. It is not worth the effort to create standard costs for this purpose if a company's inventory levels are extremely low, or if a just-in-time manufacturing system is in use, since the amount of time that will be saved in valuing inventory is small, given the minor quantities of stock that will be kept in the warehouse. However, manufacturers with large inventory balances will find that this is still an effective way to rapidly determine the value of inventory.

Unfortunately, the use of standard costs for inventory valuation is also subject to control problems, for deliberate manipulation of standards can result in large changes in the value of inventory, which in turn impacts the reported level of company profits. For example, the standard cost for a finished goods item can include an assumption for the amount of production setup costs allocated to each item, which is heavily influenced by the assumed number of units produced in a manufacturing run. By shifting the assumed length of the production run downward, the amount of cost allocated to each unit goes up. This type of interference with standard costs can result in wildly inaccurate reported financial results.

If standard costs are used for inventory valuation, the accounting staff will periodically compare standard to actual costs to ensure that there are not excessively large differences between the two. If a company is audited at year-end, then the auditors will require a comparison to actual costs, and a write-off of the difference to the cost of goods sold (if standard costs are higher than actual costs) or an increase in the inventory balance (if actual costs are higher than standard costs). Since a significant difference between the two types of costs can result in a startling change in the reported level of income during the period when this adjustment is made, it is wise to review some of the large-cost items on a regular basis in order to ensure that there will be no surprises at the time of reconciliation to actual costs.

Consequently, we can see that there are still several areas in which standard costs can be used to create greater efficiencies in selected areas of activity. However, the number of viable applications has fallen with the advent of new computer systems and production methodologies, so one should carefully review the proposed applications for standard costs before conducting an implementation.

PROCESSING: DIRECT COSTING

A direct cost is a cost that is directly associated with changes in production volume. This usually restricts the definition of direct costs to direct materials and direct labor (and a strong case can be made for *not* using direct labor, since this cost tends to be present even

Revenue		$1,000,000
Cost of Goods Sold		
Direct Materials	$320,000	
Direct Labor	170,000	
Total Direct Costs		$ 490,000
Gross Margin		
Operating Expenses		
Production Department	325,000	
General and Administrative	115,000	
Total Operating Expenses		$ 440,000
Net Profit		$ 50,000

EXHIBIT 5.7 INCOME STATEMENT FORMATTED FOR DIRECT COSTING

when production volumes vary). For example, the materials used to create a product are a direct cost, whereas the machine used to convert the materials into a finished product is not a direct cost, because it is still going to be sitting on the factory floor, irrespective of any changes in production volume. The use of direct costing results in a slightly different income statement, as shown in Exhibit 5.7.

The only difference between the income statement shown in Exhibit 5.7 and a more traditional format is that all nondirect costs have been shifted below the gross margin line and into the production department's costs. Though this seems like a subtle change, it focuses the attention of the management team on the incremental changes in the cost of goods sold that are usually masked by a large and relatively fixed amount of overhead costs.

By focusing solely on the direct cost of a product or activity, a controller can provide valuable information to management regarding prospective changes in costs that will arise as a result of some management action. For example, if a change to a more efficient type of processing equipment is contemplated, then the direct cost of a product may be lowered if this will result in less material usage. This may also result in less direct labor cost if the machine takes over some tasks previously performed by employees—this will cut direct costs, but may increase overhead costs if the cost of the machine is higher than that of the machine it is replacing. Yet another example is when a customer wants the lowest possible price for a product, and the company has some free capacity available for producing what the customer needs; the use of direct costing will reveal the lowest possible cost that must be covered by the price charged to the customer in order to break even. Direct costing can also be used to determine which customers are the most profitable, by subtracting the direct cost

THE SIMPLICITY OF DIRECT COSTING

When managers want cost information for a decision, the accounting staff may require multiple days to return the required information, due to the complexity of developing an overhead cost assignment. However, managers have a tendency to focus only on direct costs, and are likely to throw out the overhead costs when making decisions. Consequently, the new controller can save time all around by issuing only direct costs, but be sure to warn recipients of the absence of overhead costs in the presented information, and issue a general warning about the impact of ignoring the missing information.

of their purchases from the prices paid, which yields the amount they are contributing toward the company's coverage of overhead costs and profit. Another very good use for direct costing is to include the concept in the budgeting system, where it is used to change budgeted variable costs to match the actual sales volumes achieved; this approach achieves a much closer match between the budgeted and actual cost of goods sold, because the budget now flexes with the actual volume level experienced. For all of these reasons, direct costing is a highly recommended costing system.

However, there are a number of situations in which direct costing should *not* be used, and in which it will yield incorrect information. Its single largest problem is that it completely ignores all indirect costs, which make up the bulk of all costs incurred by today's companies. This is a real problem when dealing with long-term costing and pricing decisions, since direct costing will likely yield results that do not achieve long-term profitability. For example, a direct costing system may calculate a minimum product price of $10.00 for a widget that is indeed higher than all direct costs, but which is lower than the additional overhead costs that are associated with the product line. If the company continues to use the $10.00 price for all product sales for well into the future, then the company will experience losses because overhead costs are not being covered by the price. The best way to address this problem is to build strict boundaries around the circumstances where incremental prices derived from a direct costing system are used.

Another problem with direct costing is that it assumes a steady level of unit costs for the incremental costing and pricing decisions for which it is most often used. For example, a company receives an offer from a customer to buy 5,000 units of product X at a fixed price. The cost accounting staff may determine that the proposed price will indeed yield a profit, based on the direct cost per unit, and so recommends that the deal be approved. However, because the staff has focused only on direct costs, it has missed the fact that the company is operating at near full-capacity levels, and that to process the entire 5,000-unit order will require the addition of some costly machinery, the acquisition of which will make the proposed deal a very expensive one indeed. To avoid this problem, anyone using a direct costing system must have access to company capacity information, and should coordinate with the production scheduling staff to ensure that capacity levels will permit their incremental pricing and costing scenarios to be achieved.

A subtle issue that many users of direct costing systems miss is that the types of costs that fall within the direct costing definition will increase as the volume of units in a direct costing decision goes up. For example, the only direct cost involved with a single unit of production is the direct materials used to build it, whereas a larger production volume will likely involve some change in the related number of manufacturing employees needed on the production line; these are well-accepted concepts. However controllers frequently forget that additional direct costs will be included when the production volume rises to even higher levels. For example, if the direct costing decision involves an entire production line, then all of the equipment and supervisory costs that are tied to that production line are now also influenced by the decision to produce or not produce, and so should be included in the direct costing system. At an even larger level, the decision to use the production of an entire facility should include every cost needed to run that facility, which may include utilities, rent, and insurance—costs that are not normally included in smaller-volume production decisions. Consequently, direct costing analysis must be conducted within narrowly defined volume ranges, with careful attention to what costs are likely to vary with the volumes that are under review.

Direct costing cannot be used for inventory valuation, because it is disallowed by GAAP. The reason for this is that, under a direct costing system, all costs besides direct costs are charged to the current period. There is no provision for capitalizing overhead costs and associating them with inventory that will be sold off in future periods. This results in an imbalance between the reported level of profitability in each period and the amount of production that occurred. For example, a manufacturer of Christmas ornaments with a direct costing system may sell all of its output in one month of the year, but be forced to recognize all of its nondirect production costs in every month of the year, which will result in reported losses for 11 months of the year. Under GAAP, these nondirect costs would be capitalized into inventory and recognized only when the inventory is sold, thereby more closely matching reported revenues and expenses. Given the wide disparity between the reported results, it is no surprise that GAAP bans the use of direct costing for inventory valuation.

PROCESSING: THROUGHPUT COSTING

A costing methodology that focuses on capacity utilization is called throughput accounting. It assumes that there is always one bottleneck operation in a production process that commands the speed with which products or services can be completed. This operation becomes the defining issue in determining what products should be manufactured first, since this in turn results in differing levels of profitability.

The basic calculation used for throughput accounting is shown in Exhibit 5.8. This format is a simplified version of the layout used by Thomas Corbett on page 44 of *Throughput Accounting* (Great Barrington, MA: North River Press, 1998), though all of the numbers contained within the example have been changed.

The exhibit shows a series of electronic devices that a company can choose from for its near-term production requirements. The second column describes the amount of throughput that each of the products generates per minute in the bottleneck operation; "throughput" is the amount of margin left after all direct material costs have been subtracted from revenue. For example, the 19″ Color Television produces $81.10 of throughput, but requires ten minutes of

Maximum Constraint Time: 62,200					
Product	Throughput $/Minute of Constraint	Required Constraint Usage (min.)	Unit Demand/ Actual Production	Cumulative Constraint Utilization	Cumulative Throughput/ Product
19″ Color Television	$8.11	10	1,000/1,000	10,000	$ 81,100
100-Watt Stereo	7.50	8	2,800/2,800	22,400	168,000
5″ LCD Television	6.21	12	500/500	6,000	37,260
50″ High-Definition TV	5.00	14	3,800/1,700	23,800	119,000
			Throughput Total		$405,360
			Operating Expense Total		375,000
			Profit		30,360
			Profit Percentage		7.5%
			Investment		500,000
			Return on Investment		6.1%

EXHIBIT 5.8 THROUGHPUT ACCOUNTING MODEL

Reprinted with permission: Steven M. Bragg, *Cost Accounting: A Comprehensive Guide,* Wiley, 2001, Chapter 15.

processing time in the bottleneck operation, resulting in throughput per minute of $8.11. The various electronic devices are sorted in the exhibit from top to bottom in order of largest throughput per minute. This ordering tells the user how much of the most profitable products can be produced before the total amount of available time in the bottleneck (which is 62,200 minutes, as noted at the top of the exhibit) is used up. The calculation for bottleneck utilization is shown in the "Unit Demand/Actual Production" column. In that column, the 19" color Television has a current demand for 1,000 units, which requires 10,000 minutes of bottleneck time (as shown in the following column). This allocation of bottleneck time progresses downward through the various products until we come to the 50" High-Definition TV at the bottom of the list, for which there is only enough bottleneck time left to manufacture 1,700 units.

By multiplying the dollars of throughput per minute times the number of minutes of production time, we arrive at the cumulative throughput dollars resulting from the manufacture (and presumed sale) of each product, which yields a total throughput of $405,360. We then add up all other expenses, totaling $375,000, and subtract them from the total throughput, which gives us a profit of $30,360. These calculations comprise the basic throughput accounting analysis model.

Now let's reexamine the model based on a re-juggling of the priority of orders. If the cost accounting manager were to examine each of the products based on the addition of allocated overhead and direct labor costs to the direct materials that were used as the foundation for the throughput dollar calculations, she may arrive at the conclusion that, when fully burdened, the 50" High-Definition TV is actually the most profitable, while the 19" Color Television is the least profitable. Accordingly, she recommends that the order of production be changed to reflect these "realities," which gives us the new throughput report shown in Exhibit 5.9.

The result is a significant loss, rather than the increase in profits that had been expected. Why the change? The trouble is that allocated overhead costs have no bearing on throughput, because allocated costs will not change in accordance with incremental production decisions,

			Maximum Constraint Time: 62,200		
Product	Throughput $/Minute of Constraint	Required Constraint Usage (min.)	Unit Demand/ Actual Production	Cumulative Constraint Utilization	Cumulative Throughput/ Product
50" High-Definition TV	$5.00	14	3,800/3,800	53,200	$266,000
100-Watt Stereo	7.50	8	2,800/1,125	9,000	67,500
5" LCD Television	6.21	12	500/0	0	0
19" Color Television	8.11	10	1,000/0	0	0
			Throughput Total		$333,500
			Operating Expense Total		375,000
			Profit		−41,500
			Profit Percentage		−12.4%
			Investment		500,000
			Return on Investment		−8.3%

EXHIBIT 5.9 REVISED THROUGHPUT ANALYSIS BASED ON ALLOCATED COSTS
Reprinted with permission: Steven M. Bragg, *Cost Accounting: A Comprehensive Guide,* Wiley, 2001, Chapter 15.

such as which product will be manufactured first. Instead, the overhead cost pool will exist, irrespective of any modest changes in activity levels. Consequently, it makes no sense to apply allocated costs to the production scheduling decision, when the only issue that matters is how much throughput per minute a product can generate.

Capital budgeting is an area in which throughput costing analysis can be applied with excellent results. The trouble with most corporate capital budgeting systems is that they do not take into consideration the fact that the only valid investment is one that will have a positive impact on the amount of throughput that can be pushed through a bottleneck operation. Any other investment will result in greater production capacity in other areas of the company that still cannot produce any additional quantities, since the bottleneck operation controls the total amount of completed production. For example, the throughput model in Exhibit 5.10 shows the result of an investment of $28,500 in new equipment that is added later in the production process than the bottleneck operation. The result is an increase in the total investment, to $528,500, and absolutely no impact on profitability, which yields a reduced return on investment of 5.7 percent.

A more profitable solution would have been to invest in anything that would increase the productivity of the bottleneck operation, which could be either a direct investment in that operation, or an investment in an upstream operation that will reduce the amount of processing required for a product by the bottleneck operation.

As another example, the cost accounting staff has conducted a lengthy activity-based costing analysis, which has determined that a much higher amount of overhead cost must be allocated to the high-definition television, which results in a loss on that product. Accordingly, the product is removed from the list of viable products, which reduces the number of products in the mix of production activity, as shown in Exhibit 5.11.

The result is a reduction in profits. The reason is that the cost accounting staff has made the incorrect assumption that, by eliminating a product, all of the associated overhead cost will be eliminated, too. Though a small amount of overhead might be eliminated when the production of a single product is stopped, the bulk of it will still be incurred.

Maximum Constraint Time: 62,200					
Product	Throughput $/Minute of Constraint	Required Constraint Usage (min.)	Unit Demand/ Actual Production	Cumulative Constraint Utilization	Cumulative Throughput/ Product
19″ Color Television	$8.11	10	1,000/1,000	10,000	$ 81,100
100-Watt Stereo	7.50	8	2,800/2,800	22,400	168,000
5″ LCD Television	6.21	12	500/500	6,000	37,260
50″ High-Definition TV	5.00	14	3,800/1,700	23,800	119,000
			Throughput Total		$405,360
			Operating Expense Total		375,000
			Profit		30,360
			Profit Percentage		7.5%
			Investment		528,500
			Return on Investment		5.7%

EXHIBIT 5.10   REVISED THROUGHPUT ANALYSIS BASED ON ADDITIONAL INVESTMENT
Reprinted with permission: Steven M. Bragg, *Cost Accounting: A Comprehensive Guide,* Wiley, 2001, Chapter 15.

	Maximum Constraint Time: 62,200				
Product	**Throughput $/Minute of Constraint**	**Required Constraint Usage (min.)**	**Unit Demand/ Actual Production**	**Cumulative Constraint Utilization**	**Cumulative Throughput/ Product**
19" Color Television	$8.11	10	1,000/1,000	10,000	$ 81,100
100-Watt Stereo	7.50	8	2,800/2,800	22,400	168,000
5" LCD Television	6.21	12	500/500	6,000	37,260
			Throughput Total		$286,360
			Operating Expense Total		375,000
			Profit		−88,640
			Profit Percentage		−30.9%
			Investment		500,000
			Return on Investment		−17.7%

EXHIBIT 5.11 REVISED THROUGHPUT ANALYSIS WITH ONE LESS PRODUCT
Reprinted with permission: Steven M. Bragg, *Cost Accounting: A Comprehensive Guide,* Wiley, 2001, Chapter 15.

Throughput accounting does a very good job of tightly focusing attention on the priority of production in situations where there is a choice of products that can be manufactured. It can also have an impact on a number of other decisions, such as whether to grant volume discounts, outsource manufacturing, stop the creation of a product, or invest in new capital items. Given this wide range of activities, it should find a place in the mix of costing methodologies at many companies. We now shift to a discussion of activity-based costing (ABC), whose emphasis is the complete reverse of throughput accounting—it focuses on the proper allocation of overhead.

So When Do You Process the Order?

The basic concept of throughput accounting is that profits can be improved by shuffling production orders to give high priority to high-margin items going through a bottleneck operation. However, this perpetually moves low-margin items to the bottom of the priority stack, which ignores the fact that real customers are waiting for those orders! Though a company can eliminate these products in the long run and improve their profits, the short-term need to maintain responsiveness to customers makes throughput concepts somewhat impractical.

PROCESSING: ACTIVITY-BASED COSTING

An ABC system is designed to match overhead costs as closely as possible with company activities. By doing so, overhead costs can be reasonably associated with products, departments, customers, or other users of activities, which tells managers where overhead costs are being used within a company. This results in much better control over overhead costs.

There are several ways to allocate overhead costs. Some overhead costs, such as utilities, are associated with specific machines. For example, a machine may require ten cents of electricity per minute. If so, this overhead cost can be charged out to those products that are run through the machine, based on the time spent being worked upon it. Other overhead costs are associated with a specific product line, and can reasonably be allocated to the activities performed within that product line.

For example, there is typically a supervisor who is assigned to a single product line. If so, the fully burdened salary of this person can be charged to such related activities as production and maintenance scheduling. Still other overhead costs may be grouped by commodity used in the production process. For example, each member of the purchasing staff may be responsible for the procurement of a specific commodity. If so, this overhead cost can be distributed to individual products based on their usage of the commodity. Clearly, there are many valid ways to allocate overhead costs to various activities, and from there to users of those costs. An ABC system creates a structured approach to the accumulation, storage, and allocation of overhead costs using many of these activity measures.

An ABC system is a difficult and complex one to create, because of the wide variety of costs that must be accumulated, tracked in relation to different types of activities, and charged off. Here are the primary steps involved in creating such a system:

1. *Determine the scope of the system.* A fully developed ABC system that encompasses all costs throughout a company is a massive undertaking that may not yield any results for several years. A better approach is to conduct a gradual rollout of the system that produces results more quickly. Accordingly, a key factor is limiting each incremental rollout of the system to a carefully defined segment of the business. The determination of scope should also include a review of the level of detailed analysis that the system is to produce, since an excessive focus on detail may result in a system that is too expensive in relation to the utility of the information produced.

2. *Set aside direct costs.* There will be several direct costs that can be clearly and indisputably traced to specific products. These costs should be identified early in the design phase, so that they will not be erroneously added to the ABC allocation system.

3. *Locate costs in the general ledger.* The next step is to identify each of the overhead costs in the general ledger that will be allocated by the ABC system. This can be a difficult undertaking, for the required costs may be lumped together in the ledger, and must be segregated through a new data collection system that involves the creation of a new general ledger account number. Alternatively, the split may be achieved less accurately by allocating a percentage of the cost in a single general ledger account to several overhead cost items that will then be allocated.

4. *Store costs in cost pools.* All of the costs that have been identified within the general ledger must now be stored in a series of cost pools. Each cost pool accumulates costs that are similar to each other. For example, a building cost pool will include the costs of insurance and maintenance for a building, whereas a product line cost pool may include the marketing and supervisory costs that can be traced to a specific product line. A third type of cost pool is one that is related to a specific production batch, and can include such costs as production control labor, tooling, materials handling, and quality control. The total number of cost pools used will have a direct impact on the maintenance costs of an ABC system, so the design team must balance the increased allocation accuracy associated with more cost pools with the extra labor needed to maintain them.

5. *Determine activity drivers.* Having summarized overhead costs into a set of cost pools, we must now allocate them, which we do with an activity driver—this is a variable that reasonably explains the consumption of costs from a cost pool. For example, some accounts payable costs are closely associated with the number of checks printed and mailed, while some engineering costs vary directly with the number of design changes

added to a product. Examples of other activity drivers are the number of machine set-ups, the number of maintenance work orders, the number of purchase orders, and the number of customer orders processed. Whichever activity driver is chosen as the basis for cost pool allocation should be easy to calculate, require minimal data collection, and have a reasonably close cause-and-effect relationship with a cost pool.

6. *Spread costs from secondary to primary cost pools.* Some of the cost pools include costs that are, in turn, distributed to other cost pools. These costs are usually for internal company services, such as management information systems services that are provided to other departments. These secondary cost pools must be allocated to primary cost pools.

7. *Calculate the overhead cost per activity unit.* We then divide the total number of occurrences of each activity driver into the total amount of costs in the primary cost pools for the accounting period, which results in a dollar figure per unit of activity.

8. *Assign activity costs to cost objects.* The final step is to calculate the usage of each activity driver by a cost object (which is anything that uses activities, such as products or customers). For example, if a product requires the creation of two purchase orders (which are activity drivers) and the ABC system has determined that each purchase order requires $32.15 to create, then the amount of overhead charged to the product will be $64.30.

In brief, the ABC process involves taking costs out of the general ledger and assigning them to either secondary or primary cost pools, which are then distributed to cost objects through the use of activity drivers. The overall process is shown in Exhibit 5.12.

PROCESSING: TARGET COSTING

Most of the costing methodologies described in this chapter are primarily concerned with the interpretation of costing data after it has already been incurred. Target costing differs from them in that it describes the costs that are expected to be incurred, and how this will impact product profitability levels. By describing costs in a proactive and future-oriented manner, managers can determine how they should alter product designs before they enter the manufacturing process in order to ensure that the company earns a reasonable profit on all new products.

To use this methodology, the controller is assigned to a new product design team, and asked to continually compile the projected cost of a product as it moves through the design process. Managers will use this information not only to make product alterations, but also to drop a product design if it cannot meet its cost targets.

There are four basic steps involved in target costing. First, the design team conducts market research to determine the price points that a company is most likely to achieve if it creates a product with a certain set of features. The research should include information about the perceived value of certain features on a product, so that the design team can add or subtract features from the design with a full knowledge of what these changes probably will do to the final price at which the product will be sold. The second step is to subtract from the prospective product price a gross margin that must be earned on the product; this can be a standard company-wide margin that must be earned on all new products, or perhaps a more specific one that management has imposed based on the perceived risk of the project. By subtracting the required margin from the expected price, we arrive at the maximum amount that the product can cost. This total cost figure drives the next step.

The design team then uses value engineering to drive down the cost of the product until it meets its overall cost target. Value engineering requires considerable attention to the

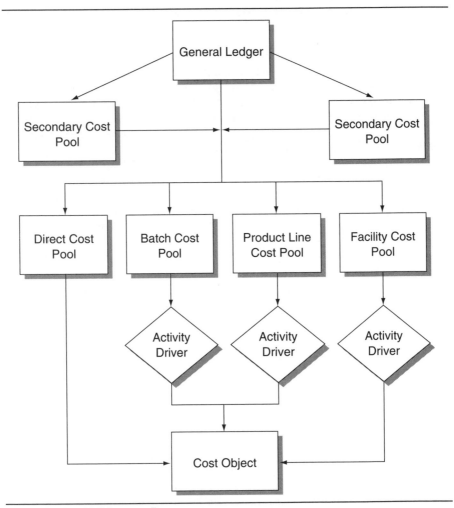

EXHIBIT 5.12   ABC PROCESS FLOW
Reprinted with permission: Steven M. Bragg, *Cost Accounting: A Comprehensive Guide,* Wiley, 2001, Chapter 17.

elimination of production functions, a product design that is cheaper to manufacture, a planned reduction of product durability in order to cut costs, a reduced number of product features, less expensive component parts, and so on—in short, any activity that will lead to a reduced product cost. This process also requires the team to confirm costs with the suppliers of raw materials and outsourced parts, as well as the processing costs that will be incurred internally. The controller plays a key role at this stage, regularly summarizing costing information and relaying it not only to the team members, but to the managers who are reviewing the team's progress. A standard procedure at this point is to force the team to come within a set percentage of its cost target at various milestones (such as being within 12% of the target after three months of design work, 6% after four months, and on target after five months); if the team cannot meet increasingly tighter costing targets, then the project will be canceled.

Once these design steps have been completed and a product has met its targeted cost level, the target costing effort is shifted into a different activity, which is follow-on activities that will reduce costs even further after the product has entered its production phase. This final step is used to create some excess gross margin over time, which allows the company to reduce the price of the product to respond to presumed increases in the level of competition. The sources of these cost reductions can be either through planned supplier cost reductions or through waste reductions in the production process (known as *kaizen* costing). The concepts of value engineering and *kaizen* costing can be used repeatedly to gradually reduce the cost of a product over time, as shown in Exhibit 5.13. In the exhibit, we see that the market price of a product follows a steady downward trend, which is caused by ongoing competitive pressure as the market for the product matures. To meet this pricing pressure with corresponding reductions in costs, the company initially creates product A, and uses value engineering to design a preset cost into the product. Once the design is released for production, *kaizen* costing is used to further reduce costs in multiple stages until there are few additional reductions left to squeeze out of the original design. At this point, the design team uses value engineering to create a replacement product B that incorporates additional cost savings (likely including the cost reduction experience gleaned from the *kaizen* costing stages used for product A) that result in an even lower initial cost. *Kaizen* costing is then used once again to further reduce the cost of product B, thereby keeping the cost reduction process moving in an ever-downward direction. The entire target costing process, incorporating all of the preceding steps, is shown in Exhibit 5.14.

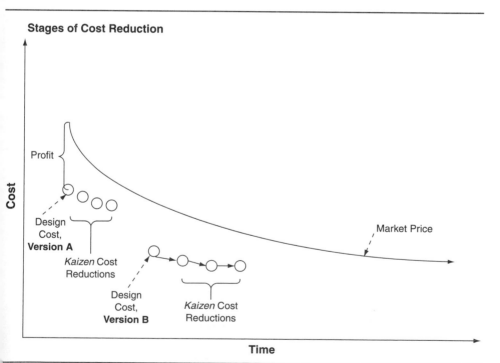

EXHIBIT 5.13 STAGES IN THE COST REDUCTION PROCESS
Reprinted with permission: Steven M. Bragg, *Cost Accounting: A Comprehensive Guide,* Wiley, 2001, Chapter 18.

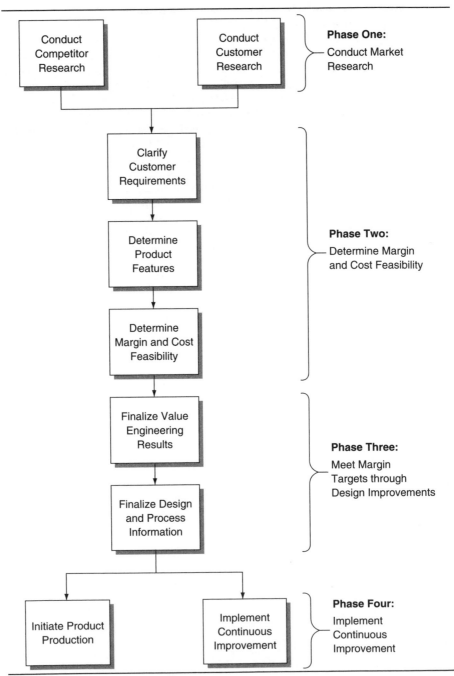

EXHIBIT 5.14 TARGET COSTING PROCESS
Reprinted with permission: Steven M. Bragg, *Cost Accounting: A Comprehensive Guide,* Wiley, 2001, Chapter 18.

OUTPUTS: COST VARIANCES

A costing methodology of any type is not of much use if there is no output from it that gives valuable information to the management team. One of the primary outputs that is expected is a listing of costing variances, which are actual costs that depart from expectations. There are a number of standard variance calculations that can be summarized into a report, and which we will cover in this section.

Variances fall into three categories. The first is a price variance, and is the difference between the standard purchase cost of an item and the actual cost at which it was purchased, multiplied by the actual number of units purchased. It can be used to describe the variances in the general cost categories of purchased parts, direct labor, and overhead, and so is seen in three different places on cost variance reports.

The second type of variance is the efficiency variance. This is the difference between the actual quantity of resources needed to manufacture something, less the standard quantity, multiplied by its standard cost. This variance can also be broken down into three sub-variances: a direct labor efficiency variance, a yield variance that relates to materials usage, and a variable overhead efficiency variance. There is no efficiency variance related to fixed overhead costs, since they are not expected to change with volume, and so have no targeted level of efficiency against which to compare.

The final variance is the volume variance. It applies to only one cost type, as opposed to the other variances; this is fixed overhead costs. Fixed overhead costs are charged to the cost of goods sold, or other parts of the income statement, as a fixed amount per accounting period, rather than as a percentage of the volume of production. Because of this difference in the method of cost allocation, a change in the actual production volume from the level that was expected when the allocation was set will result in a volume variance. It is calculated by multiplying the fixed overhead portion of the overhead rate by the number of units produced, and then subtracting this amount from the total fixed overhead cost pool.

An example of these variances, and the calculations used to derive them, is shown in Exhibit 5.15. In the upper-left corner of the variance report, we see that there is a total variance of $61,725. The block of costs immediately below this shows the cost categories in which the variance arose, which sum to $61,725. Below and to the side of these variances are subsidiary variances that are linked back to the four major cost categories. For instance, the materials price variance in the upper-right corner reveals that the price paid for materials is $1.25 higher than expected, while the material yield variance located directly below it shows that 1,500 more units of materials were used for production than had been anticipated. The total variance from these two calculations is $26,000, which traces back to the total direct materials variance on the left side of the report. All of the variances trace back through the report in a similar manner. This is a good format for showing how variance calculations are derived, and how they flow through the accounting reporting system.

A company may not choose to report on all of these variances, since the detailed investigation of each one can be extremely time consuming. Thus, the variance for the direct labor price may not be reported on the grounds that management has little control over it when pricing is ruled by a formal agreement with a labor union. Similarly, the fixed overhead volume variance may not be reported because it relates more to ongoing production volumes than to management's ability to control the size of the overhead cost pool. Variances that are more commonly reported on are the material price variance and all types of efficiency variances; the material price variance is used to monitor the performance of the purchasing staff, while efficiency variances are used to oversee the entire manufacturing process.

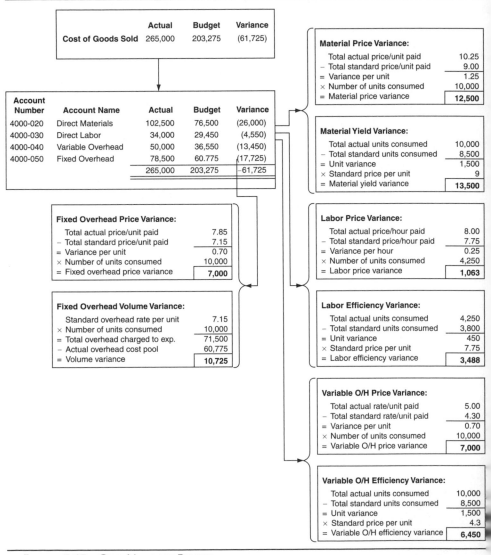

EXHIBIT 5.15   COST VARIANCE REPORT
Reprinted with permission: Steven M. Bragg, *Cost Accounting: A Comprehensive Guide,* Wiley, 2001, Chapter 16.

Some variances are not worthy of regular reporting, because they require an inordinate amount of data collection work in exchange for information that is not of much use to management. For example, a detailed scrap variance that itemizes every item that was thrown out during a reporting period, alongside the reasons for each one, calls for a very large amount of investigative effort. The resulting report will contain information that may result in some long-term savings, but probably not enough to justify the work required to create the report. Thus, report compilation work should be considered when reporting on variances.

Once the cost variance report has been completed, the accounting staff either will be asked to conduct an investigation into the causes of specific variances, or should do so on its own. If so, it is useful to know in advance what types of problems are most likely to cause variances, so that investigative work can be first targeted at these items. The most common causes of each major variance are:

- *Fixed overhead spending variance*
    - Suppliers have increased their prices for products and services that fall into this expense category. Review related supplier contracts for scheduled price increases.
    - The company has increased its usage of the products or services recorded in this category. If so, the costs may actually be variable, and should be shifted to a variable overhead account.
- *Labor price variance*
    - The standard rate has not been altered to match changes in the union's labor contract.
    - The standard does not include extra charges, such as shift premiums, bonuses, or overtime.
    - The people actually conducting work are at different pay rates than those that were assumed to be doing the work when the labor standards were created.
- *Material price variance*
    - The actual price paid is based on a different purchasing volume than what was assumed when the price standard was originally set.
    - The standard price was erroneously copied from a similar product that has a significantly different price.
    - The purchasing staff is now buying replacement parts that have a different price than the parts that were the basis for the standard.
- *Selling price variance*
    - Products were sold with different options than the products used to set selling price standards.
    - Customers have ordered in different unit volumes than those used to determine the standard price.
    - Customers have paid prices different from the invoiced prices (which will require investigation to resolve).
    - Customers were given promotional discounts on prices paid.
- *Variable overhead spending variance*
    - The supplier has changed its per-unit pricing. Look for a contractually mandated change in the per-unit price.
    - The company is purchasing in different volumes, which alters the per-unit price paid.
    - There are misclassifications in costs between the variable overhead and other accounts.

Though there are certainly other causes for variances, these are among the most common ones, and so should be investigated first. Also, the accounting staff will find that the same causes are likely to crop up over and over again, so it is useful to develop and continually update a list of variances caused from previous reporting periods. This becomes the accounting staff's "short list" of variance causes that can be used to track down similar problems in the future.

6

RATIO AND TREND ANALYSIS

IMPORTANCE OF THIS CHAPTER

Frequently, the new controller walks into a situation where there is no consistently applied ratio analysis of any kind. If so, this is a great opportunity to formulate a company-wide measurement system that she can use as the basis of a new set of management reports within a few days or weeks of starting work. This chapter is chock-full of ratios from which to make selections.

This chapter describes the analysis of a business by using ratios and trends. The most common accounting measurements are included here; these are good for analyzing the balance sheet, the income statement, and relationships between the two. In addition, there are a number of performance measurements in this chapter that do not directly relate to accounting, but rather to other functional areas, such as customer service, engineering, and materials management. These additional measures are necessary, because a controller cannot do an adequate job of maintaining systems, reporting on operating results, or recommending changes without a complete understanding of all company operations and how they interact. Consequently, the controller is well advised to develop a set of ratios and trend analyses for measurements that step beyond the usual accounting measurements to encompass the operating aspects of all departments. This chapter not only shows how to calculate each ratio, but also describes why each one is useful as well as any shortcomings it may have. The chapter concludes with a discussion of how ratios interrelate, as well as their limitations. The chapter is intended to give a controller enough information to set up a complete system of ratios and trends for the continuing analysis of all company operations.

HOW TO USE RATIOS AND TRENDS

Ratios are very useful for determining the interrelationships between numbers. For example, without a ratio, a manager has no way of knowing if the amount of accounts receivable is an acceptable one or if there should be a major collection effort underway to bring in old accounts receivable. Similarly, only a comparison of inventory to the cost of goods sold will tell if there is an excess amount of inventory on hand. Finally, one must compare interest expense to earnings to see if there is a risk of not paying for at least the interest on debt, which could result in corporate liquidation. All of this information is critical, and ratios are the best possible tool for determining it.

Ratios do not have to be used solely for analyzing financial information. For example, a ratio can reveal the extent to which a company has become top-heavy by comparing the number of indirect labor people to the number of direct labor employees. Another example is a comparison of sales to salespeople to see how many sales are being obtained, on average, by each salesperson. These measures are just as important as financial ones, but their components are not all found in the financial statements.

Despite their uses, there is a problem with ratios—they give no historical perspective on a measurement. For example, a ratio may reveal the amount of inventory turnover, but this does not tell a controller how the ratio is changing over time. For this information, one must list a series of measurements on a trend line. This can be listed on a simple bar chart or a more complex three-dimensional one, or even on a primitive numeric table—the format is important only in that it must clearly show the reader any changes in the ratio. When using ratios and trend lines together, a controller has a powerful analytical tool.

A trend line does not have to contain only ratios. They are commonly used to plot revenues or specific expense line items. This information is also useful, because management can see general trends that may require correction. The most common trend line uses only revenue data, because the sales and marketing manager wants to know the trend of sales for various divisions, product lines, and products. Once armed with this information, the sales and marketing staffs can take action to either continue hot sales growth or bolster flagging growth. Trend lines do not have to be plotted with only ratio information.

An important consideration when using ratios or trend lines is that they must be used consistently. There is nothing more confusing to a management team than to receive an entirely different set of measurements every month. Some measures may be so difficult to understand that management does not have the time to interpret the newest batch of measurements, and so ignores them; this does not assist in management's control of the business! Another problem is that inconsistent use of measurements eliminates one's ability to create any trend lines; after all, a trend line requires a series of measurements, not just one. A trend line does not provide a sufficient degree of information if it contains less than a half-dozen data points, which will not happen without a consistent measurement program.

A CAVEAT

The majority of this chapter covers the measurements that give a controller a better idea of the status of company operations. The key word is *better*, for one should not rely solely on these measurements to judge company operations. It is unfortunate that many controllers manage their departments strictly "by the numbers," and make recommendations for changes elsewhere in the company based solely on that information. A good manager uses measurements only as part of the body of knowledge required to do a thorough job of effectively and efficiently running a business. Other items that a controller should know about in order to plot a strong management course in the sea of business uncertainty are:

- *Branding.* Some companies, such as Coca-Cola, PepsiCo, or any automobile manufacturer, spend enormous amounts of money on marketing activities to build up the public's image of their brands. This may seem like a waste of money to a typical cost-conscious controller, but it has been proven time and again that consumers will pay a significant premium for branded products. Consequently, a controller should have a sufficient knowledge of corporate branding activities before releasing a report to management that recommends deep cuts in marketing costs in order to save money.

- *Company organization.* There may be quirks in how a company is organized that have a direct impact on the measurements that a controller sees. This is especially common for a large, multidivision company, where constant reorganizations result in reallocations of reporting relationships. For example, a controller may find that the sales department expenses for a division are rapidly surpassing the budget; a knowledge of the organizational structure might reveal that there is no one in that position due to a recent reorganization. This changes the controller's action from a stinging memo to the general manager of the division regarding cost controls to a strong request to the human resources staff to hire a new sales manager.

- *Competitors.* The actions of competitors have a profound impact on company operations. A competing product may be priced sharply lower than the company's product, resulting in a matching price drop that is initiated by the marketing staff. Alternatively, a sudden drop in sales may simply be caused by the entrance of a new competitor, while a rapid sales increase may be caused by the demise of a competitor, sending all of its customers to the company. For example, a controller may strongly recommend a doubling of production capacity based on a sudden up-tick in revenues, though a knowledge of the industry would have revealed that a close competitor has gone out of business, and the up-tick should be expected to only roughly match the sales of that defunct business, which is not sufficient to warrant the expense of more production facilities.

- *Goals.* If a company has established stretch goals that will be difficult to reach, a controller should expect strains on the organization that will appear in measurements. For example, an aggressive production plan will probably result in excessive levels of overtime and extra machine repair and maintenance; knowing about the goals would keep the controller in this example from spending too much time reviewing those measures that were clearly altered by the higher levels of production.

- *Labor relations.* Several of the measurements in this chapter require close tracking of direct labor hours. However, a controller may find that labor relations are so tense that additional measurements might be seen as an excessive (and unacceptable) level of control. Also, poor labor relations may mean that employees are deliberately charging their hours to incorrect activities. The first problem voids the controllers' ability to create measurements, while the second issue weakens their reliability even if they can be created. For example, a controller may see that measurements show a very low gross margin for a product line and launch a major cost investigation, only to find that the labor component is wildly incorrect. Previous knowledge of labor problems might have allowed the controller to restructure the components of the gross margin calculation, so that a trend line would have immediately shown that labor costs were the problem.

- *Management team.* The character of the management team has a profound impact on measurements. If it is unethical, there may be problems with the period-end cutoff, because this is a prime area for manipulating the volume of sales. The problem may pervade the organization, creating difficulties due to loans to owners and managers, incorrect commission payments, or difficulties with missing assets. For example, a measurement may reveal that inventory turnover is much worse than the historical average; based only on that measurement, a controller might enter into all sorts of calculations and investigations to root out the problem, whereas the knowledge that the owners are trying to inflate inventory values to underreport the cost of goods sold will lead the controller straight to the warehouse for an in-depth audit of inventory quantities.

- *Marketplace.* The market for a company's products is rarely a completely stable one. It may be seasonal, resulting in wide revenue swings depending on the month, or it may be going through a period of rapid expansion or contraction. For example, a controller may be tracking a trend line of revenue levels and notice a sudden, sharp drop in revenues for a product line. A frantic call to the sales staff might not have been so frantic if the controller realized that the product line was lawn mowers, and that sales always drop by the middle of the summer.

- *Monopoly situations.* It is not uncommon for a company to have a small number of products in its product portfolio that have no significant competition. This minority of products typically carry prices and correspondingly high margins, which may generate sufficient cash flow to make a significant difference to a company's bottom line. A controller must know enough about a company's competitive situation to know which products are in a monopoly situation, because these "breadwinner" products are critical. For example, a controller should carefully track price points, unit volume, and gross margins on all monopoly items in order to warn management of any price or margin erosion; controllers who do not know which products are breadwinners will probably not segregate them for measurement, possibly resulting in no one knowing about market changes that will have a major impact on company profits.

- *New market activities.* Most companies attempt to enter new markets from time to time. This is a very expensive activity, because potential new customers must be educated about the company, research and development costs must be incurred to create new products for the market, a distribution system must be created, and a variety of policies and procedures realigned to better service the new markets. Many controllers take the conservative approach and protest these activities because of the large up-front cost. However, a more knowledgeable controller will realize that new markets drive company sales, and the expenses needed to enter those markets are the necessary costs of getting into them.

- *Policies and procedures.* A company collects information in a more uniform manner if there are policies and procedures to cover all major transactions. If not, information may be accumulated into the wrong revenue and expense accounts, which plays havoc with a controller's measurements. For example, telling employees to break out all entertainment expenses on their travel reports resulting in all these expenses being recorded as travel expenses. A controller who does not know about this problem may be led to believe that the high travel costs are caused by excessively high air fares, and recommend a clamp down on corporate travel.

- *Product pricing.* A company may base its sales strategy on having the highest or lowest product price in the marketplace. This is not something that a controller typically measures, because the most common sales-related measures track only total revenues, not the component parts, which are prices and unit volumes. However, if the strategy is to maintain the highest or lowest price, then the controller must track this information and compare it to competing prices, so that management can maintain the appropriate price points.

- *Recruiting methods.* A company that is situated in an industry in which there is only a small available pool of qualified applicants, such as an engineering or software design company, incurs tremendous recruiting costs. This may involve overseas trips to recruit foreign candidates, or perhaps paying exorbitant fees to outside recruiters to locate potential employees. In these industries, very high recruiting costs are simply a part of doing business. If a controller does not know this, the human resources staff may be on the receiving end of a series of complaints, accusing them of using the most expensive recruiting approaches, when in fact they may be doing a very cost-effective job of locating new employees.

- *Training.* Poor employee training leads to poor transaction completion; because transactions are the basis for many measurements, this results in poor measurements. For example, poor training of the billing clerk may result in revenues being charged to an incorrect product line, which will skew both the revenues and cost of goods sold for the product line. If a controller knows where the training weaknesses lie in the organization, this makes it much easier to identify the problem and correct it, rather than assuming that the measurement is correct and that the gross margin for the product line is the real problem.

The previous points illustrate why a controller must know an organization's strengths and weaknesses, because they have a strong impact on measurements. This knowledge can be used in another way as well, for the measurement system can be altered to take advantage of corporate strengths, and bolstered to support the weakest areas. As discussed in "Interrelationship of Ratios" on page 125, it is clear that the peculiarities ensconced in every company require a controller to change, add to, and delete from the existing set of measurements to arrive at a measurement system that properly tracks weaknesses while only exerting the lightest control over organizationally strong areas.

MEASURES FOR PROFITABILITY

A controller needs to accurately judge the amount of profit extracted from a company's operations, which means knowing the exact margin earned by division, product line, and product. A controller must also have a good knowledge of fixed costs and how they impact company profits at different sales levels, as well as a thorough understanding of the amount of overhead and how that relates to the cost of goods sold. This section provides the ratios and percentage calculations needed to extract this information from the income statement. The measurements are:

- *Break-even point.* A crucial measurement for a controller to be aware of is a company's break-even point. This is the sales level at which, given a predetermined gross margin rate, a company will make a profit of zero. This is important, because a company may have such a high fixed-cost structure or low gross margins that it is nearly impossible to turn a profit unless there are extraordinarily high sales. By spotting this problem, a controller can push for sales of higher-margin products or a reduction in fixed costs. To calculate break-even, simply divide operating expenses for the reporting period by the company's historical average gross margin. For the gross margin figure, it is best to use a recent average, so that the measurement accurately reflects any recent changes.

- *Number of times interest is earned.* This is an excellent measure of the risk a company undertakes when it adds debt. If the continuing amount of cash flow cannot cover interest payments on existing debt, then a company is in serious trouble and must take steps to reduce the level of debt immediately. The measure is also good for companies considering acquiring more debt; a poor ratio will tell them not to do so. To calculate the measurement, determine the amount of interest charged on debt for a typical period (perhaps an average of the interest payments for the last quarter). Then obtain the net income figure from the income statement and add back any noncash expenses, such as amortization and depreciation, which yields the actual cash flow. Then divide the average interest expense by the cash flow amount to determine the number of times that interest is earned. The figure can be skewed if there are interest balloon payments that are not factored into the average interest expense.

- *Operating margins by division, segment, product line.* A company must have sufficient operating margins. Otherwise, all other management decisions become superfluous, since inadequate margins do not allow a company to throw off enough cash flow to stay in business. Consequently, the controller must calculate margins in a variety of ways—by division, segment, and product line—and pass this information along to management as frequently as possible. In particular, if the controller spots a rapid drop in margins, this information must go out to management immediately, rather than waiting until the next monthly financial reporting package. Information about operating margins is too time-critical to wait. The calculation for this measurement varies somewhat depending on the type of margin being measured, but is best calculated by creating a standard report for each variation using the accounting system's report writer to extract data from the general ledger and recast it in an income statement format. This may require some changes to the chart of accounts to ensure that there is enough segmentation of information to ensure reporting accuracy.

- *Overhead rate.* A primary area of competition is based on price, and the only way a company can succeed in that arena is to have extremely low costs. Costs are grouped into three areas, one of which is overhead. This can be a very large amount of money, especially for those organizations with bloated organizational structures. The amount of overhead is allocated to individual products, which has a major impact on the value of work-in-process and finished goods inventory. Allocation is based on an overhead rate that is calculated by compiling overhead costs for the period and dividing by the amount of direct labor expended during the period. The resulting overhead cost per direct labor hour is then allocated to inventory based on the amount of labor hours charged to the products. This method of charging costs to products can be highly inaccurate if the overhead rate per labor hour is extremely high, because a slight change in hours charged can result in a massive change in the overhead cost of the product. Also, because many products now require very few hours of work to produce, many companies are coming to the conclusion that direct labor is a poor basis for spreading overhead costs and are switching to more accurate allocation methodologies, such as activity-based costing (ABC).

- *Percentage return on net sales.* This is the single most commonly reviewed measure in most companies. It is a good indicator of how well all aspects of the business are performing in order to arrive at a profit. It is best tracked on a trend line to see how the profit percentage compares to that of previous periods, and is especially useful when tracked by product line, where there should be a considerable amount of consistency in the percentage from period to period. To calculate the measurement, simply divide the profit into net sales for the same period. However, one must be aware that the profit percentage is subject to manipulation, because it is possible to modify accruals and noncash expenses (e.g., depreciation and amortization) to fit the profit number that management wants.

TRACK PROFITS NET OF SALES ACTIVITY!

If a company has a mix of standard and custom products, the sales effort required to sell the custom work may be resulting in much worse margins than anyone suspects. This is because the typical costing system does not include the cost of sales calls. In particular, if the sales staff travels out of town to make these sales, try including the cost of their travel in the margin analysis. It is possible that the result will be negative margins.

- *Ratio of sales returns and allowances to gross sales.* This is an excellent way to determine the quality of goods sold or of the excess amount of inventory in the distribution pipeline. A company that finds customers sending back an inordinate amount of product, either has a faulty product that requires immediate corrective action, or has stuffed so much inventory into the distribution pipeline that retailers simply cannot sell it all. The latter calls for a different approach to selling the product. Tracking this information on a trend line is especially helpful, in order to see problems that may develop over several months. To calculate the measurement, divide the total sales returns by gross sales; both numbers should be aggregated separately in the general ledger. The ratio can be misleading, however, because sales returns invariably relate to sales from a previous period, not the current one against which the ratio is being measured.

- *Sales/profits per person.* Some companies have very large staffs, and, because the payroll expense is large, they choose to use it as a major indicator of internal efficiency. When they see the sales or profits per person falling, their typical reaction is to cut staff to bring the numbers back into line with expectations. To calculate the measurement, simply accumulate the number of personnel from payroll records and divide it into either sales or profits, both of which can be obtained from the general ledger. However, the measure is easily skewed if a company uses a large number of part-time workers; if so, these people must be converted to full-time equivalents. Also, the number can be drastically changed if a company outsources its more labor-intensive functions, essentially negating the value of the measure.

It is important to use all of the measures and not just a selection, for each one tracks different information that is critical to a complete understanding of a company's costs, margins, and break-even points. The measures are summarized in Exhibit 6.1.

Ratio	Derivation
Break-even point	$\dfrac{\text{Sales}}{\text{Average gross margin}}$
Number of times interest earned	$\dfrac{\text{Average interest expense}}{\text{Cash flow}}$
Operating margin	$\dfrac{\text{Revenues}}{\text{Cost of goods sold}}$
Overhead rate	$\dfrac{\text{Overhead expenses}}{\text{Direct labor}}$
Percent return on net sales	$\dfrac{\text{Net sales}}{\text{Net profit}}$
Ratio of sales returns and allowances to gross sales	$\dfrac{\text{Sales returns and allowances}}{\text{Gross sales}}$
Sales/profits per person	$\dfrac{\text{Sales}}{\text{Total full-time equivalents}}$
	or
	$\dfrac{\text{Net profits}}{\text{Total full-time equivalents}}$

EXHIBIT 6.1 PROFITABILITY MEASUREMENTS

MEASURES FOR THE BALANCE SHEET

One of the most heavily measured areas is the balance sheet. When used properly, the ratios and percentages noted in this section reveal a great deal of information about a company's financial health, as well as its financial strengths and weaknesses. For example, several measures cover the size of a company's debt holdings, as well as how this bears on the firm's overall level of financial risk. Other ratios deal with the relative proportions of assets needed to create revenues and profits, which an astute controller can use to compare company performance to that of competitors as well as to that of "best practices" organizations that may lie outside the industry. Other measures can be used to determine a company's short-term liquidity (which is of particular concern to lenders), as well as the age of assets. Finally, more advanced organizations are now trying to relate their assets to market valuations to determine their success in creating value in excess of the worth of their assets; there are several ratios here to assist in these calculations. The measurements are:

- *Debt/equity ratio.* To a lender, one of the most important measures is the debt to equity ratio. This reveals the degree of leverage that management has imposed on the balance sheet by acquiring debt. If the amount of debt in relation to equity is excessively high, it may be difficult for a company to service the debt or to pay it off. When a lender sees this high ratio, it may be reluctant to issue additional debt without some other assurances from management, such as personal guarantees. To calculate the measurement, simply add up all long-term and short-term debt and divide it by total equity. However, management can play with the degree of leverage by moving some debt into operating leases, which are not recorded on the balance sheet.

- *Return on assets.* This is an excellent measurement when a controller wants to know how well a company is utilizing its assets to generate revenue. If the amount of assets required in proportion to revenues is increasing, then there are inefficiencies, or at least unnecessary assets, in the organization that the controller should investigate. The components of the return on assets are shown graphically in Exhibit 6.2. Note in the exhibit the large number of components that a controller can investigate in this complicated measurement; problems can occur in such diverse areas as sales or accounts receivable that have a direct impact on the measurement. To calculate it, divide total sales by total assets, the major components of which are usually cash, accounts receivable, inventory, and fixed assets. However, this measure is not useful and can be downright misleading, when applied to a fixed asset-intensive business, such as an oil refinery, where there is a large investment that cannot be reduced, irrespective of the amount of sales generated.
- *Return on shareholder equity.* This is one of the most important measurements for a shareholder. When a shareholder has a choice between investing funds in a company or doing so elsewhere, it makes sense to compare this measure to alternative investments,

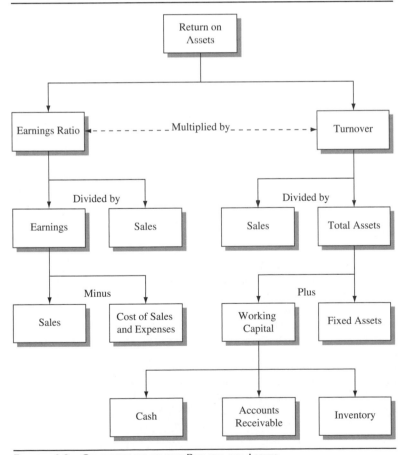

EXHIBIT 6.2   COMPONENTS OF THE RETURN ON ASSETS

and to choose the higher of the two, while factoring in various risk issues. To calculate it, simply divide net income by shareholder's equity, both of which can be found in the general ledger. The trouble with this measure is that it does not delineate changes in risk that may go hand-in-hand with changes in net income. For example, a company can increase its return on equity by incurring debt to buy back shares; however, the increased debt makes the investment more risky, so investors should also consider the debt/equity ratio alongside this one, in order to match changes in returns to changes in risk.

- *Current ratio.* A common way to measure a company's liquidity is to use the current ratio. This compares the amount of short-term assets to short-term liabilities. A good ratio is one that yields enough liquidity to pay off all current assets. If the ratio does not reveal this ability, it is possible that the company has a sufficient degree of liquidity difficulty that it is in danger of going bankrupt. To calculate this measurement, divide all current assets by all current liabilities. It can be misleading if there is a disproportionately large amount of inventory in the current assets figure, because this measure is primarily designed to track liquidity, and inventory is not a very liquid asset.

- *Quick ratio.* A controller who regularly uses a quick ratio instead of a current ratio probably has a problem with inventory. This is because the primary difference between the two ratios is inventory. The reason why inventory is dropped from the quick ratio is that it is not a very liquid asset, whereas the other components of the ratio are usually easily liquidated. This ratio gives one a good idea of how quickly a company can convert its current assets into cash to pay for current liabilities, which makes it an excellent measure of short-term liquidity. To calculate the measurement, add together all cash, accounts receivable, and temporary investments, and divide by current liabilities.

- *Ratio of sales to accounts receivable.* A controller should keep a close watch over the proportion of sales to accounts receivable, since a change in the historical rate may be indicative of worsening collection problems. To calculate the measurement, divide the amount of credit sales by the accounts receivable balance for the reporting period (both numbers should be recorded in the general ledger). The ratio should be tracked on a trend line, so that problems are more easily revealed in comparison to previous periods. The measure can be inaccurate if there is a large dollar volume of cash sales included in the sales figure; also, if the accounts receivable balance is primarily composed of a few large invoices, having even one invoice moderately overdue will severely skew the measurement.

- *Accounts payable turnover.* This ratio indicates the number of times that accounts payable were paid, or turned over, in a reporting period. It is an effective means for tracking the timeliness of payments. When tracked on a trend line, it is easy to spot when a company is entering financial difficulties, for the ratio will clearly worsen as the company delays payments. The ratio is also useful for predicting future accounts payable balances based on expected levels of purchasing. To compute the measurement, divide total purchases during the period by the ending accounts payable balance (though the average balance for the entire period is more accurate). This measure can be skewed if a company changes to or from taking early payment discounts, especially if this impacts a significant proportion of the accounts payable.

- *Ratio of repairs and maintenance expense to fixed assets.* It is extremely useful to determine the condition of a company's fixed assets, because one can thereby determine the need for expensive replacement equipment that may significantly cut into cash or borrowing reserves. The best way to do this without making a physical inspection of the equipment is to compare the size of the repairs and maintenance expense to the amount of fixed assets. When tracked on a trend line, one can easily spot any jumps in the ratio compared to previous time periods, which indicates an aging set of fixed assets. To calculate the measurement, obtain the repairs and maintenance expense from the general ledger, and divide it by the gross fixed asset cost (i.e., before depreciation). The ratio will be much more accurate if the accounting staff splits off unrelated repair and maintenance expenses, such as for grounds upkeep, and stores this information in a different general ledger account.

- *Ratio of depreciation to fixed assets.* It is important to know the age of a company's fixed assets, because an excessively old asset base may soon require replacement. One of the best ways is to simply compare the amount of accumulated depreciation to the amount of assets; a large amount of depreciation is a good indicator of old assets. To calculate the measurement, obtain the accumulated depreciation figure from the general ledger and divide it by the total fixed asset valuation (also obtained from the general ledger). The measure can be skewed if a company uses highly accelerated depreciation methods, such as double declining balance depreciation, because this appears to show an older asset base than is really the case.

- *Fixed-asset turnover.* This measurement is most useful when plotted on a trend line. It shows how much of a fixed-asset investment is needed for management to achieve a specific level of sales. If the ratio increases, then the amount of assets required has gone up, which will probably also lead to a reduced return on assets (unless margins increase). To compute the measurement, divide sales by fixed assets. Both of these numbers are located in the general ledger.

- *Ratio of retained earnings to capital.* A lender or investor uses this measurement to see how many earnings have been allowed to accumulate in the company. This is an especially important factor in a privately held company, where it is common for the owners to extract as much of the retained earnings as possible in the form of distributions, leaving few assets for continuing operations; this requires constant infusions of debt to keep the company afloat, and effectively shifts much of the risk from the owners to the lenders. To compute this measurement, divide retained earnings by total stockholder's equity, both of which are found in the general ledger.

- *Economic value added (EVA).* Many controllers do not track the returns on capital that their companies are achieving. If a company's return is lower than its cost of capital, then it is making inefficient use of that capital. In fact, it may be better for investors to take their money out of such a company and invest it elsewhere. To calculate the measurement, multiply the amount of net investment (the amount of cash invested in the business, net of depreciation) in the company by the difference between the actual return on assets and the required minimum rate of return. Shrinking the amount of working capital or fixed assets, or increasing the rate of return on those assets will improve the EVA.

- *Market value added (MVA).* From the perspective of a shareholder, a company is successful if its market value in terms of the value of its shares on the open market is in excess of the amount of capital invested in the business. If its market value is less than the amount of invested capital, then management has done a poor job of generating adequate returns. To calculate the measurement, multiply the number of shares outstanding by the share price, add in the market value of preferred stock and debt, and then subtract the total amount of invested capital.

- *Working capital productivity.* It is becoming increasingly important for companies to operate their businesses on the leanest possible asset base. Not only does this improve the return on assets, but it also reduces the risk of losing assets by investing too much in a business. Much of a typical company's investment goes into working capital, which is accounts receivable plus inventory, minus accounts payable. However, the amount of dollars in working capital is not a good way to judge it, because there is no way to compare it to some other measure of activity. This is where working capital productivity is useful. To calculate it, simply divide the amount of working capital into annual net sales. The resulting number is most useful when tracked over time and when compared to the similar number for competitors, for it tells the amount of working capital needed to support each incremental dollar of sales.

THE IMPACT OF WORKING CAPITAL

At a minimum, the new controller should track the dollar volume of working capital. This area tends to absorb excess cash due to changes in other areas, such as a looser credit policy, or an effort to stock more finished goods inventory. By refining this information to determine exactly what is causing working capital increases, the controller can keep the management team from using up more cash than necessary.

These measurements are used to create an understanding of a company's level of financial risk, liquidity, age of assets, and ability to leverage assets into revenues. It is very useful to track all of this information continuously and plot it on a trend line, so that management can spot any worrisome trends and act to correct them as soon as possible. The measures are noted again in summary form in Exhibit 6.3.

Ratio	Derivation
Debt/equity ratio	$\dfrac{\text{Long-term debt} + \text{short-term debt}}{\text{Total equity}}$
Return on assets	$\dfrac{\text{Total sales}}{\text{Total assets}}$
Return on shareholder equity	$\dfrac{\text{Net income}}{\text{Total equity}}$
Current ratio	$\dfrac{\text{Current assets}}{\text{Current liabilities}}$
Quick ratio	$\dfrac{\text{Cash} + \text{accounts receivable} + \text{investments}}{\text{Current liabilities}}$
Ratio of sales to accounts receivable	$\dfrac{\text{Net sales}}{\text{Total accounts receivable}}$
Accounts payable turnover	$\dfrac{\text{Total purchases}}{\text{Ending accounts payable balance}}$
Ratio of repairs and maintenance expense to fixed assets	$\dfrac{\text{Total repairs and maintenance expense}}{\text{Total fixed assets before depreciation}}$
Ratio of depreciation to fixed assets	$\dfrac{\text{Accumulated depreciation}}{\text{Total fixed assets}}$

EXHIBIT 6.3 BALANCE SHEET MEASUREMENTS

Ratio	Derivation
Fixed asset turnover	$\dfrac{\text{Net sales}}{\text{Fixed assets}}$
Ratio of retained earnings to capital	$\dfrac{\text{Retained earnings}}{\text{Total stockholder's equity}}$
Economic value added	(Net investment) × actual return on assets − required minimum rate of return)
Market value	(Number of shares outstanding × share price) + (market value of preferred stock and debt) − (invested capital)
Working capital productivity	$\dfrac{\text{Annual net sales}}{\text{Working capital}}$

EXHIBIT 6.3 BALANCE SHEET MEASUREMENTS *(CONTINUED)*

MEASURES FOR GROWTH

Some companies find themselves on an extremely rapid growth path. When this happens, there are financial pressures on the corporation that require different measurements to discover. For example, there will be great strains on cash flow, so there must be a close watch over the percentage change in cash flow. Other issues include changes in sales and market share; these two measures can provide contraindications by moving in opposite directions, so it is helpful to track both measures side by side. Finally, investors want to know if all of the growth pains are worth it, so the controller should track changes in earnings per share. The measurements are:

- *Percentage change in cash flow.* A change in cash flow is one of the first indicators of a variety of problems elsewhere in a company. For example, a decline in cash flow can be evidence of a decline in sales or gross margins, or it may be a sign of increased sales, general and administrative (SG&A) expenses, increased fixed asset expenditures, or even of a stock buyback. Whatever the reason, this is a good first indicator of trouble, and as such, the controller should rely upon it. There are two ways to calculate the measurement. The first and more accurate way is to add profits to all noncash and fixed asset expenditures. The "quick and dirty" alternative is to simply track the current cash balance. In either case, it is best to track the information on a trend line in order to spot any period-to-period problems.
- *Percentage change in earnings per share (EPS).* A company may find that its sales, profits, and market share are continuing to improve, but that the EPS are not keeping pace. This can understandably cause concern by investors. The key factor causing this problem is the number of shares. An equity placement that adds to the number of outstanding shares can water down the EPS to the point where even enhanced profits will still result in a decrease in the EPS. The simplest way to calculate this trend is to divide net earnings by the number of outstanding shares and plot this on a trend line.
- *Percentage change in market share.* The best absolute measure of a company's performance is its market share. If the share increases, then the company is performing better than its competitors. To track it, use the market share results issued by industry trade organizations and plot the data points on a grid chart. However, a company may be gobbling up market share and still be losing sales if the overall market is shrinking, so it helps to track the *size* of the market alongside the market share trend line.

Ratio	Derivation
Percentage change in cash flow	Incremental change in cash flow / Cash flow from previous period
Percentage change in EPS	Incremental change in EPS / EPS from previous period
Percentage change in market share	Incremental change in market share / Market shart from previous period
Percentage change in sales	Incremental change in sales / Sales from previous period

EXHIBIT 6.4 GROWTH MEASUREMENTS

- *Percentage change in sales.* A controller should closely track the trend line for sales, not only for the company as a whole, but also for individual product lines. A continuing upward slant on a growth chart is obviously encouraging, but sometimes the most important trend to track is the rate of growth. Any decline in the rate of growth must not only be factored into future growth projections, but may also result in a discussion with the sales force to see if management should expect a sudden drop-off in sales volume—something that impacts lots of functional areas. To create the trend line, simply extract the periodic sales information from the computer system, usually with the use of a report writer to extract sales by product or product line, and then plot the data points on a grid chart.

These measures are necessary for determining the amount of cash required to continue growth, the degree of growth occurring, and the extent to which investors are profiting from it. Because there are so many different factors to determine, it is necessary to track all of the measures noted in this section. The measures are summarized in Exhibit 6.4.

MEASURES FOR CASH FLOW

A company may look great on paper—sales spiraling upward, surging profits, and a vast backlog—and still go bankrupt. Cash flow measurements can see through all of the favorable indicators to ascertain the true health of the organization. The measurements in this section focus on stripping away extraordinary cash flow items to see how continuing operations are doing, as well as the ability of a corporation to cover continuing expenses for items not appearing on the income statement, such as debt repayments and fixed-asset purchases. The measurements are:

- *Cash flow adequacy.* It is critical to know if the cash flow from operations is sufficient to meet all major payment commitments. These commitments do not include basic payments that are included in the income statement, such as payments for materials, utilities, or taxes; this is for non–income statement payments, such as debt payments. To calculate the measurement, divide cash flow from operations by all scheduled payments for long-term debt, asset purchases and dividends. However, this measure is not sufficient if management is in the habit of making unscheduled payments, such as for fixed assets that are not on the annual fixed-asset purchases schedule.

- *Cash flow return on assets.* Though most companies just use the return on assets, this is a variation that may be worthwhile in some situations. Rather than dividing profits by total assets, just divide cash flow by total assets. Any difference in the two measures will be due to any noncash expenses. If there is a large amount of noncash expenses, then the cash flow return on assets can be substantially higher than the simpler return on assets. This can be used to explain company performance to investors when large depreciation or amortization charges are cutting into earnings.

- *Cash flow to sales.* This is perhaps a better measure of profitability than a simple gross or net margin on sales. It reveals the total amount of cash flow attributable to each sales dollar. To compute it, divide cash flow from operations by revenues. Because the measurement strips out all noncash expenses, such as depreciation, it gives a good view of actual cash flows to be expected from operations.

- *Dividend payout ratio.* An investor who relies on company dividends wants to know the likelihood of the company's being able to continue paying out at the same rate. This measurement provides that information. By comparing the amount of cash flow to the dividend payout rate, one can easily track the proportion of cash that goes to dividends; if the ratio worsens over time, it is likely that the dividend will be cut. To calculate the measurement, divide the total amount of dividends by the total cash from operations. It is best to track this information on a trend line to spot changes over time.

IS THE OWNER CAUSING A CASH DRAIN?

When first starting in the controller position and if preliminary analysis shows that the company is losing money, turn to the equity portion of the general ledger and see if the company owner is paying himself large distributions. If so, and this is happening despite putting the company through difficult cash-flow problems, the new controller should seriously consider working somewhere else. Laboring under constant cash flow problems caused by the boss is a no-win situation.

- *Long-term debt repayment.* A controller must be able to judge a company's ability to repay debt, so that recommendations can be made to alter operations in favor of reducing debt, if the chief financial officer (CFO) decides that to be a prudent strategy. Many companies that are not fiscally sound can convince themselves otherwise, simply by continuing to pile on the debt. A controller can tell if a company is truly solvent by tracking debt levels over the course of a year to see if there are periods when short-term debt is completely paid off. If not, a company frequently rolls over short-term debt into long-term debt with a fixed repayment schedule; this too can be a sign of fiscal trouble if the controller finds that the excessive amount of debt is leading to an unfavorable debt/equity ratio or if the number of times interest is earned is dropping. If a controller just wants to see if a company is capable of paying off continuing long-term debt payments, which are composed of both interest and principal, divide the total amount of long-term debt payments by cash from operations. If the ratio is unfavorable, it is probably time to extend the terms of the debt, so that the periodic payments are smaller.

- *Operating cash flow.* There are many factors that can impact cash flow, and many of them are extraneous ones that rarely repeat. Though one would think that these extraneous factors will eventually go away, there always seem to be a few that interfere with the determination of cash flow from basic operations. This measurement is based on

Ratio	Derivation
Cash flow adequacy	$$\frac{\text{Cash flow from operations}}{\text{All scheduled payments for long-term debt, asset purchases, and dividends}}$$
Cash flow return on assets	$$\frac{\text{Cash flow}}{\text{Total assets}}$$
Cash flow to sales	$$\frac{\text{Cash flow from operations}}{\text{Total revenue}}$$
Dividend payout ratio	$$\frac{\text{Total dividend payments}}{\text{Cash flow from operations}}$$
Long-term debt repayment	$$\frac{\text{Total long-term debt payments for the period}}{\text{Cash flow from operations for the period}}$$
Operating cash flow	Profits + noncash expenses ± changes in working capital

EXHIBIT 6.5 CASH FLOW MEASUREMENTS

only operating elements, excluding all other factors. This gives a controller the best information about the true status of cash flows. To compute the measurement, add noncash expenses to profits, and then adjust for changes in working capital (accounts receivable, accounts payable, and inventory). Just as important, the measure excludes any changes caused by investment income, fixed-asset sales, or extraordinary items such as income from legal or insurance settlements.

Compiling cash flow measurements should be at or near the top of the controller's "to do" list when the true health of a company needs to be obtained. If there is a problem, the controller can immediately get to work on fixing the underlying problems. If a controller does not regularly review this information, there is a risk that the company will find itself in a difficult cash position simply because the controller did not exercise enough foresight to accumulate the necessary information in advance. The measures are summarized in Exhibit 6.5.

MEASURES FOR NONFINANCIAL PERFORMANCE

This section deals with measures that a controller is not so accustomed to measuring—nonfinancial performance. These measures can cover an extraordinarily wide range of activities, ranging from engineering to sales and marketing. Many companies are now realizing that nonfinancial performance in these other areas is just as important to corporate success as the purely financial measures that they are more accustomed to perusing. This section divides nonfinancial performance measurements into the traditional departmental functions. (e.g., accounting, production, etc.), and describes a variety of measurements for each area that are extremely helpful for determining their efficiency, effectiveness, speed, and level of experience, all of which are direct contributors to corporate success.

Accounting

This section covers the performance measurements that a controller should use to manage the accounting department. The most heavily reviewed item is the average collection period for accounts receivable, because inattention to this area can lead to severe cash flow problems.

It is also common to closely review the percentage of accounts payable discounts taken, so that the accounting department is not inadvertently responsible for extra expenses that could have been avoided. In addition, it is increasingly common to track the number of days required to release financial statements, with many companies even tying a controller's bonus to this measure. Finally, an increasingly common set of measures is to track the efficiency of the accounting staff, much as the production staff has historically been tracked, by determining the number of errors committed and transactions completed per person. These are the primary measures used by a controller to manage the accounting department:

- *Average collection period.* This is one of the best ways to determine the quality of accounts receivable. It shows the number of days that the average account receivable has gone unpaid. If the number of days resulting from the calculation is close to the number of days before which invoices are due (e.g., payable in 30 days), then it is unlikely that there are very many old accounts receivable, which highlights the ability of the accounting staff not only to issue error-free bills that are promptly paid, but also to rapidly collect overdue invoices. Conversely, an excessive number of collection days points to probable issues on the same topics. To calculate the measurement, divide average annualized receivables by average daily credit sales.

- *Percentage of accounts receivable.* One of the primary measurements on which the controller is judged is the ability of the accounting staff to collect accounts receivable on time. If this does not happen, a company ends up with an excessive investment in accounts receivable, which is a poor use of funds. Also, older accounts receivable are at a greater risk of not being collected. To calculate this measure, print out an aged accounts receivable report, which should list at the bottom the total receivable amount in 30-day time buckets. Add up the summary totals for those time buckets that are considered to be overdue (e.g., everything over 60 days old), and divide it by the total of all accounts receivable.

- *Ratio of purchase discounts to total purchases.* A company can save a fair amount of money by taking advantage of early payment discounts. Only a small percentage of suppliers offer early payment discount options, but if a company takes advantage of them all, the savings can add up to a tidy sum. The amount saved as a percentage of all purchases does not change much over time, so tracking the percentage of discounts taken is an easy way for the controller to discover if the accounts payable staff is missing out on some discounts. To calculate it, track the purchase discounts in a separate general ledger account, and divide this monthly figure by total purchases. Then track the resulting percentage on a trend line.

- *Time to produce financial statements.* In today's competitive environment, it is no longer acceptable to wait a month to receive the results of the previous month's performance. Most managers need financial information as fast as possible, so that they can rapidly spot problems and correct them. The calculation is an easy one; just add up the days from the end of the month to the point when financial statements are issued. However, the measure is less meaningful if the accounting staff is already issuing interim reports before the financial statements that contain the most critical operating and financial information.

- *Transaction error rate.* One of the most time-consuming activities in the accounting area is fixing errors. If something is wrong, the best person to find the error and fix it is a senior staff person or manager, and this type of person is usually already in short supply and certainly overworked. Consequently, there tends to be a long backlog of problems that the accounting department has in its queue, which may involve wait time by other departments, suppliers, or customers. Clearly, the controller must pay close attention to the transaction error rate, since it has such a major impact on workflows in the accounting area. This is not a measure that can be easily tracked by an automated system. Instead, the best approach is to review the transaction journals at the end of each month and add up the number of special debits and credits that were entered in the system—each one usually represents the correction of a previous problem. Then divide the number of errors by the total number of transactions, which also comes from the transaction logs. The main issue with this measure is that it only tracks items that have been corrected, not those that are still pending (which may be far larger than the number being corrected).

- *Transactions processed per person.* Above all others, the accounting department is driven by the need to process large quantities of transactions, such as billings and payments to suppliers. Because of the large volume, this calls for extremely high levels of efficiency. By tracking the number of transactions processed per person, the controller can benchmark internal performance against that of other organizations to see if there are grounds for revamping processes to increase efficiency. The calculation varies somewhat by type of transaction, but it essentially requires that the controller accumulate data on the number of transactions processed during a specific time period, and the effort required to process them. It is easiest to do this with a periodic study, which may call for the services of a consultant.

All controllers must be efficient in producing financial statements, collecting accounts receivable, taking purchase discounts, and processing transactions, and these measurements are the primary control point over those activities. The measures are summarized in Exhibit 6.6.

Customer Service Measurements

If there is a separate customer service department (or even if not), the measurements noted in this section are useful for determining the degree of customer satisfaction. Customer turnover shows the extent to which a company can retain its existing customer base, while two

Ratio	Derivation
Average collection period	$\dfrac{\text{Average annualized accounts receivable}}{\text{Average daily credit sales}}$
Overdue accounts receivable	$\dfrac{\text{Total of overdue accounts receivable}}{\text{Total accounts receivable}}$
Ratio of purchase discounts to total purchases	$\dfrac{\text{Total purchase discounts taken}}{\text{Total purchases}}$
Time to produce financial statements	(Financial statement issue date) – (First day of the month)
Transaction error rate	$\dfrac{\text{Number of errors}}{\text{Total number of transactions}}$
Transactions processed per person	$\dfrac{\text{Number of transactions completed}}{\text{Number of full-time equivalents required to complete transactions}}$

EXHIBIT 6.6 ACCOUNTING MEASUREMENTS

other measures note the types and quantities of complaints received, as well as the company's speed in responding to them. The measurements are:

- *Customer turnover.* A company expends a vast amount of resources to acquire new customers. It is much more inexpensive to simply retain the ones it already has than to find new ones, but this is sometimes lost on aggressive sales managers who celebrate acquiring new customers; the loss of an old one tends to pass unnoticed. The controller can point out this problem by reviewing the billing records to see which customers have not done business with the company for a long time. To calculate it, compare the billing database to the list of customers to whom the company has sold products or services in the past year and determine how many have not been invoiced in the last quarter (or some other time period, as determined by management). Divide the number of noncurrent customers by the total number of customers to determine turnover.

- *Number of customer complaints.* Any well run company should know exactly how many customer complaints have been received, as well as the issues to which they pertain and how they were resolved. This information should be contained in a customer complaints database that is accessible to as many employees as possible. Only by tracking this information and taking corrective action as necessary can a company fix those problems that irritate customers enough to lead them to contact the company. To calculate the number of complaints, simply access the complaints database and summarize the number of complaints by time period. It is even more effective to summarize the complaints by *type* of complaint, which tells management what areas need the most corrective action.

- *Response time to customer complaints.* If a customer complains and then does not receive a response within a reasonable time period, that customer is probably gone for good. By closely tracking the time it takes to respond to customer problems, management can alter the response system, which results in more satisfied customers who will continue to buy from the company. To calculate it, create a complaints database in which all contacts are logged; then subtract the response date from the initial contact date. An even better measure is to track the time it takes to completely resolve each complaint, rather than just the time to make an initial contact.

These measures are summarized in Exhibit 6.7.

Distribution Measurements

Many companies seem to think that their jobs are complete once they have manufactured products; however, there is an art to delivering products to customers as quickly and with as little

Ratio	Derivation
Customer turnover	$\dfrac{\text{(Total customer list)} - \text{(Invoiced customers)}}{\text{Total customer list}}$
Number of customer complaints	Summarize complaints from complaints database for specified date range
Response time to customer complaints	(Response date) – (Initial contact date)
	or
	(Final resolution date) – (Initial contact date)

EXHIBIT 6.7 CUSTOMER SERVICE MEASUREMENTS

damage as possible. This section covers the primary measurements to use when evaluating this key function. The first measure covers the time needed to deliver products to customers, while the second explores the proportion of deliveries that meet expectations. The final measure is useful for discovering the amount of damage to products during transit. The measurements are:

- *Average delivery time.* The distribution function is responsible for picking products, packaging them, and delivering them to the customer. If the customer is in a hurry to receive the product, the time needed to get the product into the mail is critical. To calculate this measurement, note in the company's computer system the date and time when an order is sent to the shipping area, and compare this to the date and time when the order was listed in the shipping log as having been shipped. This is an easy calculation if the ordering and shipping functions are linked in the computer system, but otherwise very difficult. It rarely makes sense to track the time required to actually deliver the product to the customer, because the customer may specify a slow delivery method that will skew the measurement.

- *Percentage of on-time deliveries.* It is very important that the company deliver products on the date requested by the customer. Many customers are now using just-in-time (JIT) manufacturing systems, and so they want deliveries on a specific date,. which means that they cannot be delivered early or late. To calculate this measurement, there must be a requested delivery date entered into the computer system for each customer purchase order; otherwise, it is impossible to determine when an order is supposed to ship. Next, there must be a shipment date recorded, against which the controller can match the required date. The computer system can then subtract the delivery date from the required date and summarize the difference for all deliveries. However, there must also be an adjustment to the calculation for the estimated shipment time to the customer. It is very useful to add a detailed listing of all "problem" shipments to this measurement, so that management can see where problems have occurred and correct them.

- *Percentage of products damaged in transit.* Most companies do not deliver their own products to customers; a third-party carrier does it for them. The company must know if the carrier is damaging any of the delivered products, because this is not exactly good customer service, so that it can take steps to switch to a new carrier. This is a difficult measure to calculate unless customers tell the company about the damage; consequently, the best measurement point is customer complaints, which should be logged into a complaints database. The controller can then select only those complaints pertaining to damaged products, and divide this number by the total number of products shipped.

If these measures are not tracked regularly, management will have no way of knowing the performance of its distribution function. The measures are summarized in Exhibit 6.8.

Ratio	Derivation
Average delivery time	(Delivery date) – (Date order was sent to shipping area)
Percentage of on-time deliveries	(Required date) – (Actual delivery date)
Percentage of products damaged in transit	$\dfrac{\text{Damage-related complaints in complaints database}}{\text{Total complaints in complaints database}}$

EXHIBIT 6.8 DISTRIBUTION MEASUREMENTS

Engineering Measurements

The engineering department has a direct impact on product costs, as well as the efficiency of other departments, such as materials management and production. The measurements in this area are necessary to ensure that the key engineering functions are running properly, thereby improving the efficiency of other downstream operations. The bill of materials accuracy measurement is mandatory for ensuring that the correct quantities and types of parts are available for production. There are also several measurements, which can be used together or separately to determine the engineering department's speed in completing new product designs as rapidly as possible, which is of considerable importance in an economy where market windows open and close very fast. A parts usage measure is crucial for determining the engineering staff's ability to use existing parts in new products, greatly easing the work of the materials management staff, which must procure and store new parts. Finally, another measure determines the ability of the engineering staff to meet target costs; this skill is crucial for ensuring that a company prices its products at a price point that gives it a profitable share of the market. The measurements are:

- *Bill of materials (BOM) accuracy.* The engineering department has a major impact on the efficiency of the materials management department, in that it must specify in advance the materials needed to produce products. Without this information, the materials management personnel are reduced to guessing about the contents of new products, which commonly results in purchases of items that are never used, which contributes to an excessively large inventory. The materials list is commonly known as a bill of materials. To calculate its accuracy, review a bill of materials with the engineering, warehousing, and production staffs to ensure that all parts are actually needed. Each mistake, either in terms of quantities or item codes, is an error. Divide the number of accurate parts by the total list of parts needed to derive the accuracy percentage.

IS THERE A BILL OF MATERIALS?

A major concern for every controller of a manufacturing company is the accuracy of inventory records. If they are inaccurate, this greatly impedes all efforts to create accurate financial statements. An excellent clue to the accuracy of the inventory is the existence and frequency of updates to bills of material. If none are maintained, this is excellent evidence of minimal management attention to a key area of operations.

- *Number of patent applications filed.* Leading-edge research gives a company a good basis for building products that no one else can match. A good sign of this research is the number of patent applications filed during the period. It is easily tracked by the legal staff, which usually assists in creating and filing the necessary documents. However, filing a patent application and translating this into new products that generate sales requires lots of other activities, so patent activity is not a sure sign of future success.

- *Percentage of sales from new products.* The previous measurement showing the number of new products is not as important as the percentage of sales being derived from them, since this is a more sure measure of corporate health. To calculate it, summarize the sales from new products (it is helpful to arrange the chart of accounts in advance to track this information) and divide by total sales.

- *Percentage of new parts used on products.* The engineering staff should always strive to reduce the number of new parts in each product design to the absolute minimum, because not doing so entails buying from additional suppliers, as well as stocking extra parts in the warehouse, which requires an additional investment. To track it, compare the bill of materials for each new product to the existing list of parts in inventory to see which items are new. Then divide the number of new parts by the total number of parts used in the product.

- *Percentage of new products introduced in the period.* A key measure of a company's ability to thrive in the marketplace is the percentage of its products that are new. An old product line generally leads to declining sales, so the reverse is also true—constantly replenishing the product line leads to more revenues. To calculate the measurement, add up the number of new products introduced during the period and divide by the number of products available at the beginning of the period. This measure can be significantly skewed by how one defines a new product; if a minor product enhancement is defined as a new product, the company is only fooling itself into believing that it is creating new products.

- *Percentage of products reaching market before competition.* It is not very useful to a company to release fabulous products to the market long after the competition when there is no one left to buy them. Instead, a company must tightly focus on bringing products to market as soon as possible, even if they are not quite as perfect as the designers would like. A good way to measure this is to manually track the product release date, and then keep abreast of release dates by competitors to see when they release similar or competing products. However, the measurement is quite judgmental, because it is sometimes difficult to determine if a competitor's product is really similar to what a company has already released.

- *Percentage of released designs matching target costs.* A new product will not be very profitable if the costs designed into it are so high that the company either cannot obtain a profit when selling at a competitive price, or must sell at an exorbitant price in order to obtain a profit. Instead, the controller should verify that product designs are being released that have costs matching expectations (the target cost). To calculate the measurement, simply summarize all actual costs for a product and divide them by the original target cost, which should be noted in the engineering documentation. It may also be useful to track the percentage by which released designs are missing their targets, so that management can work on gradually dropping costs down to target levels.

- *Time from design inception to production.* The engineering staff must be able to produce new product designs as rapidly as possible in order to beat the speed with which competitors are introducing products. This is an ever-declining time period, so it is best to track the design time on a trend line, working toward extremely short design periods. To calculate it manually, note the design start and end dates and subtract the former from the later to derive the total number of design days. The design time will vary greatly by product, of course, since they may vary greatly in complexity, so it is best to track this information separately for each product line.

Many companies treat their engineering departments as something of a "black hole"— they feed money into it, and new products come out from time to time, though no one knows their exact configurations, nor when they will be released. A better approach is to use the measurements in this section to determine the speed with which new products are being created, the efficient use of old parts in new products, and the level of detail that the department is providing the materials management personnel in terms of the parts needed to

Ratio	Accuracy
BOM accuracy	$\dfrac{\text{Number of accurate parts per BOM}}{\text{Total list of parts on BOM}}$
Number of patent applications filed	Number of applications logged in as having been sent during the period
Percentage of new products introduced in the period	$\dfrac{\text{Number of new products introduced in the period}}{\text{Number of products available at the beginning of the period}}$
Percentage of sales from new products	$\dfrac{\text{Revenues from new products}}{\text{Total revenues}}$
Percentage of new parts used on products	$\dfrac{\text{Number of new parts in BOM}}{\text{Total number of products released}}$
Percentage of products reaching market before competition	$\dfrac{\text{Number of products released before competition}}{\text{Total number of products released}}$
Percentage of released designs matching target costs	$\dfrac{\text{Summary of actual product costs}}{\text{Summary of target costs}}$
Time from design inception to production	(Completed design and signoff date) − (Design start date)

EXHIBIT 6.9   ENGINEERING MEASUREMENTS

build each product. The measurements can also be used to determine the impact on sales of new product introductions. Finally, the department must be responsible for hitting prearranged target costs; there is a measurement here for determining that information. In short, this section provides the tools to attain a high level of control over the engineering department. The measures are summarized in Exhibit 6.9.

Human Resources

The human resources department fulfills a wide variety of tasks, some of which must be completed properly if a company is to avoid government fines, promptly fill new positions, and avoid excessive levels of overhead. The measure that is central to the needs of a growing firm that has an insatiable need for new employees is the time needed to fill requested positions. Other firms with lesser hiring needs may concentrate on fulfilling government requirements, such as the percentage of minorities on the payroll. There are several other measures covering the trend of fringe benefits or indirect labor to direct labor, which are useful for determining the trend of employee-related costs. For a more progressive company that wants to have a highly trained staff, there is also a measurement for tracking the percentage of employees with certifications. Some combination of these measurements will fulfill the requirements of most human resources departments. The measurements are:

- *Average time to fill requested positions.* One of the human resources department's most important tasks is to assist in finding good candidates for requested positions throughout the company. In an explosive growth company, where continued growth is almost entirely dependent on finding additional staff, this is the department's most critical function. To calculate it, create a log book in which the date of all new position requests are received by the human resources staff, as well as the date on which offer letters are accepted by recruits; the difference between the two dates is the average time to fill requested positions.

- *Average yearly wage per employee.* It is of moderate use to management to know the average annual pay of its employees, since this gives it some idea of the company's pay levels as compared to the industry. For example, if the employee turnover rate is high and the average pay rate is low, this may be an indication that the company must start offering higher pay rates in order to retain staff. To calculate it, use a report writer to create a standard report listing everyone's pay rate; this usually requires two lists, one for the hourly staff and one for the paid staff. Then summarize each list. Multiply the total on the hourly employee list by the total number of standard hours worked in a year (usually 2,080), and multiply the total on the salaried employee list by the total number of pay periods. Then add the two lists together and divide by the total number of employees. This calculation may be slightly skewed if there are many part-time employees, since this will translate into a very low annual pay rate.

- *Employee turnover rate.* By far the most important measurement in the human resources area is employee turnover. It is exceedingly expensive to recruit and train new employees, so management must tightly focus on retaining all current staff. To calculate it, add up the number of people who have left the company, and divide by the number of employees at the beginning of the measurement period. It may be useful to subdivide this measurement so that the most critical departments, such as engineering, are tracked separately.

- *Indirect to direct personnel ratio.* Management may want to know if a company is becoming top-heavy with an excessive number of people in the overhead areas, such as administration, accounting, or engineering. Changes in this proportion are most clear when tracked over time (perhaps annually). To calculate it, summarize the number of personnel in overhead positions (the easiest way is to use the payroll system to list personnel by department) and divide that number by the total in direct labor positions (i.e., the production department). Another way to measure this is to use payroll dollars instead of headcount, which gives a more accurate picture of a company's proportional investment in indirect labor.

- *Minorities percentage.* Depending on the size of a company, there may be federal government reporting requirements for the percentages of various types of minorities in a company. If so, the best way to track this information is to record a minority code in the payroll or human resources computer systems for each person, so that a simple computer query can extract the information needed for various government reports.

- *Percentage of employees with certifications.* A company with many certified employees is a company with a great knowledge base that will contribute toward constant system improvements. Certifications fall into nearly every functional area, from certified management accountants to certified engineers. This information can be recorded in the human resources database with a code, and can be extracted with a simple query. To calculate it, divide the total number of people with certifications by the total number of employees. This measurement can be subdivided into departments, so that management can determine the skill levels by functional area.

- *Ratio of fringe benefits to direct labor.* The human resources staff is responsible for the cost (though not necessarily the types) of fringe benefits offered to the staff, which is principally comprised of medical insurance. Senior management sometimes looks at the ratio of fringe benefits to direct labor to see if too much is being spent on fringe benefits, and may cut back in this area if they perceive that to be the case. To calculate it, manually summarize the fringe benefit cost per person (or else accumulate the information through general ledger accounts) and divide it by the direct labor cost, which is usually obtained through the payroll system.

- *Trend of headcount.* Some managers like to review the number of people in each department, preferably on a trend line, to spot unusual changes in headcount. This is most informative when tied to various activity measures (usually revenues), so that there is a direct relationship between an activity and headcount. Headcount is easily extracted from the payroll database, though one must be careful to translate any part-time staff to full-time equivalents to ensure comparability across time periods.

There are many measurements available to track the performance of the human resources staff, or of the employees for whom they are responsible. Not all of these measurements should be used at one time, however. For example, a rapidly growing company will focus primarily on the department's ability to rapidly recruit new people and will want to know about employee turnover, but a more staid organization may be more interested in obeying rules and regulations, and so will focus on minority percentages. For this area, the controller must fit the measurements to the circumstances. The measures are summarized in Exhibit 6.10.

Materials Management Measurements

Recent developments in the materials management area can make this one of the most streamlined operations in a company. Measurements are needed to verify the extent of the department's efficiency. For example, inventory accuracy is needed to ensure that a material requirements planning (MRP) system operates properly. Also, an inventory turnover measurement is needed to verify the outcome of MRP and JIT systems. In addition, there are several measures for determining the department's success in shrinking the number of suppliers, as well as of switching to more efficient electronic commerce systems. It is also

Ratio	Derivation
Average time to fill requested positions	(Date offer letter is accepted by recruit) − (Date of receipt of position request)
Average yearly wage per employee	$\dfrac{\text{(Summary of all hourly wages} \times \text{number of annual working hours)} + \text{(Summary of all salaries)}}{\text{Number of employees}}$
Employee turnover rate	$\dfrac{\text{Number of employee departures}}{\text{Number of employees at beginning of period}}$
Indirect to direct personnel ratio	$\dfrac{\text{Number of personnel in overhead positions}}{\text{Number of personnel in direct labor positions}}$ or $\dfrac{\text{Total payroll of overhead positions}}{\text{Total payroll of direct labor positions}}$
Minorities percentage	Summarize by minority code in payroll or human resources systems
Percentage of employees with certifications	$\dfrac{\text{Number of employees with certifications}}{\text{Total number of employees}}$
Ratio of fringe benefits to direct labor	$\dfrac{\text{Total fringe benefit expense}}{\text{Total direct labor expense}}$
Trend of headcount	(Total full-time employees) + (Total full-time equivalents for part-time employees)

EXHIBIT 6.10   HUMAN RESOURCE MEASUREMENTS

important to track the percentage of on-time parts delivery, since this impacts the ability of the production department to complete new products on time. The measurements are:

- *Inventory accuracy.* The inventory database must accurately reflect the quantities, part numbers, and locations of all inventory in stock. If not, the materials management staff cannot be sure about what materials are in stock, and will probably purchase extra materials to cover this level of uncertainty, which increases the inventory investment as well as the potential level of obsolescence. To measure it, print out a listing of the inventory and its locations and audit a significant sample from the listing. Divide the number of test items with correct information by the total number sampled to obtain the accuracy percentage.

- *Inventory turnover.* An extremely important measure is inventory turnover. This tells management the proportion of inventory in stock (as raw materials, work-in-process, and finished goods) as compared to the cost of goods sold. A high proportion of inventory indicates that there is an excessive investment in working capital that is a good target for reduction. To calculate it, add up the cost of all inventory and divide by the annualized cost of goods sold. This calculation can be skewed if there is a large amount of finished goods on hand (which can fluctuate widely if sales are highly seasonal).

- *Number of suppliers used by commodity code.* The materials management staff can become overwhelmed if it is managing too many suppliers. It is better to utilize the services of a smaller number of suppliers, so that a company has enough time to implement supplier rating systems, electronic data transfers, and mutual product designs with a limited group of business partners. An excessive number of suppliers in each commodity code is a clear indicator that some shrinkage of the supplier base is in order. To calculate it, use the accounts payable database to create a list of all suppliers from whom the company has made purchases in the last year, and sort the list by commodity code.

- *Obsolete inventory percentage.* An excessive amount of obsolete inventory is an indicator of too much inventory on hand (since not all of it is being used), an inadequate materials management system (since it is not using up in-house parts), or of the unwillingness of management to dispose of old parts. In any of these cases, a controller needs to emphasize that eliminating the root causes of obsolescence are a primary method for reducing materials costs. To calculate it, use the materials management system to extract all inventory records for which there has been no inventory movement for a long time (which can vary from a few months to years, depending on the industry); when the costs of these inventory items are divided by the total inventory cost, this yields a rough measure of total obsolescence. The measure can be skewed by items that are old, but which can be sold—a review by management will easily uncover these items.

- *Percentage of on-time part deliveries.* The most important function for the materials management staff is to ensure that materials arrive on time, so that the production process is not held up. This requires tight control over the arrival of needed materials. To calculate this measurement, create a report in the computer system that compares the requested arrival date on all company purchase orders to the dates on which parts were actually received (which should be entered by the receiving staff). If these portions of a company's systems are not run with computers, the measurement is nearly impossible to calculate.

- *Percentage of suppliers using electronic data interchange (EDI).* The materials management staff can operate more efficiently if it conducts electronic purchasing and other transactions with suppliers. By doing so, it reduces the time required to transfer information, and, depending on the interfaces used, can even lead to the near-automation of most transactions. To measure it, manually summarize the number of suppliers with whom the company has EDI links, and divide by the total number of suppliers with whom the company did business in the past year (which is obtained from accounts payable records).

- *Total number of components.* Many companies are overwhelmed with an excessive number of parts, many of which have not been used in a very long time, but which the materials management staff must still track. If there is an excessive amount, the best management action is to undertake a detailed review of parts usage to see what can be eliminated from stock. To calculate this measurement, simply run an inventory listing for all items currently in stock, and add up all the line items. It is also helpful to compare the number of parts to sales, since the number of parts will probably increase with revenues. It is also useful to create a "where used" report that shows the products for which each part is used; if a part is in stock but is not used on any current products, then it is a prime candidate for elimination.

Today's competitive pressures almost always result in some changes in the materials management area, either to electronically link to suppliers and customers, or to increase the speed or efficiency with which materials are procured and sent to the shop floor. The amalgam of measurements in this section will serve the controller in determining departmental performance for almost any performance improvement project. The measures are summarized in Exhibit 6.11.

Production Measurements

The production department has been greatly impacted by JIT production methods, and to a large extent the measurements in this section are needed to identify its success. A key JIT concept is reducing equipment setup times, so there is a measurement for that. Also, there is a measure for tracking the proportion of successfully completed products; under JIT, this should be very nearly 100 percent. The turnover of work-in-process inventory should also

Ratio	Derivation
Inventory accuracy	$\dfrac{\text{Number of accurate test items}}{\text{Number of items sampled}}$
Number of suppliers used by commodity code	Sort accounts payable list of suppliers by commodity code
Obsolete inventory percentage	$\dfrac{\text{Cost of inventory items with no recent usage}}{\text{Total inventory cost}}$
Percentage of on-time part delivery	(Actual arrival date) − (Requested arrival date)
Percentage of suppliers using EDI	$\dfrac{\text{Number of suppliers with EDI linkages}}{\text{Total number of suppliers}}$
Total number of components	Summary of all inventory line items

EXHIBIT 6.11 MATERIALS MANAGEMENT MEASUREMENTS

increase under a JIT system, so there is a supporting measurement here for that. There are also more traditional measures that are not used in JIT, such as the percentage of scrap, and labor productivity. The measurements are:

- *Average equipment setup time.* In a just-in-time manufacturing environment, it is critical to only produce what is immediately needed. However, most companies still make long production runs, even though this generates more products than are needed. They do this because the production equipment takes so long to set up that it is only cost-effective to make long production runs. The solution, then, is to reduce the length of the equipment setup times. This is tracked separately for each piece of equipment, and is usually done by either the production or process engineering staffs. The calculation is simply the time (in hours, minutes, or seconds) required to switch a machine over from one type of production to another.

- *Percentage of acceptable products completed.* Management should know what proportion of every production run results in good products that are acceptable for sale. This is absolutely critical in an industry such as chip wafer manufacturing, where yield rates may be as low as 20 percent. To calculate the measurement, create a system for collecting and counting all unacceptable products from a production run, and then divide this amount by the total of all products created in the run (either acceptable or not). It may only be necessary to aggregate this information for a single monthly measurement, but it is more common to run the measurement by product line, since yield may vary dramatically by type of product.

- *Percentage of scrap.* A good way to determine if the production department is making efficient use of materials is to track the amount of scrap falling out of the manufacturing process. An excessive scrap amount is an indicator of a variety of items, such as improper machine setup (which requires extra material to test it), employee theft of materials, and faulty products that are detected during the production process and thrown away. Due to the large number of underlying problems, this measure should be considered only a symptom of the real problem, with much additional work required to discover the underlying issues. There are several ways to calculate the measurement. The most inaccurate is to throw all scrap into scrap bins, and then periodically weigh the bins to estimate the cost of what is inside. A more accurate approach is to use an MRP system to determine the material cost that should be required for scheduled production, and then compare this to the actual cost to determine the difference. It can be especially difficult to determine the cost of products that were scrapped after some amount of labor and overhead had already been applied to them.

- *Unit output per employee hour.* A company that operates along traditional lines, using long production runs, wants to know about the ability of its employees to churn out products at the highest possible speed. This measurement is no longer used in a JIT environment, where the emphasis is on only producing what is needed, rather than producing at the fastest possible rate. Also, focusing on this measure tends to increase the production error rate, since employees will complete products irrespective of problems, because they are being judged on their speed, not their accuracy. Nonetheless, if a controller still wants to calculate this measurement, the best approach is to aggregate all personnel in an assembly line or on a specific job, add up the hours worked from payroll records, and divide this amount by the number of products completed during the same time period. This number will be inaccurate if the payroll hours include a holiday for which employees are being paid. The number will also be incorrect if the output is based on direct labor dollars (instead of hours), because the dollar amount can be considerably increased by overtime or shift differentials.

- *Work-in-process (WIP) turnover.* A company that is focusing on improving its JIT manufacturing systems uses the WIP turnover rate as one of its primary measures of success. This is because a properly functioning JIT system requires very little inventory in the manufacturing process, so the WIP turnover rate should be very high. To calculate the measurement, take the period-end work-in-process figure from the general ledger and divide it by the cost of goods sold for the year. This measure should be tracked on a trend line, since anyone involved in a JIT system will want to track it as direct evidence of the success of the system.

Traditional production systems focus on improving the speed of output, while newer systems tend to focus on product error rates and the amount of work-in-process. This section has the measurements a controller needs to track the performance of either type of system. The measures are summarized in Exhibit 6.12.

Sales and Marketing Measurements

The sales department represents the controller's leading edge of information about conditions in the marketplace. Measurements for this area must be constructed that yield as much market information as possible. One is market share, which reveals a company's share of the market "pie." Another key factor is a company's ability to convince customers to sole source their purchases through it. Also, several other departments depend on the sales staff to keep a steady flow of orders coming into the company; a backlog measurement is a prime advance indicator of potential trouble. Finally, there are several sales trend lines to watch that indicate problems with the rate of sales growth (or decline) that are of use when planning for new products or upgrades to existing products. These measurements follow:

- *Market share.* Sometimes an upward trend in sales volume disguises a decline in market share. For example, upward sales growth in the computer industry means little, when everyone's sales are growing; only growth that exceeds the growth of competitors matters, because this allows a company to exercise economies of scale, thereby lowering costs and reaping greater profits than competitors. Market share is a difficult item to measure; the best calculation is to fund an industry trade group that releases an

Ratio	Derivation
Average equipment setup time	(Start time for new production run) − (Stop time for last production run)
Percentage of acceptable products completed	$\dfrac{\text{Number of rejected products}}{\text{Number of products in production run}}$
Percentage of scrap	$\dfrac{\text{(Actual cost of goods sold)} - \text{(Standard cost of goods sold)}}{\text{Standard cost of goods sold}}$
Unit output per employee hour	$\dfrac{\text{Aggregate output per production area}}{\text{Total hours worked in production area}}$
WIP turnover	$\dfrac{\text{Total work-in-process}}{\text{Annual cost of goods sold}}$

EXHIBIT 6.12 PRODUCTION MEASUREMENTS

annual or quarterly market share survey. If there is no trade group, the marketing staff must conduct its own research, which will probably be moderately inaccurate; none-theless, either method will reveal changes in market share over time that management should act on as necessary.

- *Number of major accounts for which the company is the preferred supplier.* The ulti-mate goal of any sales department is to make the company the sole supplier to the best customers. This allows it to incrementally raise prices enough to reap good margins, while at the same time avoiding an excessive number of sales contacts, which merely increase overhead costs. To calculate it, the sales staff must contact suppliers to deter-mine company sourcing status; the total number of these customers must then be divided by the list of active major customers. This is a difficult measurement to con-struct, for there may be some debate regarding what constitutes a major account; the best approach is to set a hard limit on sales volume from each customer during the previous year—if a customer exceeds that level, it is designated a major account.

- *Ratio of backlog to sales.* The sales department must support the production depart-ment in having enough sales on hand to avoid a significant slippage in the flow of pro-duction, which may result in major layoffs in the production area. It helps to maintain a consistent pattern of sales, too. A good control point is to constantly compare the dollar volume of backlog to a short-term record of sales to see if there are sudden changes in the backlog that require immediate action by the sales force. To calculate it, summarize the dollar value of all orders not yet in production (which is usually avail-able on the production backlog report), and divide it into a rolling average of the last three months' sales.

- *Sales trend by product line.* The sales and engineering staffs need to know when the trend of product sales is beginning to slow or decline, so that they can either run pro-motions to increase sales (a function of the sales and marketing staffs) or renew sales with replacement products. To do this, there should be a trend line, preferably in graphic form, for each product line. To calculate it, accumulate product sales under different sales codes or general ledger accounts, and transfer the monthly sales infor-mation to a graphical display. It is dangerous to report this information on an exces-sively summarized level, since it may hide a multitude of sales variations for separate products or product lines that are being grouped into a single trend line.

A controller should track all of the measurements in this section, because each one shows a different aspect of the sales and marketing functions, and all of them are important. One must track market share, as well as the trend of sales by product line, while it is always prudent to determine the size of the backlog. Finally, the sales staff should always strive to achieve sole-source status with suppliers, and the controller should remind them of this responsibility by tracking that information and reporting it back to them. All of these mea-sures are key to controlling the sales and marketing department. The measures are summa-rized in Exhibit 6.13.

Cycle Time

There is one measurement that cuts across all departmental boundaries. That is cycle time, which is used to determine the time taken to complete a transaction. Because many transactions cut across departmental boundaries, the measurement is placed here, rather than under the pre-vious department headings. This is also done to emphasize the importance of the measurement.

Ratio	Derivation
Market share	$$\frac{\text{Dollar volume of company shipments}}{\text{Dollar volume of industry shipments}}$$
Number of major accounts for which the company is the preferred supplier	$$\frac{\text{Number of major sole-source customers}}{\text{Number of major customers}}$$
Ratio of backlog to sales	$$\frac{\text{Dollar volume of all orders not yet in production}}{\text{Average of sales for last three months}}$$
Sales trend by product line	Summary of sales by product code or $$\frac{\text{(Summary of current period sales by product code)} - \text{(Summary of previous period sales by product code)}}{\text{Summary of previous period sales by product code)}}$$

Exhibit 6.13 Sales and Marketing Measurements

Poor cycle time leads to very slow customer service, which is bad for customer retention and therefore revenues. This is a very important item for a controller to track.

Major processes, such as order fulfillment, run through multiple departments, and so are not actively tracked by individual departments (they just blame problems on the other departments that are also involved in the process). However, these are frequently the cause of major inefficiencies in a company, and so the controller should periodically review the time required to process transactions through them, so that management has a clear understanding of the time interval (or "cycle time") needed. The calculation will vary depending on the process, but the basic method is to create a set of standard transactions and run them through a process, taking note of the beginning and ending dates (or times). The average transaction length becomes the official cycle time for the process.

It is very important not only to know the time needed to process transactions, but also to constantly strive for better performance. Thus, a controller should continually track cycle times to enhance a company's level of performance and competitiveness. The measure for cycle times is summarized in Exhibit 6.14.

INTERRELATIONSHIP OF RATIOS

Focusing on a problem ratio and resolving the underlying issues can create problems with other related ratios. For example, a company's debt covenant may specify a current ratio of 2:1. If the ratio is 1.5:1, the controller can borrow money and retain the cash to improve the current ratio. However, the controller's action also worsened the company's ratio of long-term debt to shareholder's equity. The controller must be aware of changes to other ratios that may result from fixing seemingly unrelated measurements. A number of impacts on related ratios are noted in Exhibit 6.15.

Ratio	Derivation
Cycle time	(Process end time) − (Process start time)

Exhibit 6.14 Cycle Time Measurement

A Change in This Ratio	Impacts These Ratios
Current ratio	Management improves the ratio by borrowing money and retaining the cash: *the ratio of long-term debt to shareholder's equity* worsens because debt has increased.
Ratio of long-term debt to shareholder's equity	Management improves the ratio by liquidating short-term investments to pay down the long-term debt; the *current ratio* worsens because investments have been reduced.
Ratio of net sales to receivables	Management improves the ratio by factoring receivables: the *ratio of net profits to net sales* worsens because there is a service charge associated with factoring the receivables.
Turnover of inventories	Management improves the ratio by selling off inventories; the *ratio of gross profit to net sales* worsens because management must pay premium prices to buy raw materials on short notice and ship it to the company by express freight.
Ratio of net sales to working capital	Management improves the ratio by extending payables; the *ratio of gross profit to net sales* worsens because suppliers will not ship additional raw materials, so management must pay premium prices to buy raw materials on short notice and ship it to the company by express freight.
Ratio of repairs and maintenance to fixed assets	Management improves the ratio by cutting the amount of maintenance work on equipment; the *ratio of net income to net sales* worsens because production capacity drops when equipment breaks down.
Number of times fixed charges are earned	Management improves the ratio by using cash on hand to pay down debt; the *current ratio* worsens because the cash is used.
Ratio of gross profit to net sales	Management improves the ratio by increasing prices; the *ratio of net income to net sales* worsens because fewer people buy the product at the higher price.
Ratio of operating expenses to net sales	Management improves the ratio by reducing the accounting department's payroll; the *ratio of gross profit to net sales* worsens because there is no cost accountant to review increased product costs.
Ratio of net income to net sales	Management improves the ratio by selling manufacturing equipment and recording a gain on the sale; the *ratio of gross profit to net sales* worsens because production capacity is reduced, and production must be given to subcontractors at a higher cost.

EXHIBIT 6.15   IMPACT ON RELATED RATIOS

SETTING UP A SYSTEM OF RATIOS AND TREND ANALYSES

There are enough measurements in this chapter to keep even the most analytical controller happy. However, there are so many that issuing all of them will drown the management team in a flood of data that it has no time to read. The controller must select only a portion of all measures for perusal by management. The controller must know how to pick the correct measures and how to present them in a clear and understandable format.

The first step is to match the measurement system to company objectives. Some management teams are driven by strong revenue growth, because they have a tight focus on grabbing as much market share as possible; this is common in a new industry. For this situation, there should be a preponderance of measures that closely track all changes in revenue streams.

Other companies are in slow-growth industries where the focus is on gaining a slight edge in profitability over the competition. In this case, the bulk of the measures should track gross and net margins and the key components thereof. Another common occurrence, especially in high technology industries, is for corporate success to be largely driven by the organization's ability to acquire and retain the best employees. In this case, the most important measurements may not even be financial—they are human resources related, such as employee turnover percentages and the time needed to fill open positions. Consequently, company objectives play a strong role in a controller's choice of measures to report.

Another important consideration for creating a measurement system is the strengths and weaknesses of a company's controls. For example, if there are many divisions, all of which handle a large amount of cash, it is reasonable for a controller to create many cash-related measurements that track cash receipts and disbursements, as well as the company's ability to collect the cash from all divisions and properly invest it. Another example is inventory systems; if there is a strong JIT manufacturing system in place, then there is little need to expend an excessive amount of company resources on measuring the small amount of inventory needed to maintain it. However, a befuddled manufacturing system may call for a considerable amount of inventory measuring—perhaps weekly or even daily—as well as constant tracking of obsolete inventories. If there are strong controls already in place, such as a billing system that creates perfect customer billings, then there is little need to measure it. However, strong controls frequently become strong because employees know that they are being measured; completely removing the measurement tells employees that the control is no longer important, so they do not expend the same effort to keep the control strong. Consequently, it is less necessary to measure strong control points than weak ones, but these measurements should not be completely eliminated; instead, they should be conducted less frequently.

A key consideration that is all too frequently ignored is the time needed to collect information that forms the basis for a measurement. If the data collection systems needed to calculate a measurement are not in place, a controller should seriously consider abandoning the measurement unless it is absolutely critical or it is only needed for a single measurement, not to be repeated. For example, if a controller receives a request for sales broken down by product but finds that the accounting system will not easily divulge this information, the only option in the short term may be to go through all invoices issued for the month and manually summarize the information. Clearly, this is not a viable option for the long term. If the controller cannot find a more automated approach to collecting the information, it is time to discuss the cost of collecting the data with the person requesting the information to see if it is really needed. Too often, a controller simply goes on wasting time month after month, issuing measurements that require vast amounts of manual labor, when the information was only needed once. Continual communications with management is the key to keeping away from using labor-intensive measurements.

Another approach is for a controller to track all possible measurements, but to only report those results to management that do not meet expectations. For example, the accounting staff can track every conceivable measurement related to the engineering department, but only reveal those measurement results that show problems. Though this approach will tightly focus management attention on problem areas, there are several reasons for not using it. One is that, even though only high-variance measures are being reported, some of these measures may be in areas so unimportant that management is simply being distracted from more important tasks. For example, high employee turnover among the distribution personnel may not be an issue if the company is a newspaper, where high turnover among the newspaper delivery people is an expected part of the business. Another reason is that this approach puts a large burden on the accounting staff. Many measures must be manually calculated, and doing this for a very large number of measures is not a good use of staff time. Finally, management can become confused when it is presented with a different set of measurements every reporting period; some measures may be unfamiliar, so the controller must retrain management to understand the new measures. This not only wastes the controller's time, but it also interferes with the orderly conduct of management work. Consequently, tracking all measures and reporting by exception is probably too labor intensive and complicated to be an effective measurement presentation approach for most companies.

An example of how to determine what ratios to track follows: Leforto Electronics designs circuits for other manufacturing companies. It has no inventories, and most of the staff is in the engineering department. The company is growing at a very rapid rate through increasing sales to a small number of key accounts. In this case, the controller can safely avoid measurements for inventory. Because engineers are generally hard to come by, there should be a measurement to track employee turnover, as well as one to track the time needed to acquire new recruits. Given the small number of customers, a customer turnover statistic may be of some importance. Also, since the company does nothing but design circuits, it is reasonable that profitability is closely tied to the speed with which the engineers complete their design work, so a measurement should track the percentage of design jobs completed on time. Finally, given the small number of customers, it is possible that there are a few large invoices to customers, which makes cash receipts very "lumpy." Given this issue, there is a strong need to monitor the age of accounts receivable, as well as short-term cash forecasts. This is a simple example, but it is evident that the measurement systems needed for Leforto Electronics will vary considerably from companies in other industries, where the underlying operating conditions might make all of Leforto's measurements useless, while calling for a completely different set of measures.

A good example of a company that must use an entirely different set of measurements is a manufacturing company. This one we shall call Manfred Manufacturing. This company builds a large number of products, which requires a large number of component parts. It sells them to a large number of distributors, most of whom buy in small quantities; some are old friends of the owners. The industry is a mature one, so profit margins are low. The direct labor content of most products is high. In this case, there is no need to track engineering variances at all. Instead, there must be a strong emphasis on inventory tracking as well as obsolescence, since this probably constitutes a large part of the balance sheet. In addition, there must be careful margin tracking for all products and product lines in order to find and correct the prices of products with low margins. Also, because some customers are friends of the owners, it seems likely that their credit standing is being ignored, so close tracking of overdue accounts receivable is critical. Finally, because of the large labor component in product costs, the controller should adopt measurements for tracking labor efficiency as well as hours charged to specific jobs. In comparing these two examples, it is evident that a controller must take into account such disparate items as a company's industry, number of customers, preponderance of certain departments, and even owner friendships when devising a good set of performance measurements.

7

INTERNAL CONTROL SYSTEMS

IMPORTANCE OF THIS CHAPTER

With the advent of the Sarbanes–Oxley Act and its considerable emphasis on control systems, the new controller must be especially careful to ensure that corporate controls are adequate. This chapter includes many examples of internal controls and fraud situations, and so serves as the starting point for a detailed corporate controls examination.

Historically, the reason a company places emphasis on its internal control systems is to keep fraud from occurring. Although reducing fraud losses is still a valid concern, more companies are now emphasizing internal controls because they monitor the consistency with which transactions are completed. This change in emphasis has been brought about by the realization that a company can generate a significant competitive advantage by improving the quality and speed of delivery of its products by tightly monitoring its systems. Thus, internal controls are used not only to combat fraud but also to monitor the consistency and completion speed of transactions.

Besides objectives, this chapter also notes how responsibility is assigned for various controls. This is not a simple issue, because controls spread across many departments, making it difficult to pin down the reason for a control failure. In addition, the chapter contains an elementary set of control points that are useful for controlling the most basic company functions. Though by no means complete, they give the reader a rough overview of the types of controls that a controller should consider installing. In addition, controls may eventually outlive their usefulness due to changes in the business. Accordingly, guidelines are provided on how to spot and eliminate these controls. Fraud is then discussed: the types of fraud one encounters, how to detect it, and how to prevent it. Most controllers will encounter a case of fraud at some time in their careers, though it may be as minor as petty cash pilferage, so these sections serve as a good reference point for how to identify, prevent, and deal with such problems. Finally, the chapter notes the main points of the Foreign Corrupt Practices Act, which is a federal law that directly impacts a company's internal control systems. In short, this chapter provides an overview of controls—why they are used, how to create them, and when to eliminate them.

OBJECTIVES

It is not sufficient to scatter a large number of controls throughout a company's transaction processing systems, because this random approach may result in an insufficient number of controls over key risk factors, while adding an excessive number of controls in areas where there are few risks. The upshot of a control system that is poorly planned is a high-risk transaction environment that is nonetheless burdened with an excessive number of controls. This section discusses the primary control objectives that a controller should consider in order to implement only those controls that are most important for a specific set of transactions. The main control objectives are:

- *Authorization.* Was the transaction authorized by management? This could be evidenced in a general way by establishing related policies, contract authorization limits, investment limits, and standard price lists; or specific authorization may be needed in a given situation.
- *Reconciliation.* Periodic reconciliations of physical assets to records, or control accounts, should be made. This can include bank reconciliations, securities inventories, physical inventories of raw materials, and comparison of work-in-process and finished goods to control accounts.
- *Recording.* Transactions should be recorded, not only in the proper account, but also at the proper time (i.e., proper cutoff) and with the proper description. No fictitious transactions should be recorded, and erroneous material and incomplete descriptions should be avoided.
- *Safeguarding.* Physical assets should not be under the physical custody of those responsible for related recordkeeping functions. Access to the assets should be restricted to designated individuals.
- *Valuation.* Provision should be made for assurances that assets are properly valued in accordance with generally accepted accounting principles (GAAP) and that the adjustments are valid.

These five control objectives relate to the prevention of errors and the detection of any errors or irregularities in transactions. They must be considered when the evaluation of an internal control system is made.

RESPONSIBILITY FOR INTERNAL CONTROLS

Although the controller has a major involvement in the design and maintenance of internal controls, he or she is not the only one responsible for internal controls. This is an especially important factor to consider because of the Foreign Corrupt Practices Act (see "Foreign Corrupt Practices Act" on page 143), which can entail jail terms for senior company management if there are inadequate control systems. In addition to this factor, there are many control systems that extend beyond the reach of a typical controller's jurisdiction; therefore, other people within a company must take a hand in creating and maintaining those systems.

This section discusses the various positions within a company that are responsible for internal controls, as well as the extent of that responsibility. They are noted as follows, in descending order by position:

1. *Board of Directors.* This group is ultimately responsible for a company's control systems, as it is responsible for total company performance. Unfortunately, it operates at such a high level that it cannot adequately monitor, or even have a knowledge of, all key control systems. It can alleviate this problem by forming an audit committee to which the internal audit department reports; this allows the Board to closely monitor all reviews of the control system, which allows it to mandate changes that are deemed necessary by the internal audit staff.

2. *Senior management.* Although the Board of Directors is theoretically responsible for the adequacy of controls, it is senior management that actually has this responsibility from a practical perspective. This is because senior management is "closer to the action," with a much more detailed knowledge of operating conditions. Accordingly, the senior management team must ensure that there is an efficient and effective system of internal controls that results in accurate financial information, as well as the safeguarding of assets. Senior management must:

    ○ Assume responsibility to shareholders for the accuracy of financial reporting.
    ○ Create and maintain a properly documented internal control system.
    ○ Create and maintain the proper environment to enforce the necessary controls. This may require the use of policies, procedures, and statements of ethical standards to enforce.
    ○ Identify the risks inherent in the business and the potential for errors and irregularities in various parts of the transaction processing systems.

3. *Financial management.* Though other members of management have responsibility for the adequacy of controls, this burden falls heaviest on the members of the financial management team, for they are presumed to have the highest degree of training and experience in this area. Also, the majority of control points are typically installed in areas that are under the direct control of the financial managers. Consequently, from a practical perspective, these employees have the bulk of the real responsibility for controls. The financial management team must:

    ○ Know the technical requirements of a sound financial control system and how to create such a system based on the nuances of the existing business.
    ○ Verify that a sufficient number of controls are installed and that they operate in a satisfactory manner.
    ○ Enforce conformance to all controls, as noted in policies and procedures.
    ○ Assume direct responsibility for the accuracy of the information contained in periodic financial statements and accompanying notes.

4. *Internal audit staff.* This group has a major impact on the presence of adequate control systems. It is responsible for reviewing the existence and effectiveness of control systems in a variety of areas, and reports to management on the adequacy of those controls, as well as any deficiencies. However, the audit program followed by this group is usually approved by the internal audit committee, which is a subset of the Board of Directors. If this program is inadequate, the internal audit staff will not conduct a sufficient

number of reviews to ensure the adequacy of internal control systems. Also, this group is not empowered to change any control systems; instead, it only reports on problems. This limits the effectiveness of the internal audit staff in forcing necessary changes to control systems.

5. *Independent auditor.* This position is listed as the lowest of the management positions, although in reality it is located here simply because it is the only position in the list that falls outside of the corporate hierarchy. As part of an outside auditor's audit of a company's financial statements, it is customary to determine the strength of the underlying control systems that support those statements. If weaknesses in the control systems are discovered, the auditor is in a unique position to report this information to senior management as well as the Board of Directors as part of a management report that frequently accompanies the audited financial statements. The reported weaknesses can also be accompanied by recommendations to improve the situation. If management wants additional assistance from the auditors, they can be called on to provide educational materials or training to the company, as well as a more complete review of the control systems. However, a controls review is considered only to be part of the audit work for a full audit, and not for a review or compilation; these two lesser forms of financial review are increasingly common for many companies, so in these cases, the external auditor has minimal impact on or responsibility for the state of a company's control systems.

READ YOUR AUDIT REPORTS!

A good source of information about control weaknesses is prior management reports issued by the external auditors. The new controller should peruse all of these reports that have been issued for the past few years to see what problems the auditors uncovered, and which ones have not yet been resolved.

Responsibility for the adequacy of a control system is spread throughout a company, with theoretical responsibility residing in the Board of Directors and practical responsibility sitting squarely on the shoulders of the financial and senior managers. This group is assisted by the internal and external auditors, who can recommend changes to existing controls but do not have the authority to make any changes.

EXAMPLES OF INTERNAL CONTROLS

This section provides a "laundry list" of controls that are commonly used. Controllers can pick from this list when creating control systems for their companies. However, do not be misled into believing that the only crucial controls are noted below. On the contrary, there are many controls that are industry-specific that will not be found anywhere in this book. To gather information about these special controls, it is useful to consult with an external auditing firm that has experience in a specific industry, or obtain advice from an industrial trade group with similar expertise. Conversely, it is not necessary to implement every control listed in this section, because this would introduce a great deal of inefficient control redundancy. The best use of this section is as a reference for carefully selecting controls that can be shaped and altered to fit a company's specific needs. The controls are grouped by balance sheet and income statement category. They are:

- *Cash*
    - Compare check register to actual check number sequence.
    - Control check stock.
    - Control signature plates.
    - Perform bank reconciliations.
    - Review uncashed checks.
- *Investments*
    - Impose investment limits.
    - Require authorizations to shift funds among accounts.
    - Verify that investments do not exceed federally insured limits.
- *Accounts receivable*
    - Require approval of bad debt expenses.
    - Require approval of credits.
    - Require constant review of old accounts receivable.
- *Inventory*
    - Conduct inventory audits.
    - Require approval to sign out inventory beyond amounts on pick list.
    - Restrict warehouse access to designated personnel.
- *Employee advances*
    - Continually review all outstanding advances.
    - Require approval of all advance payments to employees.
- *Fixed assets*
    - Ensure that fixed-asset purchases have appropriate prior authorization.
    - Verify that correct depreciation calculations are being made.
    - Verify that fixed-asset disposal are properly authorized.
    - Verify that fixed assets are being utilized.
- *Accounts payable*
    - Compare payments made to the receiving log.
- *Notes payable*
    - Require approval of the terms of all new borrowing agreements.
    - Require supervisory approval of all borrowings and repayments.
- *Revenues*
    - Compare all billings to the shipping log.
- *Cost of goods sold*
    - Compare the cost of all completed jobs to budgeted costs.
    - Pick from stock based on bills of material.

- ○ Purchase based on blanket purchase orders and related releases.
- ○ Reject all purchases that are not preapproved.
- ○ Require approval of all overtime expenditures.
- *Travel and entertainment expenses*
  - ○ Audit expense reports at random.
  - ○ Issue strict policies concerning allowable expenses.
  - ○ Require supervisory approval of all expense reports.
- *Payroll expenses*
  - ○ Require approval of all overtime hours worked by hourly personnel.
  - ○ Require approval of all pay changes.
- *Occupancy expenses*
  - ○ Compare the cost of employee furnishings to company policy.
  - ○ Compare the square footage per person to company policy.
- *General*
  - ○ Audit credit card statements.
  - ○ Impose a total monthly dollar limit on credit card purchases.
  - ○ Impose single transaction limits on credit card purchases.
  - ○ Impose supplier exclusions on credit card purchases.
  - ○ Require supervisory approval of credit card statements.
- *Other: Contracts*
  - ○ Require monitoring of changes in contract costs.
  - ○ Require monitoring of when contracts are due for renewal.
  - ○ Require specific authorizations for various levels of monetary commitment.

The controls noted in this section are among the most common ones used, irrespective of the type of industry. Although a controller may select the majority of his or her controls from this list, it is important to consider special controls that are indigenous to specific industries and do not appear on this list.

WHEN TO ELIMINATE CONTROLS

Most controllers are good at imposing new controls, but few give any thought to eliminating them. This is an extremely useful exercise, because fewer controls translate into less work by the staff and (sometimes) quicker transaction processing times. This section discusses how to set up an orderly system for reviewing controls at regular intervals and eliminating those that are no longer necessary.

In order to review the need for controls, one must first know what they are. Many controllers have no idea of the types of controls a company uses, because they have inherited an informal mass (or mess) of controls from the previous controller, and never trouble themselves to understand the system. Accordingly, the first step is to conduct a broad-ranging series of interviews with employees to understand the flow of transactions throughout the company, and then convert this information into a set of easily understandable flowcharts. A quarterly control review can be scheduled in which the controller scans the existing controls to see if any controls have become unnecessary; this happens when changes in business conditions, such as new operating procedures, outsourcing, or reengineering, render existing controls obsolete. Any additions to or deletions from a company's control systems must be reflected in the flowcharts, so they must be updated regularly, even if the formal control review takes place only quarterly. Using flowcharts and a scheduled control review allows a controller to eliminate unnecessary controls.

Although flowcharts are an excellent method for tracking control points, a controller can take the concept too far. It can take an enormous amount of time to convert every conceivable process into a flowchart, and more time to ensure that it stays correct. To avoid too large a time investment, those systems that have no significant financial impact, such as the scheduling for janitorial services, should be ignored and concentration should be on key transactions, such as order fulfillment.

Once key controls have been documented, the controller should determine how much it costs to have them in place. This step is very important, for a controller is responsible for installing controls that are *cost effective,* not ones that require so much effort that company operations are severely burdened by them. To determine control costs, a controller should observe controls in action to see how much labor and material costs are required to maintain them. This is a very inexact science, and a controller may be forced to rely on nothing more than the opinions of the employees who use the controls. Still, even estimates of costs are better than no information at all.

A controller should also categorize each control as being a major or secondary control. Most control systems have multiple controls that focus on solving a control problem, with a few controls being extremely important and others being relatively unimportant. For example, a primary control over inventory is installing a fence around the warehouse to eliminate pilferage, while a secondary control is bonding the warehouse staff so that a company can obtain reimbursement if an employee is caught stealing inventory. By categorizing controls in this manner, a controller can see which controls are necessary and which can be deleted.

The final step in determining which controls can be eliminated is to add control costs (as previously determined) to the chart that categorizes controls as being major or secondary. This allows a controller to quickly skim through the list of controls and see whether there are any secondary control points that are very expensive. If so, these are prime candidates for elimination. Before deleting these controls, however, a controller should first make a determination of the risk of not having them. Even an expensive secondary control point may have some value if it provides control over a potential asset loss that is so large that the control is still worth having. Risks that fall into this category include loss of investment accounts due to embezzlement or the loss of entire facilities due to fire damage. For these situations, which are admittedly few in number, it may still be worthwhile to retain controls that would otherwise be eliminated.

A simpler, though less effective, way to review controls is to constantly review the need for control reports. All companies rely on a large number of reports that list transactions; when regularly reviewed, these reports act as controls over a large number of activities. A controller can determine whether these reports are needed by tracing them to report recipients and quizzing them regarding the need for the reports. This can result in a major reduction in the number of reports used, which is a major time savings if the reports are being manually prepared.

A more common method of reducing the number of controls is to conduct an intensive review of controls whenever there are significant changes to the business, such as reengineering projects, outsourcing of major functions, or downsizing. When these events occur, the controller should be heavily involved in examining proposed system changes, which will likely result in the elimination of large numbers of controls. It is common to enroll the internal audit staff in these reviews, because it is largely concerned with the adequacy of existing controls. However, although there will almost certainly be some reduction in the number of controls as a result of these changes, there may be a need for an entirely new set of controls that are just as, if not more, expensive than the controls being eliminated.

INVOLVE YOURSELF IN BEST PRACTICES IMPLEMENTATIONS

Unfortunately, the presence of control points can make any process less efficient, since it may require labor to complete them. Consequently, best practices projects tend to focus on their elimination on the grounds that efficiency can thereby be improved. In order to avoid hard feelings when the new controller recommends against a new best practice because of control weaknesses, it is useful to monitor the progress of best practices teams to see what recommendations they are likely to make.

When a controller decides to eliminate a control, it is best to review the decision with anyone who may be using the control for other reasons. This is a major concern when the control point is a report that contains valuable information. For example, a control report that lists all fixed assets may also be used by an accounts payable person to determine the value of assets to be reported to the government for the calculation of property taxes. When these types of controls are eliminated, there may be so much extra work required by other parts of the company to "fill the gap" of the information that is no longer available that the cost of stopping the control may exceed the cost of leaving it in place. Thus, checking with potential users is key prior to stopping a control point.

Finally, it is common to order the elimination of a control point, only to find that the controller's order is ignored by the staff. This happens when employees are so overwhelmed with work that there is a strong predilection toward keeping systems the way they are, rather than working through the details of system changes. It is also common when control changes are not properly thought out; the staff frequently realizes that there are unresolved issues and balk at making changes until these issues have been resolved. In the first case, the controller should request the assistance of the internal audit staff, which can conduct periodic reviews of processes to see if changes have actually been implemented. In the second case, the controller is well advised to listen to staff objections and work through changes with them, which usually results in altered systems that are more clearly understood and which have greater staff acceptance. Proper follow-up and attention to staff objections are critical to ensuring that control system changes are completely implemented.

In short, a controller can eliminate unnecessary controls by conducting a periodic review of existing controls, itemizing why they are used, and including the cost of each one as well as the changes in risks if they are eliminated. A detailed review of this information will usually reveal a number of control points that are too expensive for the level of incremental control they provide. It is important to review proposed control eliminations with other employees to ensure that there are no undocumented uses for the controls that may justify their continued existence; this review may also uncover objections to changing the system, which the controller should deal with prior to making alterations. By following these steps, a controller can keep the number of controls to a minimum, while still ensuring that a company's major control objectives are met.

TYPES OF FRAUD

All controllers must be aware of the primary types of fraud. By knowing them, a controller can design effective control systems for their prevention. This knowledge is also useful for those controllers who are interested in increasing transactional efficiency by reducing some control points—only by knowing how employees can take advantage of a reduced set of controls to commit fraud can a controller judge which controls can be safely eliminated.

All types of fraud involve the theft of company assets. However, within the broad category of "assets" lie a large number of subcategories, such as fixed assets, employee advances, and cash. The type of fraudulent activity needed to take each of these subcategories of assets away from a company differs for each category, and is described in the following list by subcategory:

- *Expense account abuse.* Employees run extra expenses through their expense reports that are not allowed by company policy, or use false receipts to charge extra expenses that did not actually occur. Employees may also charge expenses that are higher than allowed by company policy. For example, employees may take first-class plane trips, charge through exorbitant meals, and expect reimbursement for nonbusiness expenses, such as gifts or clothes.

- *Nonpayment of employee advances.* Employees who have requested an advance payment of their paychecks or an advance to cover trip expenses will not pay back the company for these expenses. This tends to be a passive activity, for they do not actively try to bilk money from the company—they just do nothing to pay back what they have already been paid.

STORE EMPLOYEE ADVANCES IN AN ASSET ACCOUNT

It is difficult to collect an employee advance almost every time one is paid out, making this one of the most common forms of fraud. To create an automatic monthly reminder, be sure to record each advance in an asset account, and then insert an account reconciliation reminder for that account in the monthly closing checklist; by doing so, someone has to review outstanding advances every month.

- *Purchases for personal use.* Employees can take advantage of the authorization systems built into the purchasing system to order items for their personal use. This is most common when a company has high approval limits, so that employees can order items with no fear of review by their supervisors. This is also common when companies exercise little control over company credit cards, so that employees can charge through purchases that are not in any way related to company business.

- *Supplier kickbacks.* Employees in the purchasing function can arrange with suppliers to buy their products and services at inflated costs in exchange for direct payments back to the employees. Depending on the quantities purchased, the amount of these kickbacks can be enormous.

- *Theft of cash and investments.* The primary target of many employees who commit fraud is cash. This can be done in a variety of ways. One is to steal a blank check and make it out to the employee. Another is to gain control of bank account authorization codes and wire large amounts of funds to an employee-controlled bank account. Yet another approach is to steal cash. However, from a practical perspective, this tends to be the most difficult area in which to steal a large amount, for most companies tend to focus their controls on this asset area.

- *Theft of fixed assets.* Fixed assets that are not bolted down, are small in size, and have a high resale value are subject to theft. This is especially true if the assets are rarely used or stored in out-of-the-way locations, so that no one will notice a theft for some time. This type of fraud is especially common in companies in which there is minimal tracking of assets. Conversely, large and heavy equipment that requires immense effort to move is practically immune to theft.

- *Theft of inventory or supplies.* Employees can remove supplies and inventory from the company, either for personal use or for resale. Supplies are especially easy to remove, because they are not tracked as carefully as inventory items and are not normally stored in a restricted area. This is an especially large problem if inventory items have a high street value, are small enough to be easily concealed, and are not rigorously tracked. Large and inexpensive inventory items are much less likely to be stolen.

These asset areas correspond roughly to the asset section of the balance sheet. The most commonly recognized fraud areas involve cash and investments, but it is actually much easier for an employee to steal assets in other areas, such as inventory, because the greatest concentration of controls cover the cash area, with much weaker controls elsewhere.

PREVENTING FRAUD

According to the Association of Certified Fraud Examiners, the cost of fraud is now $400 billion per year. For some firms, the amount is so crippling that at a minimum it takes a large bite out of profits, and in some cases takes down the entire company. Even if the amount being stolen is small, most controllers feel as though fraudulent activities are a personal affront, for it means that someone has found a way to circumvent the control systems that were personally installed by the controllers. Accordingly, this section is designed to give a controller a list of warning signs for how to spot fraudulent activities, and what to do about it.

There are two sets of fraud indicators. The first is at a high level: How management acts and its way of running the company are either direct indicators of fraud by management or indicate a general pattern of behavior that, if duplicated lower down in the company, will create an environment in which fraud will flourish unchecked. The high-level indicators are frequently missed, because the controller is so wrapped up in managing at this level that the signs are too close to see. It is best to ask the company auditors for their opinions regarding fraud indicators at this level, for they can provide a more balanced, outside view of the situation. The high-level fraud indicators are:

- *Management creates an overly complex organizational structure.* If there are so many interlocked organizations that it is difficult to track transactions through the myriad of entities, it is possible that senior management has purposely created this level of complexity in order to hide fraudulent transactions.

- *Management has an excessive emphasis on meeting profit goals.* If the management team cares for nothing but meeting profit goals, this channels everyone's activities in that direction. This may seem innocuous, but if the goals are extremely hard to reach, there is a considerable temptation for employees to fabricate profits by any number of means in order to meet their goals. This is particularly a problem when large bonuses are awarded when profit goals are met.

- *Management has an aggressive attitude toward financial reporting.* The management team may use the loosest possible interpretations of the accounting rules in order to recognize revenue and income. When this is present, it is possible that management is also engaged in other activities that are beyond the accounting rules. Surprisingly, controllers do not always see this, because they may have been in the accounting department so long that they accept the loose accounting interpretations as normal.

- *Management is unwilling to pay for good controls.* A management team with an undue focus on profits may not want to pay for the more expensive control points that will prevent large-scale fraud. Employees will eventually determine where there are no controls or weak ones, and some will be tempted to exploit the situation.

- *Management is dominated by one person.* If there is a strong owner or chief executive officer (CEO) running the company who brooks no discussion of decisions made, there is a strong risk of fraud, probably by that person. The risk is especially high in this situation, because the CEO has absolute authority to do anything—no controls will be effective in this situation.

- *Management prefers excessive decentralization.* The management team may have a preference for minimal control from the headquarters facility; instead, it favors a "hands off" approach for all subsidiaries. This is a laudable approach in many situations, but there should be a sufficient level of oversight to at least ensure that adequate control systems are in place at all subsidiaries.

- *Management turnover is high.* When there is a large amount of churning among the management ranks, it may indicate that there are ongoing activities that are questionable, and that the departing people have chosen to leave rather than be associated with the company.

- *Customers or suppliers are suing the company.* There may be lawsuits pending related to not paying suppliers or not providing complete services to customers, and which may be caused by fraud on the part of senior management. These lawsuits frequently escape the attention of the controller, because they are handled through the legal department.

- *Management is forcing a rapid pace of growth.* If a company is going through a period of explosive growth, it is extremely difficult to maintain control systems. Also, because so many people are being hired during this period, it is difficult to conduct an adequate level of screening of incoming employees, so there is a greater likelihood of hiring someone who has committed fraud in the past.

- *Management is acquiring a large number of companies.* When management acquires a series of companies at high speed, it is possible that it will buy into a company where fraud is present. This is because a newly acquired company may have poor control systems that allow this to happen. The real problem is that, because of the pace of acquisition, the controller may not have sufficient time to create and monitor controls at each newly acquired company, which means that there is an environment in which fraud can continue to flourish.

SHOW MANAGEMENT THE ERROR OF THEIR WAYS

As noted above, the management team can be indirectly responsible for a weak control system. When this happens, collect all information about fraud losses into a summary document and present it to the management team, noting what types of controls could have been imposed that cost less than the resulting losses.

There are a number of warning signals to look for at an employee level that may be indicators of fraud. These indicators require no special control system; a controller simply needs to be aware of them in order to identify situations in which there is a stronger likelihood of a possibly fraudulent situation. If a number of the following factors are present, a controller is justified in conducting an especially careful audit to determine whether there are fraudulent activities occurring. The warning signs are:

- *401k withdrawals.* An employee is more likely to commit fraud if short on cash. One sign of this is repeated withdrawals from a 401k plan or reductions in the amount of paycheck withdrawals that go to the plan. Another sign of this is a long history of asking for advances on paychecks.

- *Bad debt write-offs.* There appears to be a large proportion of bad debt write-offs occurring. There may not be any increasing trend line indicating this, since fraudulent write-offs may have been going on for a long time, so an alternative way to tell is to compare the rate to industry standards.

- *Inventory discrepancies.* If there are constant discrepancies between expected inventory records and actual counts, this is a sign of possible inventory theft; this also applies to manufacturing tools, which are especially easy to sell. Continuing losses of small quantities of easily salable items are a major indicator of theft.

- *Invoicing discrepancies.* A common type of fraud is to intercept incoming checks and hide the theft by constantly modifying customer invoices with adjustments of various kinds to make them match a smaller amount of customer payment. A large number of invoice adjustments is a sign of this problem.

- *Lack of supervision.* Some employees, for whatever reason, have not been subjected to close management for a long time, which gives them an opportunity to devise fraudulent activities in the absence of any oversight.

- *Large personal expenditures.* Some employees spend their fraudulently acquired funds in a very public manner; seeing an employee arrive in a new and expensive car is an indicator of this, especially when combined with a change of home address (which they usually give to the payroll person so that paychecks are mailed to the correct location), which may indicate the purchase of a more expensive home.

- *No competitive bidding.* A number of contracts are being awarded without any competitive bidding, which indicates that suppliers may be paying purchasing personnel to do this. However, this is increasingly difficult to prove, because just-in-time manufacturing principles dictate that sole sourcing is a better purchasing technique than using competitive bidding.

- *No payment from the sale of assets.* When a controller notices that there are fewer assets, either from sale documents or a fixed asset audit, it is useful to see if cash was received as part of the transaction. If there does not appear to be any compensation for transferring the asset to the recipient, the controller should suspect that funds were pocketed and investigate further.

- *No vacations.* Key staff people somehow never manage to take any vacation time for years on end, which may indicate that they are afraid of having their activities detected in their absence.

- *Supplier addresses match employee addresses.* A virtually certain indicator of fraud is when an employee sends in invoices from a fictitious company and has the payments sent to his or her home address. Though it can be difficult to compare the list of employee addresses to the same information for suppliers, it may be worth the effort if a controller suspects that there are problems with supplier payments.

Though these indicators of fraudulent activities are legitimate, a controller must realize that there are also real reasons for many of the same activities, so it is easy to receive a false impression that someone is committing fraud. For example, an employee may not have taken vacation during the past year, but this may be due to a workload that was so severe that there really was no way to take it. To avoid false indicators, it is better to rely on a combination of factors. For example, if a billing clerk suddenly arrives in a new sports car, and this is coincident with a number of billing irregularities, then there are excellent grounds for conducting an investigation.

While noting that several indicators in combination represent a reasonable warning of the presence of fraud, it is even more likely that the vast majority of fraud cases leave no warning signs at all. Many perpetrators conduct their activities on such a low level, taking assets worth very small amounts, that it is very nearly impossible for anyone to spot them. In these cases, the controls that would be necessary to prevent or find fraud would be so onerous that the cost of the controls would very likely exceed the cost of the fraud. For example, employees may be using the company postage machine to send out personal mail. The control over this might require installing a lock on the machine as well as direct supervision when it is in use. Doing this may be more expensive than the cost of any lost postage. In short, many fraud cases involve losses on such a small scale that it is not worth the effort of installing controls to ensure that it does not happen.

Other fraud cases *do* involve potentially large losses. A controller must act to prevent these situations from occurring, since they can have a large impact on company cash flow and profits. The best way to determine the extent of potential fraud is to review all areas of the company and estimate the largest amount of fraud that can possibly occur in each function. To use the previous example, the upper limit on losses through a postage machine is the amount of postage stored in it, which rarely exceeds $1,000 and is usually considerably less. However, the potential for inventory theft in a large warehouse area may run into millions of dollars. Another example is sending wire transfers; if a person can send one for all available company funds to a numbered Swiss bank account, this can bankrupt a company. Of the three examples, it is clear which areas require a broader range of controls. Accordingly, a controller should first evaluate all functional areas to determine the degree of potential loss and hone in on those areas in which the company can lose large sums.

When a controller reviews a business to locate potentially high-risk fraud situations, there is a great likelihood that the review will miss some potential situations if the controller does not have a strong knowledge of the business. For example, if a manufacturing company hires a controller from one of the service industries, that controller will not have a good knowledge of internal controls over manufactured goods, and of how materials can be removed from the system without detection. In this situation, a controller can flowchart the main processes of the company, which also yields an excellent knowledge of operations. However, many controllers, especially new ones, do not have time for such an in-depth review. In these cases, the controller can bring in the company auditors, who have presumably audited many similar companies, and who have a great store of knowledge of control systems. The auditors can conduct the review and make a large number of recommended system changes in a very short period of time. In short, assessing the existing control environment requires a good knowledge of systems, which may call for outside assistance in conducting the review.

Aside from the use of control systems to combat fraud, there are other ways to detect it, such as notification by fellow employees. In many cases, other employees are well aware of fraud situations and make the (false) assumption that management knows about it too and has chosen to take no action. The best way to clear up this level of employee uncertainty as well as to be on the receiving end of information about fraud problems is simple accessibility. It is very helpful if a controller or someone on the controller's staff is a gregarious type who mixes constantly with other people in the company. By making themselves available, the accounting staff puts itself in a better position to be trusted by other employees, which results in information about improprieties. Notification by employees is an important second source of information about fraud.

There are many warning signs that indicate the presence of fraud. A controller is well advised to review this information from time to time to determine whether there are conditions at a company that make it easy for fraud to occur. In addition, there should be a continual review of control systems to monitor the risk and amount of loss at various points in the company. If there have been changes in these factors since the last review, a controller should consider altering the controls. Finally, it is almost as important to keep lines of communication open between the accounting staff and the rest of the company, for hints from employees run a close second as a good method for spotting fraud cases. By using general indicators and good control points, and by being receptive to employees, a controller will have a much better chance of finding fraud in the company.

HOW TO DEAL WITH A FRAUD SITUATION

A controller faces difficult choices when confronted with a fraud situation—should the company go public and push for criminal charges against the perpetrator, or is it better to reach a private resolution? Some companies even accept payment back from the problem employee and then *retain* that person! This section discusses the factors in favor of and against each option.

The following list notes the primary options available to a company when resolving a fraud situation. The first point is the most drastic resolution, with succeeding options declining in severity. For each item, there is a discussion of the likely results of each action, as well as any moral considerations.

- *Bring criminal charges.* This option sends the clearest message to employees—that the company will not tolerate fraud under any circumstances. Therefore, it tends to have a positive impact on reducing subsequent fraud. Also, from a moral standpoint, it is the correct action to take, because there is now a public record that a person has committed an illegal act, which gives adequate notice to other companies that may hire the individual. However, publicly held companies tend not to take this route, because a public display of corporate incompetence that originally allowed the fraud to take place does not give the company a positive public image, and may even lead to the firing of top management by the Board of Directors. Consequently, and unfortunately, many companies tend to shy away from this option.

- *Demand restitution and fire the employee.* This option is the most common one. A company is certainly justified in demanding restitution, and should always fire anyone committing fraud, as this avoids the chance of any recurrence of the situation. Also, because there are no legal proceedings, stockholders will not find out about the fraud situation, which upholds the reputation of the company as well as senior management. However, this does not create a public record that the wrongdoer has committed fraud, so other companies that hire this person will have no way of knowing that they are hiring a "bad apple." Thus, this option is not as morally acceptable as the first option.

- *Dismiss employee for cause.* Many companies take this approach if there is no reasonable chance of recovering missing funds or other assets. This approach also avoids any legal controversy that may result in adverse publicity. However, it creates no public record of wrongdoing, so the perpetrator is free to commit fraud again elsewhere.

- *Permit employee to resign.* This approach is sometimes allowed for employees who have committed fraud but who occupy such high-profile positions that their firings would excite comment by the business community. The same option may be extended to employees who have worked for a company for such a long time that management feels it has some obligation to allow a quiet departure. However, from a moral perspective, this is one of the worst options; another company will have no reason to suspect that there was a criminal situation at a previous company, because there is no record of a firing. By selecting this option, a company allows a perpetrator to continue fraudulent acts at other organizations.

- *Demand restitution and permit the employee to stay.* Though this option allows a company to recoup its losses, it runs the substantial risk of having the perpetrator commit fraud yet again. Also, other employees will see that there was no drastic action taken, so they will either be encouraged to commit fraud themselves, or will at least have a minimal incentive for reporting future cases of fraud to management. Despite these drawbacks, companies continue to select this option for two reasons—either the person committing fraud is a member of the family that owns the company, or management feels that it has a better chance of getting its money back by having direct control over the payroll deductions that will gradually return the cash.

- *Do nothing.* Companies pick this option primarily because the person committing fraud is a co-owner of the business, which makes it difficult to take any action. This has a demoralizing effect on other employees who see illegal activities taking place without any fear of retribution, and frequently leads to excessive levels of employee turnover, as people find other companies with more upright moral standards.

The range of actions that management can take to combat fraud is very broad. The best approach is to take a stern stand against all cases of fraud, which has the multiple benefits of setting a good example for other employees to see, giving a company some chance of reacquiring lost assets, and of leaving a public record of criminal activity, which gives other companies due notice of a prospective employee's character. The other options for dealing with fraud will result in increasing levels of difficulty, such as no return of lost assets, reduced employee morale, possible increases in employee turnover, and additional fraud cases at other companies as employees emigrate to new companies and commit crimes again. In short, management should react strongly to any cases of fraud, including prosecution to the fullest extent of the law.

FOREIGN CORRUPT PRACTICES ACT

Congress enacted the Foreign Corrupt Practices Act in 1977. This Act was passed because of disclosures by the Office of the Watergate Special Prosecutor and the Securities and Exchange Commission (SEC) of the use of U.S. corporate funds for domestic political contributions and for the bribery of foreign government officials. Some of these payments were clearly illegal and others questionable, while some payments appeared to have been made by avoiding internal control systems. To prevent these problems from occurring in the future, the Act requires a publicly traded company (it does not apply to privately held companies) to keep in reasonable detail "books, records and accounts" that accurately and fairly reflect its transactions and disposition of assets, and maintain an adequate system of internal controls. The control system must have the following attributes:

- Transactions must occur under the authorization of management.
- Transactions must be properly recorded.
- There must be reasonable controls over access to assets.
- There must be periodic reconciliations of recorded to actual assets, with an investigation of any differences.

This Act is particularly applicable to multinational organizations, so the controllers of these organizations must be aware of it and its ramifications for enhanced control systems. To be in compliance with the Act, a controller should be particularly mindful of the adequacy of company control systems, as well as of subtle changes in financial results that may indicate the presence of control problems.

8

INTERNAL AUDIT FUNCTION

IMPORTANCE OF THIS CHAPTER

The new controller may initially ignore any internal audit staff that her company may have. However, as this chapter points out, internal auditors can be an excellent resource for examining a variety of problems within a company. By understanding how this function works, the controller can use it as a resource to accomplish a number of key goals that she might not otherwise have sufficient staff to accomplish.

A key factor in the internal audit function is the manager to whom the function reports, since an incorrect reporting relationship can lead to skewed audit programs that avoid the areas supervised by that manager. Another issue is the objectives that the internal audit function should follow; too narrow a set of objectives may avoid reviews of key areas that are in serious need of help, while an excessively broad range of objectives will water down the department's ability to complete a reasonable set of target programs in a timely manner. A wide range of suggested activities for the internal audit staff are listed in this chapter, which are of use when determining a set of audit programs for the upcoming period. Finally, key factors are noted to consider when creating and maintaining a management system that provides an effective degree of control over the internal auditing staff. This chapter consists of an overview of the internal audit function, why it exists, what it does, and how to manage it.

REPORTING RELATIONSHIPS

Many companies adopt a reporting relationship between the accounting and internal auditing functions that leads to strained relations between the two functions. This section analyzes the problem and suggests a solution.

Many companies have the head of the internal audit department report to either the controller or (more commonly) the chief financial officer (CFO). They do so on the grounds that the bulk of the work performed by the internal audit staff addresses accounting and finance issues, so it makes sense to cluster the departments together. In addition, the internal audit staff is usually trained in accounting and is probably looking toward a promotion into the accounting and finance staffs once they have completed a tour of duty in the internal audit area. By keeping the two departments "under one roof," the accounting and finance staffs get a close look at the internal audit staff and can use this knowledge to promote them into the most appropriate positions. There are valid reasons for having the internal audit staff report to the manager of the accounting or finance functions.

Unfortunately, this relationship does not work very well. The reason is that the job of the internal audit staff is largely to review and report on the operations of the accounting and finance staffs. Because these reports tend to focus on problems, they do not cast the management of the accounting and finance departments in an overly favorable light. Consequently, if the internal audit staff reports to this area, it is common for the controller or CFO to design audit programs that focus on relatively innocuous areas, or else to focus on other parts of the company, while ignoring the accounting and finance areas. An alternative result is for the internal audit reports to be buried, so that senior management does not review any information that is critical of the way in which the accounting and finance areas are being managed. All of these outcomes tend to focus minimal internal audit attention on key accounting and finance processes, which is the precise area in which the auditors should be spending most of their time. The reporting relationship has a direct bearing on the review work performed by the internal audit staff.

If the internal audit staff is to conduct unencumbered reviews of the accounting and finance areas, it is necessary to shift the reporting relationship away from them. This allows the internal audit staff to avoid any problems caused by managers who do not want to have deleterious results shown to senior management. However, moving management of the function to a different area of the company raises similar problems, for anyone to whom the function reports will also not want the group to conduct any internal audits on areas that may reflect poorly on the manager. Consequently, the internal audit function should only report to positions at the top of the organization, where the manager is responsible for the entire company, and thus has no reason to avoid poor results in specific areas. This position can be the chief executive officer (CEO), but if this person is engaged in questionable activities, he or she may try to quash *all* internal audit activities. The best alternative is the board of directors, which is responsible for no company functions, and who is only concerned with maintaining the most efficient and effective operations, as well as appropriate levels of control over assets. The board can direct the internal audit staff by forming an audit committee. This committee can approve suggested audit programs, besides its usual function of selecting and overseeing the activities of the external auditors. This solution gives unfiltered information to the board, while also allowing it to target those areas of the company that it feels may be in most need of a review.

Since this section has recommended that the internal audit staff not report to the controller, one might ask why this chapter is even included in this book—after all, if it is not managed by the controller, why discuss it? The reason is that the controller can still have a considerable amount of control over the annual list of audits that the department conducts. This happens for two reasons. First, the controller is the senior accounting officer in the company, and as such is in the best position to spot problem areas and request audits that will highlight any problems. Second, whether there is a direct reporting relationship or not, the manager of the internal audit staff will recognize that the controller is more senior in the corporate hierarchy, and so it is a good idea to at least listen to any recommendations for future audits. For these reasons, the controller still has a considerable amount of influence over the activities of the internal audit staff, no matter who is the manager of the function.

In short, it is inappropriate for the internal audit staff to report directly to the controller or CFO, because they can skew audit programs or hide results to show the accounting and finance areas in the best possible light. It is better to assign the audit staff to the audit committee of the board of directors, which is a much more impartial management group.

COMPOSITION OF THE AUDIT COMMITTEE

The audit committee should be a standing committee of the Board of Directors, and should be comprised primarily of non-officer directors. These directors should not be involved in the management of the company, nor have previously been its officers. These restrictions are intended to create the most independent overview environment possible for the committee.

The committee is generally comprised of between three and five members, not all of whom must have an accounting, auditing, or finance background. It can be more useful to have some directors with a solid operational knowledge of the industry in which the company operates; these people can spot potential control weaknesses, based on their knowledge of how transactions flow in an industry-specific environment. Nonetheless, at least one committee member should have considerable training or experience in the accounting and finance arena. The committee should be expected to meet on at least a quarterly basis.

The CFO is rarely a member of this committee. Instead, sometimes she will be asked to attend its meetings in order to advise committee members on specific issues, or to answer questions about problems that the committee has uncovered through its review activities. The CFO should certainly maintain a strong line of communication with committee members, in order to inform them of possible accounting rule changes or prospective policy changes that may impact the reporting of financial information. The CFO should also educate committee members about key financial topics, such as corporate lines of business, accounting policies, legal obligations, regulatory filings, and industry accounting practices.

The director of the internal audit function usually reports to the CFO, but can report instead to the audit committee. The most common reporting relationship is for the internal audit director to be supervised by the CFO, but to have unimpeded access to the audit committee at any time; this reporting system is designed to give committee members direct access to the results of internal audits, while at the same time giving the internal audit director the ability to go around the CFO if that person appears to be obstructing the dissemination of internal audit results.

In short, the audit committee's structure is intended to be as independent of the management team as possible, while still giving it direct access to key accounting and audit personnel within the management team.

ASK TO ATTEND

The controller is not normally invited to meetings of the audit committee, since the CFO represents the accounting department. However, the committee discusses a number of topics relevant to the controller's job and is also attended by several company directors. In order to keep abreast of audit problems and meet several directors, it is worth asking to attend as an observer.

ROLE OF THE AUDIT COMMITTEE

The goal of the audit committee is to assist the Board of Directors by providing oversight of the financial reporting process and related controls. The committee is not empowered to make any decisions—rather, it recommends actions to the full Board, which may then vote on its recommendations. The exact range of tasks granted to the audit committee will vary, but are generally confined to the following issues:

- *Tasks related to company management:*
  - ○ *Review expenses incurred by the management team.* Used to spot any excessive use of corporate funds by managers.
  - ○ *Review business transactions between the company and the management team.* Used to ensure that managers are not enriching themselves at the expense of the company, as well as not holding their personal interests above those of the company.
- *Tasks related to external auditors:*
  - ○ *Recommend the hiring of external auditors.* Used to ensure that a truly independent auditor is used, rather than one having connections with the company in some way that may influence its review of the company's financial statements. The audit committee should also base this recommendation on the auditor's expertise in the industry, the quality of its services, the extent to which it performs other services for the company, and the amount of its quoted fees for the audit.
  - ○ *Review auditor recommendations.* Used to ensure that control issues spotted by the auditors are properly dealt with by the management team, resulting in a stronger control environment.
  - ○ *Review disputes between the external auditors and management.* Used to determine if the management team is attempting to force the auditors to agree with an alternative accounting treatment for transactions.
  - ○ *Review the use of external auditors for other services.* Used to determine if the external auditor has obtained such a significant amount of extra business with the company that it may be less inclined to issue an unfavorable audit opinion, due to the risk of losing the additional business.
- *Tasks related to internal audits:*
  - ○ *Review the replacement of the internal audit director.* Used to verify that the internal auditor director is being replaced for reasonable cause, rather than because the CFO wants to install a more malleable director.
  - ○ *Review the internal audit staff's objectives, work plans, training, and reports.* Used to verify that the internal audit staff is appropriately targeted at those areas of the company that are at greatest risk of control problems, and that the audit staff is appropriately trained to handle the audits. A detailed review of the annual work plan will reveal if the internal audit director has allocated a sufficient amount of time to each audit, or has sufficient staff available to complete all goals.
  - ○ *Review the cooperation received by the internal auditors.* Used to spot possible areas of fraudulent activities, since minimal cooperation is a signal that an auditee may be hiding information from audit teams.
  - ○ *Review disaster recovery plans.* Used to ensure that adequate recovery plans have been created and tested for the most likely disaster scenarios.

- *Tasks related to financial systems:*

  ○ *Investigate fraud and other forms of financial misconduct.* Used as the grounds for a direct investigation of any situation possibly involving deliberately inaccurate financial reporting or the misuse of company assets.

  ○ *Review corporate policies for compliance with laws and ethics.* Used to ensure that all corporate policies, irrespective of their relationship to financial systems, are constructed in accordance with local regulations, and meet the restrictions of the corporate statement of ethical activities.

  ○ *Verify that financial reports address all information requirements of lenders.* Used to ensure that lender-required financial information is reported to them at the appropriate times and in the correct formats, so there is minimal risk of losing vital credit lines as a result of missing information.

  ○ *Review all reports to shareholders, including special reports, for consistency of information.* Used to verify that all reports present a consistent picture of corporate financial health to investors. This is of particular concern for special reports, which tend to include different types of measures (such as EBITDA instead of the net income figure found on financial statements) and bullish statements by management that do not always match the tenor of information presented in the standard set of financial reports.

Of special interest is the audit committee's emphasis on the *review* of a wide range of financial activities—with the exception of one item: The audit committee is empowered to *investigate* fraud and other forms of financial misconduct, rather than review the results of such an investigation by someone else. The reason for this direct action is that employees are probably involved in the fraudulent activities, which may possibly involve members of management, so the audit committee can obtain an unbiased review of the situation only by doing so itself.

Thus, in all cases besides the investigation of financial misconduct, the audit committee's role is to examine the results of a variety of audits and other investigations to ensure that the company's system of financial reporting fairly represents actual operating results.

INTERNAL AUDIT OBJECTIVES

It is extremely important to determine the correct set of objectives for the internal audit staff. These objectives are used as the framework for constructing audit programs, as well as for determining the most appropriate skill set for the staff, plus the number of people needed to staff the department. Devising the correct set of objectives has a direct bearing on both the structure and work of the department. This section describes a typical set of objectives, as well as some changes to the list that are appropriate under certain circumstances.

There is a broad range of internal audit objectives that a company can adopt. The exact number and type of objective can vary greatly, depending on the anticipated size and skill of the audit staff, as well as the perceived need for audit reviews (which is frequently based on the past history of the company) by the management team that creates or approves the list of objectives. For example, a company may have had a great deal of trouble convincing its staff to follow a specific set of procedures, and so it will place great emphasis on an objective that hones in on the consistent use of policies and procedures. Another company may have had trouble with fraud or harrassment in the past, and so one of its key objectives will be to ensure that the company's code of ethics is being followed. Yet another company may have been burned by inconsistent financial reporting, which calls for an objective that tracks this issue. The most common minimum objectives for the internal audit department will address the need to safeguard assets and create accurate financial statements. These objectives are strictly financial in nature, and can be handled by an audit staff with a traditional financial background and a minimum training in company procedures. These are also useful objectives when the audit staff is so small that there is no room to pursue a wider-ranging set of objectives. These objectives are:

- That control systems will adequately safeguard company assets
- That company financial statements follow generally accepted accounting principles (GAAP) and are accurate

These objectives can be widened to include reviews of operating policies and procedures. This is a very common objective if there are perceived problems in this area. Also, problems in operations tend to have an impact on the accuracy of the financial statements, so many companies take the view that this objective goes "hand in hand" with the earlier objective for financial statements and therefore must be included. However, this requires a broader range of skills and a much larger work plan, so this objective tends to result in a larger and more experienced audit staff. This objective is:

- That the company is following operating policies and procedures

Given the prevalence of computer systems and the degree to which they are now integrated into a company's most crucial operations, it is also common to specify an objective that addresses this area. By doing so, a company must add a highly skilled group of computer system auditors to the internal audit staff. Any review work involving computer systems requires a considerable degree of knowledge, primarily of systems design and testing. Some more detailed reviews may even require a knowledge of programming languages, though it is customary to contract out this more specialized audit work, since it is difficult to find and retain personnel with such unique skill sets. It is sometimes necessary to contract out virtually *all* computer-related audit work, given the difficulty of finding qualified staff people to conduct the work. This objective is:

- That computer systems are accurately processing data

It is common for companies to also require reviews of ethical standards by the internal audit group. This requirement is frequently a result of a highly public scandal that has damaged the company's reputation or of a large lawsuit settlement that could have been avoided if there had been higher ethical standards (e.g., kickbacks, sexual harassment, etc.). Since this type of audit tends to fall outside of the experience of a typical internal auditor, it is customary to bring in a consultant to advise on how to construct and follow through on ethics audits (with the primary focus being on audits of scheduled ethics training of employees). This objective is:

- That the company is following an approved set of ethical guidelines

There should be an objective that requires the internal audit staff to support the activities of the external auditors. This objective is necessary because the fees charged by the outside auditors can be reduced by supplementing their work with that of the internal auditors. There is a limit to how much work the inside auditors can perform, because an excessive degree of assistance by them would interfere with the independence and objectivity of the external auditor's work. Nonetheless, the outside auditors may rely on them for a significant volume of work. This objective is:

- That the department adequately supports the activities of external auditors

The previous objectives have addressed key areas of a company that must be reviewed. In addition, there should be an objective that requires the internal audit manager to prepare an annual internal audit plan for reviewing the previous objectives. This is important, because it forces the manager to address such issues as the importance of various audits, the degree to which some objectives are being addressed at the expense of others, and the adequacy of the department's staffing and expense budget. This objective is:

- That it creates an annual audit plan that addresses all of these objectives

The final objective relates to the output from the work of the internal audit department. While the previous objectives have established a direction for the audits to be conducted or the management of that work, there is no provision for what the department is supposed to do with the results of all this work. Accordingly, the final objective requires the department to create reports that detail all findings and make recommendations to resolve problems. In addition, the objective should require that the reports be distributed to those levels of management that can use the information to resolve the problems. This final objective closes the loop on all activities required of the internal audit department. This objective is

- That it provides written reports of its findings to those levels of management needing the information in order to correct faulty systems

The bulk of these objectives relate to the types of audit work to be conducted by the department, with the key areas including the safeguarding of assets, accuracy of financial statements, and reviews of operations and computer systems. Many of these objectives are discussed again in the next section, where we derive internal audit activities based on each of the objectives.

INTERNAL AUDIT ACTIVITIES

This section is based on the objectives that were described in the previous section. Though there are a few activities noted here, the reader should not rely on this list to create a comprehensive set of activities for an internal audit department. The reason is that there will certainly be additional activities that are unique to each company; also, there may be a number of activities that are specific to particular industries. A manager who is compiling activities for this department should talk to consultants, external auditors, and trade associations that have considerable experience in specific industries to obtain input on additional activities for the department. This will yield a more comprehensive set of tasks for the internal audit department.

RECRUIT FROM THE INTERNAL AUDIT STAFF

Internal auditors do not necessarily have to be CPAs or even earn a degree in accounting, since they are called upon to conduct audits in a variety of areas well away from the controller's department. However, as evidenced by a number of the following bullet points, many of them have considerable accounting experience. If so, use an internal audit of the accounting department as an excuse to evaluate them, and extend job offers for an internal transfer to the department if they appear likely to be a good addition.

The eight internal audit objectives noted below are all followed by a variety of related audit activities.

1. *Objective: That control systems will adequately safeguard company assets*
   - Cash: Verify that there are adequate controls over petty cash.
   - Fixed assets: Verify that there is a sufficient degree of control over borrowed assets. Verify that there is a sufficient degree of control over the acquisition and disposal of assets.
   - Inventory: Verify that there are sufficient safeguards against the loss of inventory. Verify that there is a sufficient degree of control over consigned inventory.
   - Supplies: Verify that there is a sufficient degree of control over the purchase, storage, and use of supplies.

2. *Objective: That company financial statements follow GAAP and are accurate*
   - Cost of goods sold: Verify that product bills of material are accurate. Verify that the cost of goods sold is correctly computed. Verify that there is a proper cutoff of receipts and shipments at the end of the reporting period.
   - Expenses: Verify that all expense accruals are correctly calculated. Verify that all prepaid expenses are expensed in the correct periods. Verify that expenses are incurred only up to budgeted levels. Verify that paychecks are only calculated and paid for current employees. Verify that payroll amounts are correctly calculated. Verify that the assumed resale values of fixed assets are reasonable, based on a current review of asset values. Verify that the authorization for incurring expenses is appropriate. Verify that the time period over which depreciation is taken is reasonable, based on industry standards and historical usage.
   - Revenue: Verify that billings are only made for services and product sales that are actually completed. Verify that invoices are recorded in the correct periods and amounts.

3. *Objective: That the company is following operating policies and procedures*
   - Determine labor productivity.
   - Investigate and determine the cause of transactional errors.
   - Review the appropriateness of expenses for new construction.
   - Review the fixed asset purchasing goals after-the-fact to see if goals were met.
   - Review the obsolescence of existing equipment.
   - Verify the appropriateness of pay levels based on experience and education.
   - Verify from a sample of expense reports that only those approved types of travel expenses are being reimbursed.
   - Verify that bank reconciliations are regularly performed and reviewed.
   - Verify that financial statements are published within specified due dates.
   - Verify that machine run rates are within expected levels.
   - Verify that product quality levels match minimum standards.
   - Verify that production scrap rates are within expected levels.
   - Verify that shipments are made on scheduled ship dates.
   - Verify the accuracy and timeliness of all key transactions.

4. *Objective: That computer systems are accurately processing data*

   ○ Verify from a sample of transactions that the computer system is correctly calculating accounting transactions.

   ○ Verify that data from an acquired company is accurately entered into the existing computer system.

   ○ Verify that new systems under development are designed with an appropriate number of control points to ensure proper processing of transactions.

   ○ Verify that there are a sufficient number of safeguards built into the system to ensure a rapid recovery from catastrophic computer damage.

   ○ Verify that there is sufficient testing of systems and data during a conversion of computer systems to a replacement system.

5. *Objective: That the company is following an approved set of ethical guidelines*

   ○ Follow up on reported ethics cases and determine the extent to which formal ethics training programs would have avoided the situations.

   ○ Verify from training records that each employee has received at least the minimum number of ethics training hours per year.

   ○ Verify that the training materials used to teach ethics to employees contain information that matches and supports the principles described in the company's official ethics policy.

6. *Objective: That the department adequately supports the activities of external auditors*

   ○ Verify that the internal audit staff completed the tasks assigned to it by the external auditors.

   ○ Verify that the tasks assigned to the internal audit staff to support the external auditors were completed to the satisfaction of the external auditors.

   ○ Review the entire external audit program and make recommendations to increase the share of work completed by the internal audit staff, in order to reduce fees charged by the external auditors.

7. *Objective: That the department creates an annual audit plan that addresses all of these objectives*

   ○ Verify that a broad range of managers are consulted regarding the contents of the annual audit plan.

   ○ Verify that the annual audit plan contains some reviews for all of the previous audit objectives related to control over assets, ethics, operations, financial accuracy, and operations.

   ○ Verify that the key control problems pointed out by the external auditors are being addressed by the annual audit plan.

8. *Objective: That the department provides written reports of its findings to those levels of management needing the information in order to correct faulty systems*

   ○ Verify that feedback is solicited from auditees regarding the findings and recommendations made in audit reports.

   ○ Verify the degree to which recommendations have been implemented, subsequent to the release of audit reports.

This section presented a wide-ranging list of internal audit activities that are closely tied to the audit objectives described in the last section. However, this is not a comprehensive list, so other industry-specific sources should be consulted in order to compile a more complete listing of activities.

MANAGING THE INTERNAL AUDIT FUNCTION

The internal audit department is not a line function, so there are no regular outputs to examine, nor are there any direct cost savings or added revenues attributable to it. This lack of clear results makes it somewhat more difficult to manage the function. This section describes the main steps that a manager should complete in order to create a management system for the internal audit function, as well as a means for determining the status of activities, and controlling it based on that information.

The first step in managing the department is to create and disseminate a clear set of responsibilities for the internal audit staff. This gives the department definitive guidelines to follow, as well as direction in its daily activities. A typical responsibility statement should include:

- That control systems will adequately safeguard company assets
- That company financial statements follow GAAP and are accurate
- That the company is following operating policies and procedures
- That the company is following an approved set of ethical guidelines
- That computer systems are accurately processing data
- That the department adequately supports the activities of external auditors
- That it creates an annual audit plan that addresses all of these objectives
- That it provides written reports of its findings to those levels of management needing the information in order to correct faulty systems

Once these objectives are in place, the manager can focus on the primary output—the annual audit plan—as the easiest means for managing the department. The annual plan is usually a brief document that lists every audit to be completed during the year, as well as a brief description of the objectives of each audit. For example, it might include the following audit:

> *Review the method for recording additions, changes, and deletions of fixed assets to and from the accounting records for the Andersonville facility. The audit will verify that the correct capitalization limit is being observed, that there are documented and justified reasons for making alterations to the fixed asset records subsequent to additions, that deletions are recorded properly, and that the sale amounts of assets are reasonable.*

GET ON THE LIST!

A well-managed annual audit plan will leave room for a few unplanned audits, but the controller should not rely on trying to jam extra audits into the plan once it has been finalized. Instead, correspond regularly with the internal audit manager about the status and priority of various audit requests during the annual budgeting process to ensure that key accounting reviews will be included.

Division	Project	Hours	Start Date	End Date	Personnel
Denver	Fixed assets	240	01/01/XX	02/15/XX	Smith/Jones
Denver	Billings	280	01/01/XX	02/21/XX	Barnaby/Granger
Boston	Fixed assets	240	02/16/XX	03/31/XX	Smith/Jones
Chicago	Fixed assets	240	04/01/XX	05/15/XX	Smith/Jones
Chicago	Billings	280	02/22/XX	03/07/XX	Barnaby/Granger
Atlanta	Fixed assets	240	05/16/XX	06/30/XX	Smith/Jones
Atlanta	Billings	280	03/08/XX	04/21/XX	Barnaby/Granger

EXHIBIT 8.1   SAMPLE INTERNAL AUDIT BUDGET

Though this audit description gives one a good idea of what will happen during an audit, it does not yield a sufficient degree of additional information, such as the number of hours budgeted for the work, who will be assigned to the project, or when it will take place, for a manager to achieve tight control over the department. This requires a more detailed audit budget for the year, such as the one shown in Exhibit 8.1. The primary information contained in this budget are the budgeted hours scheduled for each job, and the estimated range of dates during which work will be completed.

Once armed with the internal audit budget, a manager can exercise a much greater degree of control over the internal audit department. The budget information allows a manager to use the following controls:

- Compare budget to actual hours worked.
- Compare budget to actual project start dates.
- Compare budget to actual project completion dates.
- Compare budget to actual staffing requirements.

In addition to these quantitative control points, there are a variety of other controls that a manager can use. These extra controls tend to supplement the quantitative controls, and can be "mixed and matched" to derive a set of controls that are best suited for specific situations. The extra controls are:

- Compare the written objectives of the department to its actual activities.
- Ensure that the internal audit staff coordinates its work to support that of the external auditors.
- Ensure that there is an up-to-date policies and procedures manual that clearly shows how audit work is to be conducted.
- Review audit reports for activities conducted, findings noted, and recommendations given.
- Review comments from departments that were the subject of audits.
- Review the mix of scheduled reviews to see if there is a lack of attention to specific areas, such as reviews of accounting, computer, or operational controls.
- Review work papers to ensure that audits were completed in as thorough a manner as possible.
- Verify that audit recommendations are being acted on.

- Verify that auditors have a sufficient educational background to conduct specific types of audits (some audits are so specialized that outside expertise must be brought in).
- Verify that the audit committee is satisfied with departmental performance, and follow up on any shortcomings.
- Verify that the department is reviewing the controls being built into new computer system projects.
- Verify that the department is sufficiently large to accomplish all planned goals.
- Verify that there are scheduled reviews of the company's ethical standards.
- Verify that there have been no restrictions of departmental activities due to intransigence by auditees, and bring up exceptions with the audit committee for action.

It is important to have prior knowledge of the activities of and conditions in the internal audit department before selecting from the previous list of management controls, because this information has a direct bearing on which controls are selected. How does one gather this information? There are a variety of information sources that can be consulted, including:

- *The depth and accuracy of audit planning.* An internal audit is a project, and as such must be adequately planned and then managed against that plan to ensure that audits are completed on time.
- *The image of the department.* The department manager and any staff members who are in direct contact with other departments must present a positive and professional image, especially when conducting reviews, discussing recommendations, or presenting findings.
- *The opinion of the outside auditors.* The external auditors are accustomed to working with the internal audit staff from time to time, and can usually provide an opinion regarding the quality of the department's work.
- *The quality of personnel practices.* The members of the internal audit staff should have a high level of training, possess adequate knowledge of the areas being audited, have clear career paths that are well documented, and be conversant in the use of any new technologies that assist them in conducting their jobs.
- *The reaction of departments that have been reviewed.* Any auditees should have a positive view of the internal audit department (unless it discovered massive problems!), since auditors should conduct their reviews in a professional manner and keep auditees well informed of their progress and recommendations.
- *The reaction of senior management and the board of directors.* These managers should feel that the internal audit group has provided meaningful insights on company operations, as well as made solid improvement recommendations.
- *The types of recommendations in previous audit reports.* If there is a large proportion of less important recommendations, this is a sign that the internal audit staff is either not well acquainted with the systems it is reviewing, or that the quality of work conducted is so low that no significant recommendations are likely to be found.

Only by reviewing this information can a manager determine the particular strengths and weaknesses of an internal audit department, which can then be used to select the specific control methods necessary to manage the department. In general, a successful internal audit manager should utilize all of the quantitative measures noted in this section, and supplement them with a selection of qualitative controls (also noted in this section) that are tailored to the specific circumstances of the department. Only by doing so can a manager create a management system that is both efficient and effective, which will result in a high-performance internal audit department without an excessively burdensome management system.

FUND ADDITIONAL AUDITS

If the internal auditors' schedule is completely booked for many months in advance and there is no way for the controller to schedule a key audit, consider shifting budgeted funds from the accounting budget to that of the internal audit department. Offering to pay for an audit can give an audit request a much higher level of priority.

9

GLOBALIZATION: COMPLEXITIES AND OPPORTUNITIES

IMPORTANCE OF THIS CHAPTER

Even in a smaller company, a new controller is likely to be impacted by some aspect of the global economy, perhaps in the areas of letters of credit, export/import considerations, transfer pricing, or value-added taxes. This chapter gives an overview of how global trade impacts companies, as well as how to deal with it.

INTRODUCTION: PERVASIVE NATURE OF GLOBALIZATION

Those active in business know that change is constant. It seems some subjects are emphasized, then deemphasized and later emphasized again, for example, benchmarking, reengineering, empowered workteams, leveraged buyouts, mergers and acquisitions, explosion of new technologies, the changing nature of capital markets. And now we have globalization.

In the 1970s and 1980s, international trade, in the eyes of many, focused on North America, Europe, and Japan—the most developed markets. Now vast new markets have opened for Western goods in Asia, South America, and Eastern Europe. It is these still developing areas, which include the Pacific Rim, India, Latin America, China, and Africa, that need attention. This is where the largest growth will be.

With the greatly expanded global horizon, the financial executive should be aware of these aspects:

- The expanded markets for U.S. goods and services, and the related impact on specific industries, required changes in packaging and product design, and distributions to meet local tastes.
- Potential changes in sources for raw materials and supplies.

158

- Widened financial investment opportunities, with differing rates of return and diversification possibilities in foreign stocks (including ADRs—American Depositary Receipts), bonds, and global mutual funds specific to a particular county or region.

- Possible impact on organization structure, including top management structure and related local management chain of command and financial management structure.

While the subject of globalization is currently popular, it bears mentioning that though many managements may attempt to do business globally, a very large number do not. Converting a local business to a global basis is difficult. The differences in style of management required, in control and lack thereof, and in business practices, causes some management to shy away from globalization. (See "Technical Aspects of the Controllership Function under Globalization" on page 167.) But the rewards, if successful, are great—shared resources, shared management talent, broadened markets, lessened impact of a local economy downtrend. Globalization under the proper conditions can open up a world of opportunity.

- Possible changes in corporate or entity relationships, including the virtual corporation.

- Changes in policies and procedures relating to planning and control responsibilities or other activities required by U.S., foreign national, or local laws and regulations—as well as transfer pricing guidelines.

CHANGING NATURE OF INTERNATIONAL TRADE

U.S. companies have engaged in international trade for many years by exporting U.S. produced goods or services, importing selected foreign products, and utilizing factories in foreign countries to assemble products for sale in the United States. With the emergence of huge trading blocks in North America (including the implementation of the North American Free Trade Agreement [NAFTA], Europe [the European Union], and East Asia [the Pacific Rim]) and the growth in other areas, major changes are taking place as to the manner in which global or multinational organizations are doing business. Cross-border trade and investments are both rising dramatically.

These specific developments illustrate the trend:

- Many U.S. companies are increasing their foreign capital investments in plant and equipment.

- U.S. investors are putting record funds into foreign investment—ADRs, some stocks, bonds, and mutual funds.

- Some U.S. corporations are engaging in sophisticated or advanced research and development (R&D) in foreign laboratories instead of the United States.

- U.S. owned companies are beginning to employ large numbers of foreign workers relative to the number of U.S. employees.

- Many U.S. owned corporations are exporting foreign produced goods to the United States. Conversely, some foreign-owned companies are establishing manufacturing plants and distribution facilities in the United States for the sale of their U.S. produced goods.

- Many non-U.S. companies with facilities in the United States are exporting a significant value of U.S. produced goods to foreign markets.

For many years, U.S. global companies regarded foreign plants as appendages for the manufacture and sale of products designed or engineered in the United States. Given competitive pressures, the superior knowledge that foreign nationals have about local practices or customs in their country, and perhaps a less dominant position of some U.S. products and services, there is now more of a cross flow of technology, capital, and talents in many directions. In reality, the nationality of a company is not as clear as it once was; and the chain of command may include many U.S. citizens as well as foreign nationals.

All these developments add to the complexities of doing business on a global basis.

IMPACT OF GLOBAL TRADE ON SEGMENTS OF THE U.S. ECONOMY

It should be of general interest to know how global trade affects different segments of the U.S. economy. How does it impact a particular industry or company? Because U.S. government statistics do not provide much assistance, *Business Week* made its own review after dividing the U.S. economy into three segments: (1) exporting trade, (2) import-competing trade, and (3) domestic trade.[1] The makeup of the sectors and the general conclusions are:

1. *Exporting trade.* The exporting sector consists of industries that are competing effectively in markets at home and abroad. To be included, the industry group must export at least 10% of its output. The exporting sector includes industries such as:

Aircraft	Financial services
Business services	Higher education
(e.g., consulting and accounting)	Instruments
Chemicals	International communications and
Computers	transportation
Drugs	Lumber and paper products
Electronic equipment and components	Moviemaking and other entertainment

   The *Business Week* report indicates that workers in the exporting sector are winners in the trend toward a global economy. Exporters have expanded output and sales, and they also have boosted productivity by reducing jobs and substituting capital for labor. Although employment was flat, average real wages increased by 5.2% since 1980. As one economist stated, "Export success means rising wages."

2. *Import-competing trade.* Industries in the import-competing category import no more than 10% of foreign goods into the U.S. market. This sector includes the following categories of industry:

Automobiles and motorcycles	Most industrial machinery
Cement	Screws, nuts, and other small hardware
Clothing	Shoes and luggage
Consumer electronics	Steel, aluminum, and other metals
Furniture	Tires
Machine tools	Toys
Mining	

---

1.   Michael J. Mandel, and Aaron Bernstein, "Dispelling the Myths That Are Holding Us Back," *Business Week,* Dec. 17, 1990, p. 67.

Employees in this segment have been hurt by the direct and indirect effects of foreign competition. Jobs have become scarce, and wages, once good, have fallen.

3. *Domestic.* This category includes industries that do little importing or exporting. Most are service industries, although some manufacturing is included (e.g., concrete blocks) when local tastes, standards, or economics limit international trade. The domestic sector includes these industries:

Business services	Food processing
Commercial printing	Health services
Concrete products	Personal services (e.g., hair dress-
Construction	ing and automobile repair)
Domestic transportation and communications	Publishing
Education (primary and secondary)	Rubber and plastic products
Financial services, real estate, and insurance	Wholesale and retail trade

Global competition has pushed down wages in the domestic sector. While it may be relatively easy to find work, pay has decreased and is getting lower. Moreover, as imports or increasing productivity reduce the number of jobs in other categories, many employees have migrated to the service sector, making competition a more important factor.

Global trade can affect just about everyone in every sector of the economy.

DETERMINING AND IMPLEMENTING SUCCESSFUL GLOBAL STRATEGIES

A great many factors influence whether a particular entity will be successful in the global marketplace. Perhaps no factor is more important than the selection of the proper strategies; and this includes determining the strategy decided upon in the proper manner. It is a reflection of the "NIH" syndrome—not invented here.

A key player in carrying out global strategies is the subsidiary top manager. Some research into the viewpoints of these managers revealed these conclusions as to the process by which strategies should be determined.[2]

- *It is important that the head office executives become familiar with local conditions.* Only where the subsidiary managers believe the head office executives understand how the local market operates do they respect the decisions reached, and make a greater effort to follow them.

- *Two-way communication is essential.* Subsidiary top managers value the ability to voice their opinions and exchange ideas with the home office in reaching a strategic decision.

- *Subsidiary managers must regard the decision-making practices as consistent.* In other words, strategic decision making is a *political* process as well as any *economic* and *competitive* process. Subsidiary managers must not conclude that those on the "inside track" will be heard, but that all others will be overlooked.

---

2. W. Chan Kim, and Renee A. Mauborgne, "Making Global Strategies Work," *Sloan Management Review,* Spring 1993, pp. 11–26.

- *Subsidiary managers must believe they have the ability to reflect or openly challenge the head office decision.* In such an environment, the subsidiary managers think the head office may better recognize that strategic decisions will be of a higher quality, and will be made in the overall economic interest—not primarily a political interest.
- *Subsidiary top managers think it is only fair that the head office explain the reasons for the final global strategic decisions.* When such a procedure is followed, many subsidiary managers tend to believe that the head office at least considered the subsidiary position, and that they thereby acted in a fair and impartial manner.

The existence of a fair *process* of establishing global strategies is key to making the strategy successful. It tends to cause subsidiary managers to pursue *voluntary* execution—doing more than is required—rather than *compulsory* execution—meeting minimum requirements. The traditional mechanism for strategy enforcement—incentive compensation, auditing or monitoring systems, heavy-handed disciplining by the head office, and other rewards or punishments—are of some worth. But these mechanisms are of declining value by reason of such trends or factors as these, among others:

- Increasing size of subsidiary units
- A growth in unique or distinctive skills in the subsidiaries
- Growing and extensive communication between the subsidiaries in comparing ideas (and excluding the home office)
- Growing importance of subcultures
- Increasing difficulty in monitoring efforts in enforcing the prescribed strategy—due to an inability to distinguish the cause of failure—whether the result of factors beyond the control of the manager, or poor implementation that he or she *can* control
- Growing loss of control by the central office

LOOK FOR SKILLS OUTSIDE THE HEAD OFFICE

It is entirely possible that a company has staff with excellent accounting skills who are located in other countries. If so, the controller should consider regularly visiting these facilities to evaluate staff, and persuade the best ones to move to corporate headquarters. Alternatively, consider sending corporate accounting staff abroad for short intervals in order to learn about local business conditions and requirements.

The growing complexities in the global marketplace make a participative management approach, perceived as fair and equitable, increasingly important. Aside from the psychological environment, the most important factor is the actual strategy adopted. The predominant philosophy or type of strategy will depend, among other things, upon the product, the industry, the specific market, and the nature of the competition. A study of styles of competition in the semiconductor business made by a Fordham University Graduate School of Business professor concluded that, in this instance, U.S. firms tended to develop a unique strategy while the effective Japanese competitors tended to win by implementing in a superior manner a not-so-unique strategy.[3] A comparative summary of different competitive actions in this specific market are shown in Exhibit 9.1.

---

3. See William G. Egelhoff, "Great Strategy or Great Strategy Implementation—Two Ways of Competing in Global Markets," *Sloan Management Review,* Winter 1993, pp. 37–50.

	Dominant Competitive Style	
Action	**U.S. Company**	**Japanese Company**
Securing unique product-market advantage	Attempts to develop unique advantage for each product line	Does not seek unique product-market advantage; relies on low cost and high quality
Role of process technology (which transfers a product design into marketable products)	Great variance from company to company. Large firms may attempt to stay in the forefront of process technology, whereas firms that rely most heavily on product-market differentiation may consider process technology less important	Emphasizes staying at the forefront of technology—both for product development and for capital improvement
Sources of process technology know-how	Often depends on external sources—e.g., by engaging in collaborative research, by outright purchase, or by seeking assistance from equipment manufacturers	Tending to favor internal development
Withdrawal from the market	Tends to withdraw from product-market segment when clear advantage cannot be gained, often after competitive pressures make segment unprofitable	Seldom withdraws from market; tends to remain in product segment and to strive for profitability through efficiency
Status of vertical integration	Generally values such integration only when related products contribute uniqueness	Highly values vertical integration as part of drive to self-sufficiency

EXHIBIT 9.1 COMPARATIVE COMPETITIVE STYLES

As might be expected, the dominant competitive style influences any industry structure, which in turn influences the industry's member firms, their suppliers, and their customers. Exhibit 9.2 compares the impact of the two competitive styles on some important industry factors and characteristics. Note that the impact could be either an advantage or a disadvantage for any given particular firm.

Distinguishing Characteristics	Competing Style	
	"Superior" Strategy	**More Effective Implementation**
Impact on Factor		
Strategic variety	Greater variety of strategies results in greater range of products as well as greater segmentation of markets	Fewer strategies, resulting in more direct competition between products and product substitutes, with emphasis on quality and cost
Industry concentration	Many successful competitors and low industry concentration	Only a few successful competitors and high industry concentration
Industry survival pattern	Innovative competitors survive and dominate industry, with high turnover among leaders	Efficient competitors survive and dominate industry, with lower turnover among leaders

EXHIBIT 9.2 "SUPERIOR STRATEGY" VS. MORE EFFECTIVE IMPLEMENTATION OF A NONUNIQUE STRATEGY

Distinguishing Characteristics	Competing Style	
	"Superior" Strategy	More Effective Implementation
Industry Characteristics		
Product life cycle	Strategy is most effective in early stage of product life cycle, when technological and/or environmental change is rapid and a variety of feasible product designs exist	Strategy works best in later stages of product life cycle, when technological and/or environmental change is slow and the basic designs have evolved
Risk of technological or environmental change	Entity risks losing competitive advantage when there are fewer such changes and when imitators enter market	Entity risks losing competitive advantage when technological and/or environmental change dominates market
Profit margins	Less direct competition, resulting in higher profit margins	More direct competition, resulting in lower profit margins

EXHIBIT 9.2   "SUPERIOR STRATEGY" VS. MORE EFFECTIVE IMPLEMENTATION OF A NONUNIQUE STRATEGY *(CONTINUED)*

ORGANIZATION STRUCTURE IN A GLOBAL ENTERPRISE

The removal of trade barriers and the trend toward a global economy is changing the manner in which companies do business and, as a consequence, often also causes a change in some organizational arrangements. As entities become global, new threats appear in the home market as well as the foreign market. New products enter the marketplace, and competition increases for existing as well as new customers. These competitive forces are causing these changes:

- *Increased customer demands.* Customers tend to require faster deliveries, improved quality, and more numerous other related services.

- *Quicker responses.* It becomes increasingly necessary to react quickly to competitive actions, as well as changing market conditions, and to shorten the time for development of new products and services.

- *Improved outsourcing or subcontracting.* Another frequent requirement is the developing of closer relations with key suppliers so as to facilitate just-in-time delivery of materials or parts or other fast response needs.

- *Strengthening core competencies.* With the need to assemble and strengthen core competencies, some entities are forming flexible partnerships—as discussed in Chapter 10. (See "Importance of Communications with Employees" on page 194.) These business adaptations, coupled with the changes in information technology and the inflexibility of traditional, cumbersome, and bureaucratic structures, excessive management layers, and onerous procedures, are resulting in some new organization structures. Some may be recognized in a realigned organization, and others are reflected in "new organizations" that are not usually a part of the typical organization chart. A few of these new relationships are reflected in the phenomena listed next.

- *High-performance teams.* This is a group of individuals with differing skills brought together to function as a team and to completely reengineer a process—such as filling customer orders or a manufacturing sequence. The team works as a group using shared information and groupware—especially designed software to support collaborative effort.

- *Integrated organization.* In reality this is a change in the access and flow of information. Instead of, for example, three separate resource areas (a) financial, (b) physical assets, and (c) human resources, a new integrated information system lets executives directly access the required data. This new information system removes layers of management and modifying influences.

- *The extended business.* With the help of industry standards, computer systems are extending outward and linking with both customers and suppliers. In a sense, a change is taking place from a vertical organization to a horizontal entity. Again, some of this change is seen in the virtual corporation.

We see the impetus of international competition forcing the elimination of layers of management, and effective working groups built around key processes instead of single functions or departments. Moreover, knowledge of local markets and important customers argues for a great deal of decentralization.

In the context of organization structure, two other changes are occurring:

1. *Unit headquarters.* In this increasingly global economy, many U.S. companies are transferring abroad the world headquarters of important business units. Astute managements are recognizing that they must operate near key customers and closer to competitors—not in a far-away location. Many large business are finding that a company cannot be run from a single location; several different headquarters may be required for different product lines or competitive postures. With such changes, some loss of control may result. Hence, the controller must be sensitive to these developments.

2. *The finance organization.* Just as the principle of decentralization applies to the marketing function, it could be advantageous in the finance organization. The chief financial planning and control office of the subsidiary unit should report *administratively* to the local unit manager. This structure tends to make the financial executive a member of the local management, and not be perceived as the eyes and ears of the corporate office. Also, it should make the local financial manager more responsive to the needs of local management. The corporate controller could then provide *functional* guidance, such as the financial procedures to be used, internal control procedures, and report requirements for the home office.

ADOPT A DECENTRALIZED ACCOUNTING STRUCTURE

Though a new controller may be tempted to centralize all accounting functions within a company, this is rarely possible in an organization with international locations. The intricacies of local business requirements almost always mandate that some accounting staff be present in each country. At best, one can centralize accounting operations for all locations within each country.

The staff relationship of the unit controllers to the corporate controller is illustrated in Exhibit 9.3.

VIRTUAL CORPORATION

In the context of meeting global competition, a new form of organization—the virtual corporation—is emerging to more quickly take advantage of new economic opportunities. This development in organization structure warrants discussion in a separate section. While often used in connection with outsourcing, the concept may spread to other functions.

Global Enterprise, Inc.
MASTER ORGANIZATION CHART

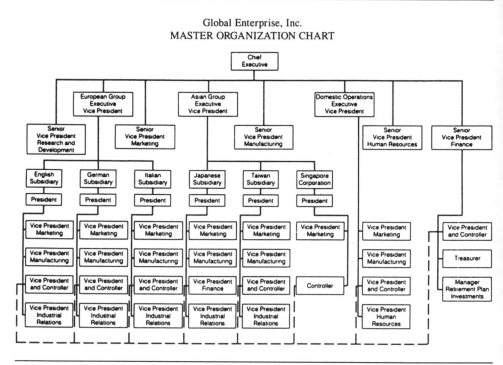

EXHIBIT 9.3   GLOBAL ORGANIZATION STRUCTURE (WITH EMPHASIS ON THE FINANCIAL ORGANIZATION)

Webster's Tenth New Collegiate Dictionary defines "virtual" as "being such in essence or effect though not formally recognized or admitted." By this definition, a virtual corporation is an entity that, although not formally recognized or admitted as a corporation, is such in effect. As typically described, it is a temporary, flexible network of independent organizations linked by information technology for the purpose of sharing skills, costs, and access to one another's markets. It is a means of quickly meeting competitive pressures. The principal characteristics of this form of organization are:

- *Excellence.* Each participant in the organization commits its "core competence" to the joint effort—with the result that each function or process can be world class in a faster time than other methods. A single corporation only rarely can achieve world class status in most of its functions.

- *Opportunistic and temporary.* The association is less likely to be either permanent or formal than other arrangements. The entities band together to meet a particular need or to take advantage of a particular opportunity. When the need no longer exists, or the benefits have been realized, then the organizations disband. But benefits have accrued for each member.

- *Existence of indeterminate borders.* With the many contacts among suppliers, customers, and perhaps competitors, the corporate boundaries often become blurred.

- *Technology dependent.* The new information technology enables the widely dispersed entities to communicate and work cooperatively. The electronics interchange reduces greatly the time required for legal decisions, or link-ups, or making changes.

- *Codependence.* The nature of the new relationship makes each participant quite dependent on the other members of the group.

- *Loss of control.* The various characteristics listed above results in some loss of control over some operations, with possible related difficulties.

This form of organization should be considered by some global entities.

TECHNICAL ASPECTS OF THE CONTROLLERSHIP FUNCTION UNDER GLOBALIZATION

The bulk of the preceding discussion in this chapter has related to those *general* aspects of globalization or international trade of which the controller should be aware. Additionally, in properly carrying out the duties of a controller in a situation involving multicountry operations, as contrasted with single country activities, these subjects are germane and specific to the task—and they are all interrelated:

- Open communications
- Need for uniformity in data definition
- Complying with international accounting requirements
- Measuring foreign operations
- Translating financial statements
- Evaluating foreign investments—capital expenditures, R&D projects, operating programs (such as designing and constructing an aircraft), and so on
- Transfer pricing
- Taxation
- Import/export regulations
- Managing currency risk
- The Foreign Corrupt Practices Act (FCPA)

Open Communications

Two factors contribute to communication problems in an international operation. They are language and distance. It is important for a controller to address these problems and develop a satisfactory solution.

The most obvious way to handle the language problem is to ensure that someone with good bilingual skills is representing the controller in the overseas operation. This individual must be able to deal effectively with the local country officials and employees and then communicate important and necessary information back to the parent. The communication can be in person, by phone, by letter, and by data transmission. In larger operations, private communications systems will allow easy teleprocessing and telecommunications. In smaller organizations, careful planning of when calls and data are transmitted will result in good communications.

However, even after placing a qualified representative in the foreign operation, the controller must remain aware of the importance of clear information exchange. The need becomes even greater as the company expands into more countries and as the foreign operations become a bigger part of the business.

One technique that has proved effective is to issue written instructions on important matters such as:

- Planning assumptions

- Accounting and reporting requirements

- Control assessments

- Disbursement practices

The instructions should be formal notification to the subsidiaries as to what is required of them. The letters or instructions should be controlled (e.g., a sequential number assigned to each one so that all recipients are aware of all communiques). It is helpful to the subsidiaries if the parent periodically issues a summary of all such instructions that are still in force.

A second, and probably invaluable, communication technique is the one-on-one meeting. It is here that all the nuances of operation are really covered. These meetings of key people (controller to controller) should take place at least once a year and probably more often if there are difficult issues to be resolved.

Another effective communication vehicle is the use of group meetings, seminars, and classes wherein the controller sponsors a meeting of international people perhaps from several countries at which specific items of mutual interest are discussed. This also allows people with the same problems to come together and informally talk about problems. There has proved to be a continuing benefit in this approach in that the people stay in touch with one another to discuss ongoing and future problems and share solutions.

New developments in groupware to provide meeting support can assist in keeping the communication lines open.

Uniform Data Requirements

When operating internationally it is essential that there be worldwide uniformity in data definitions for three reasons:

1. It simplifies consolidation of financial statements and reports.

2. It allows for comparability of results.

3. It permits timely release of reports.

The use of a standard schedule of accounts, developed and maintained centrally but responsive to country needs, is the most obvious way to achieve uniformity or reporting. It becomes simple then to define the aggregation of data in order to achieve usable reports. This results in one scorecard that is then used by all parts of the organizations within the company. To be effective, use of a standard reporting chart of accounts requires that headquarters have a knowledge of the out-of-country business and how it is to be recorded and summarized. It also requires an interpretation of U.S. accounting standards, which must be articulated and promulgated to all subsidiaries so that financial reports have a uniformity of structure and content.

To sum up, a world-class accounting operation would be organized to:

- Keep responsibility for recording at the country level.

- Provide clear instructions to the countries as to how transactions would be summarized and reported.

- Have each country prepare statements in the parent-company currency using U.S. generally accepted accounting principles (GAAP).

This structure will result in uniform accounting reports to allow comparison between units. It will also permit tighter closing schedules and the resultant earlier release of information both within the company and externally.

International Accounting Requirements

In putting together a world-class accounting operation the controller must address:

- Records of a subsidiary must be kept in the *local* currency and language and must meet local fiscal, professional, and tax requirements.

- The records must then (a) be adjusted to "generally accepted accounting principles" of the parent, and (b) be translated into the currency of the parent. (Less commonly, a second ledger may be maintained in the currency of the parent and in accordance with GAAP of the parent.)

The record keeping of the subsidiary is generally done locally. The day-to-day transactions covering payment of salaries, purchasing of goods and services, billings to customers, and collecting cash, as well as maintaining and controlling assets and liabilities all take place locally and in local currency. The accounting for these transactions is most effectively done where and when they transpire.

The accounting records must be constructed so as to provide adequate information to prepare tax returns and produce local financial statements for regulators, creditors, unions, and other interested parties, and to facilitate reporting to the parent company. The accounting standards to be followed must be those of the host country so the record keeping must be done using those standards or easily convertible to them. This conversion is necessary if the accounting standards used are not local standards but rather are those of the parent company's country.

It should be noted that the accounting standards required by the authorities vary from country to country. The International Accounting Standards Committee (IASC) is attempting to minimize alternatives by issuing international standards, but all such standards must then be adopted by the appropriate authorities in each of the countries before they become official. This could be a long and tedious process. In the meantime a broad knowledge of each country's generally accepted accounting policies must be developed and maintained by the controller of a multinational company. A listing of International Accounting Standards as issued by the IASC is available, but the acceptance by each country must be determined individually.

The translation and remeasurement of local results can be done by either the local country or the parent. If done in-house by local personnel, there will be a need for each country controller to understand U.S. GAAP. This can be accomplished in several ways: through a program of individual education, through in-house seminars and workshops, and through centrally developed and issued accounting instructions, all of which must be directed by the corporate controller. The latter provides the best opportunity for uniformity in recording and reporting and probably will be necessary even if local finance people become knowledgeable about parent-company GAAP.

If the translation and adjustments are done at the parent-company headquarters, there are several areas of concern. First, country management will not have an opportunity to review the dollar results before they are put into the consolidation process, and valuable insight into cause and effects of current operations will be missing. Second, higher management at the parent headquarters will be viewing reports that have not yet been seen at the operating level. Communications could easily become confused and important decisions delayed.

Having the translation and remeasurement work done at the country level is the more effective approach.

Measuring Foreign Operations

In most organizations, the primary control and measurement techniques are:

- Define key objectives.

- Prepare a financial plan, compare actual results to it, and take corrective action.

- Compare actual results to a prior period.

The multinational company generally uses these techniques to measure the translated results of its foreign subsidiaries. The technique is effective if the variable of currency fluctuation is recognized and adjusted for. As mentioned elsewhere in this chapter, translated results can present a very different picture of operations and financial condition than local currency results reflect. The controller should be familiar with both sets of data and the analysis supporting them. However, it is the parent-company currency that is used for external reporting; therefore, the use and understanding of translated financial statements will remain a key part of the controller's work.

As an overall summary of this task of measuring the financial performance of a global unit manager, the reports should reflect these three objectives:

1. To reflect the *financial* plan for all activities under the control or responsibility of the local manager.

2. To measure *actual results* against plan for those matters under the control of the local manager.

3. To reflect the planned results *translated* into the parent company currency; and to identify planned vs. actual results segregated between (a) those reflecting the entity manager's performance and (b) those which are due to the impact of currency fluctuations.

Comparisons with Budget or Plan.   The biggest unique planning and control problem facing the controller of an international business is that of fluctuations in the currency exchange rate. When plans or budgets are established an estimated exchange rate must be used to express in the parent's currency the budget amounts developed in local currency. The "actuals" from the accounting records are translated at the current rate, which is usually different from the rate used for the plan, for example:

In this example the parent-company currency, the U.S. dollar, has strengthened, and it now takes more local currency units to equal one dollar than was planned. The effect is that,

Currency Exchange Rates

Plan assumptions	4 local currency (L/C) = $1
Actual	5 local currency (L/C) = $1

Statement of Operations

	Actual	Budget	Variance (Unfavorable)
Sales (L/C)	1,000,000	1,000,000	-0-
Rate	5:1	4:1	
Sales ($)	200,000	250,000	(50,000)

when viewed from a local perspective, sales are on plan, but when viewed from a parent-company perspective (i.e., the dollar), the subsidiary is under plan and substantially so, requiring analysis and explanation. One way to give a better view of what is happening is to add two more columns to the report, showing the effect of currency. The report now tells the reader that the unfavorable variance is all due to a currency exchange movement.

Statement of Operations

				Amount Due to	
	Actual	Budget	Variance (Unfavorable)	Currency Translation	Business Performance
Sales $	200,000	250,000	(50,000)	(50,000)	-0-

If the example was changed to include a modest overbudget situation in local currency, it would be reported as follows:

	Actual	Budget	Variance (Unfavorable)
Sales (L/C)	1,100,000	1,000,000	100,000
Exchange rate	5:1	4:1	
Sales ($)	220,000	250,000	(30,000)

In this example the results shown in dollars portray a misleading result, but when the currency effect is shown separately, a much clearer picture emerges.

				Amount Due to	
	Actual	Budget	Variance (Unfavorable)	Currency Translation	Business Performance
Sales $	220,000	250,000	(30,000)	(55,000)	25,000

The amount of variance due to business is calculated by either: (1) taking the variance in local currency and translating it at the current rate, or (2) more commonly since local currency results are not usually transmitted early, having the countries calculate the actual results translated at the plan rates. In the examples, both budget and actual would be translated into dollars using the plan rate of 4 L/C = $1.

The analyst would keep the budget amount constant at a 4:1 translation rate and prepare an "actual" using the same translation rate to produce the following result:

	Actual	Budget	Variance (Unfavorable)
Sales (L/C)	1,100,000	1,000,000	100,000
Exchange rate	4:1	4:1	
Sales ($)	275,000	250,000	25,000

The above variance is attributed to sales being higher than planned and is therefore the variance due to business operations. The difference between the total variance in translated amounts and the business variance determined above is attributed to the effect of currency changes.

Comparisons with Prior Year.   A similar problem in plan/actual comparisons occurs when current actual results are compared to the actual results of prior periods. If the exchange rates used for the two periods are different, then the results are clouded by the change. For example, if

	Current Year	Prior Year	Increase/(Decrease)
Sales (L/C)	1,000,000	900,000	200,000
Exchange rate	5:1	4:1	
Sales ($)	220,000	225,000	(5,000)

However, if the exchange rates are normalized by translating the current period using the same exchange as the period being compared to, the following picture results:

				Amount Due to	
	Actual	Budget	Variance (Unfavorable)	Currency Translation	Business Performance
Sales $	220,000	225,000	(5,000)	(55,000)	50,000

As in the plan/actual analysis, the "actual" results in both periods would be translated at the same exchange rate to produce the following result:

	Current Year	Prior Year	Increase/(Decrease)
Sales (L/C)	1,100,000	900,000	200,000
Exchange rate	4:1	4:1	
Sales ($)	275,000	225,000	50,000

By isolating the currency exchange effect, we can see that there was a growth in the business of $50,000 or 22%, rather than a 2% decline. We can also see that the currency effect was to reduce sales, in dollars, by 25%, wiping out the operating growth and resulting in a decline in reported sales compared to the prior year.

Inflation.   In a multinational company, the impact of inflation on the business results is not different from a national company; usually it is just more volatile. The same analyses and actions taken in regard to home-country inflation generally apply to translated results. However, there are many less developed nations that experience hyperinflation (i.e., annual inflation in the hundreds or thousands of percent). For these situations, some special analysis of local currency results must be made to normalize for inflation.

Establishing a base year for currency value and then adjusting subsequent years results to that value presents a more accurate picture of growth or decline. For example, hyperinflationary country A experiences a 100% inflation rate in the current year. Its sales results for this year and last year are:

Current year	L/C	1,000,000
Prior year	L/C	750,000
Increase	L/C	250,000
Percentage		33%

However, using the prior years' currency value as 1, the current year value is 0.5 after adjusting for 100% inflation (1/+100% 1). The current year sales value when compared to last year is L/C 500,000 (1,000,000 × 0.5). So instead of a 33% gain in sales, there has been a 33% decrease—a very different result and one requiring further analysis and action. This is called constant currency and the results are:

Current year	L/C	500,000
Prior year	L/C	750,000
Decrease	L/C	(250,000)
Percentage		33%

As indicated above, this inflation move is reflected in currency translation rates and translated results therefore have only the parent-company inflation rate included.

STANDARDIZE AND AUDIT MEASUREMENT SYSTEMS

Accounting departments located in other countries have a habit of skewing reporting systems to enhance their reported performance. To prevent this, publish a standard list of all measurements, including what information is to be used for each one. Also, schedule periodic internal audit reviews of how each location is calculating the measurements in order to ensure compliance.

Evaluating Capital Expenditures

When the question "Should we invest overseas?" is raised, all the analyses used in making capital investment decisions in the home country will have to be made. Additionally the new risks of exchange rate fluctuations and political uncertainty must be considered.

Unless there are unusual circumstances (e.g., a need to maintain special know-how available in a specific location), the key consideration in the investment discussion is the return on assets or return on equity that relates to "cash flow to the parent."

Exchange Rate Fluctuations.   The impact of currency movements on financial statements and the analysis of them is discussed in detail in the section of this chapter titled "Measuring Foreign Operations," page 170. Exchange rate fluctuations will also have a significant effect on the cash flow to the parent of an investment in a foreign country and so must be recognized in the planning and assessment of investment alternatives. It should be noted that the analysis of investment returns when calculated in the currency of the country where the investment will be made results in a different answer than when it is done in the currency of the parent.

For example, using a "net present value" analysis to determine the return in both currencies shows the comparison illustrated in Exhibit 9.4.

A rule of thumb is that if this investment does not yield a positive cash flow in the parent's currency then it should not be made.

If the return is positive then the required internal rate of return and/or the hurdle rate of return must be met. Another good rule of thumb is that the rate of return should at least exceed the expected interest rate of government securities in that country.

In estimating the value in the parents' currency of future cash flows, it is necessary to forecast for each of the years included in the analysis:

- Exchange rates
- Withholding taxes
- Currency restrictions
- Political risks

This is a difficult but doable effort.

	Subsidiary Currency	Parent Currency
Present value of cash inflows over the life of the project	Net profit before depreciation	After-tax value of dividends, interest and royalties remitted by the subsidiary
Plus		
Present value of terminal value (liquidation value)	After-tax recoverable amount	After-tax amount remitted to parent
Equals		
Total present value of cash inflows	Estimated amount	Translated value of remitted amounts
Minus		
Original investment (plant and working capital)	Translated amount	Established amount in parent currency
Equals		
Net present value		

EXHIBIT 9.4   CALCULATION OF NET PRESENT VALUE IN TWO CURRENCIES

Exchange Rates.   In considering the economic exposure to future foreign exchange risk, both the cash flows in foreign currency and the value of dividends in the parent currency must be considered. For example, a devaluation of the foreign currency will result in a decrease in the value of foreign currency dividends in the parent currency. But, it may also lead to an increase in foreign currency profit as a result of increased sales volume or sales price on exports. The net impact on the cash flow to the parent is the sum of both effects.

The analysis should begin with an assessment of the most likely exchange rates anticipated by year. Then simulate what would happen to cash flows under a variety of "what-if" scenarios. For example, if it is decided that the most likely case is a 5% devaluation of the foreign currency each year, a cash flow plan using that premise should be prepared. It can then be varied by asking "what if" it is less or more than 5% and the same plan and assessment done at 3% and 4%, or 6%, 7%, 10%, etc. Another scenario that should be performed is "what if" there is appreciation rather than devaluation and the plan is assembled using +2% or +5%, etc. The relevant range of possible changes depends upon the foreign currency under consideration. Brazil can be safely expected to have its currency continually devalue, and only devalue. The range, however, is very wide and volatile, perhaps 100% to 200% per year. The Netherlands on the other hand could have its currency move in either direction but probably no more than 10% each way.

After the economic analysis is finished then a probability-of-occurrence analysis should be performed and a weighting given to the results. For example, if there are two probable scenarios—a 5% devaluation and an 8% devaluation—and the probability is judged to be 80% for the 5% case and 20% for the 8% case then the following cost estimate can be made and incorporated into the estimated results:

$$5\% \text{ devaluation} \neq \text{NPV} \times 0.80 = \quad \text{A}$$
$$8\% \text{ devaluation} \neq \text{NPV} \times 0.20 = \quad \underline{\text{B}}$$
$$\text{Expected value of exchange movement} = \overline{\text{A} + \text{B}}$$

Political Risks.   It is necessary to estimate the costs associated with the political risk of investing in a particular country. This risk can be defined as the risk that the foreign government intervenes in some unexpected way that affects cash flow to the parent. There are several exposures in this area:

- Unexpected change in repatriation restrictions. In order to force reinvestment in its country, a government may forbid any funds from leaving the country or it might severely limit the amount or percent. For example, in India the amount "repatriable" is negotiable but must be approved by the authorities.
- An unexpected change in withholding taxes on remittances
- An unexpected change in import duties
- An unexpected change in labor and wage laws
- Devaluation of currency
- Expropriation of assets

In this latter extreme situation there are two effects on the cash flow to the parent:

1. The assets are not paid for by the expropriating government, or the payment is less than fair market value.

2. Future cash flows from operations are lost.

Insurance against expropriation can be purchased in the United States through the Overseas Private Investment Corporation (OPIC), but there is a premium to be paid that represents immediate cash outflow that must be weighed against the present value of the possible future loss.

There are sources of information on each of the political risks. For example, in the United States there is Frost and Sullivan's *World Political Risk Forecasts*. This publication summarizes the expert opinions of individuals knowledgeable about each country relative to three kinds of investments:

1. Financial—loans to the country
2. Investment—direct investment in the country
3. Exporting—exports to the country

It assesses the political stability of the country, government restrictions (duties, tariffs, control of natural resources), and economic policies that affect inflation and exchange fluctuations.

This information and data like it make it possible to establish ranges of probability in estimating factors over many future years that will affect cash flows of foreign subsidiaries. It is the controller's responsibility to ensure that this analysis is done as best it can be and not ignored because it is too difficult or includes too much "soft" data.

Transfer Pricing

An international transfer price is the value given to goods or services produced or performed in one country for the benefit or use by a related company in another country. For example, the ABC Company, an American company, has subsidiaries in Germany and France. It has a manufacturing plant in Germany that supplies products to both France and the United States. It has a computer center in France that services France and Germany. Its headquarters and research and development facilities are in the United States. Transfer prices have to be developed for:

- Products shipped from Germany to France and to the United States
- Information services performed by France for Germany
- A share of R&D expense to be paid by France and Germany
- A management fee assessed by the U.S. parent on its subsidiaries

We will now examine how each transfer price could be determined.

Development of the Transfer Price.   It is usually the responsibility of the corporate controller to develop the transfer prices that will be used in dealings between subsidiaries or between parent and subsidiaries. The price used will result in a profit or loss for the exporting country and will directly influence the profit or loss ultimately realized in the importing country. Such a situation has led some multinationals to develop transfer prices that are very subjective and result in the lowest profit (or even losses) being reported in the highest tax rate countries and conversely the highest profit being realized in the lowest tax rate countries. While this approach seems logical and defensible at first glance, it is unfair and has resulted in more laws and restrictions by the countries that believe they are being taken advantage of. Furthermore, in recent years the Internal Revenue Service (IRS) has taken a more aggressive stance in its search for transfer pricing abuses. The use of subjectively developed transfer prices also complicates the measurement system and frustrates local management because it cannot control or influence a significant item of cost.

A more businesslike approach is for the controller to establish a uniform, objective system of transfer pricing that is:

- Simple and inexpensive to administer
- Understandable to the users
- Fair in its effect on measurements

An arm's-length, objective system can take two forms:

1. Cost based
2. Market based

Cost-Based System.   A cost-based system, the one usually favored by American companies, uses the output of the company's cost accounting systems and adds a markup for profit to it. This profit factor is usually established for the long term and not changed unless it becomes unrealistic. One approach to establishing the profit factor for a country that manufactures a product is to use a long-term (e.g., ten-year) average of the consolidated company's net-income-before-taxes margin. Other objective and fair methods can be identified by each company. Once established, the estimated transfer price should be published and used in the preparation of financial plans by the various units.

The markup on the transfer of services performed by one unit for another is more subjective and a flat percentage is usually established and not changed. For example, computer services could be marked up 10%, treasury services 5%, and so on. The important factor is that after a reasonable decision is made as to amount, then it should not be changed and it should be applied uniformly in all countries. If products are marked up 15% and services 10%, there should be no exceptions made based on unique facts and circumstances. To allow deviations introduces complexity and confusion into the internal system and causes consternation and distrust on the part of country regulators and tax authorities.

Market-Based System.   A market-based system, the one usually favored by many European countries, starts with the expected selling price in the importing countries and reduces it by estimated locally incurred cost, expenses, and profit, to arrive at a transfer price that is affordable to the importer. This price is then used by the exporter in billing the related company and should recover the actual costs incurred in the production of the goods and services along with a reasonable profit. In order to make a market-based transfer-pricing system effective, the transfer price must be accurately developed and then published and used until it is revised.

Royalties.   Whether a cost-based transfer price system or a market-based transfer price system is used by a multinational company it will probably also employ a "royalty" system in addition. The transfer price system is used to move goods and services between related companies. A royalty system is used to recover, from the subsidiaries, compensation for "know-how," the use of brand names, company logos, and the like. The two most common royalties charged to subsidiaries are for:

- Research and development
- Parent-company management

The royalty for R&D is traditionally a percentage of sales. It can be based on the ratio of R&D expense of the consolidated company to total sales of the consolidated company applied to the total sales of the subsidiary company. The resultant amount, less any locally incurred R&D, would be the R&D royalty due to the parent company.

A parent-company management royalty is usually not based on a ratio but is rather an apportionment of the total parent-company staff and general expense based on a relationship of the subsidiaries. One method is the percent each subsidiary contributes to gross income applied to the total parent-headquarters expense pool. Another is a negotiated fee based on number of employees, profit margin, growth, and so on, but which recovers all parent-headquarters expenses.

In applying these approaches to the example given at the beginning of this section, the transfer prices shown in Exhibits 9.5 through 9.8 would be developed.

Taxation

Tax laws in each country are extensive, complex, and changeable. Since the impact of the laws is to share a significant percentage of the company's profit (on average, 30% to 60%) with the various governments of the countries in which the firm does business, it is essential that

---

a. Product manufactured in Germany at a cost of 1,000 DM

b. ABC Company NEBT margin = 12% (for last 15 years)

c. Transfer price =1,000 + 12%
(12% × 1,000) 120

Total = 1,120 DM

EXHIBIT 9.5   DEVELOPMENT OF TRANSFER PRICE FOR PRODUCTS

---

a. Computer center work done in France at a cost of 100 FF

b. Uniform markup for all nonproduct goods and services = 10%

c. Transfer price =100 + 10%
(10% × 100) 10

Total = 110 FF

EXHIBIT 9.6   DEVELOPMENT OF TRANSFER PRICE FOR NONPRODUCT SERVICES

---

a. R&D expense for consolidated ABC Company = $10,000 (average 10 years)

b. Total gross income for Consolidated ABC Company = $200,000 (average 10 years)

c. Royalty for R&D
$\dfrac{\text{R\&D Expense}}{\text{Gross Income}} = \dfrac{\$\ 10,000}{\$200,000}$
= 5% of Gross Income

d. Germany current year gross
income	80,000 DM
Royalty at	5%
Total	4,000 DM
at 2 DM = $1 =	$ 2,000

France current year gross
income	100,000 FF
Royalty at	5%
Total	5,000 FF
at 4 FF = $1 =	$ 1,000

EXHIBIT 9.7   DEVELOPMENT OF ROYALTY FOR RESEARCH AND DEVELOPMENT

---

a. The parent-company corporate expense for current year = $20,000

b. Gross income by unit

	$	%
U.S.	100,000	63
France	20,000	12
Germany	40,000	25
Total	$160,000	100%

Management fee $20,000 ×

	%	$
U.S.	63	12,600
France	12	2,400
Germany	25	5,000
Total	100%	$20,000

EXHIBIT 9.8   DEVELOPMENT OF ROYALTY FOR PARENT-COMPANY MANAGEMENT

local tax experts be available to the company. These local tax professionals have the responsibility to understand local tax law, interpret the law as it applies to the company business, advise local management how to minimize taxes, and handle the filing and reporting of local tax returns. The local tax expert should also be aware of possible tax changes and assess the effect of such changes on the local business. He would then keep the parent's tax executive (e.g., controller) informed of important matters.

While it is essential to have local tax experts it is also important to have a coordinated tax operation. This will require an expertise that is broader but perhaps not as deep as the local requirements. It is this centralized organization that develops tax planning and strategies and thereby contributes to the overall financial plan of the company. The senior tax executive has the responsibility of:

• Estimating taxes to be paid by period
• Negotiating disputes with authorities
• Providing advice and counsel to local experts

He should also have the authority to resolve disputes and disagreements.

Aside from the complications of foreign taxes, the controller must be sensitive to the U.S. tax laws and regulations. The IRS carefully checks transfer prices. New tax laws are being enacted to eliminate loopholes. In 1993, a law was passed to eliminate "earnings stripping" by foreign companies. This occurs when a foreign entity uses large loans instead of direct equity investment to fund its U.S. activities. The interest payments on the loans become a tax deduction, thus "stripping" away U.S. tax exposure.

The controller and tax executives minimize taxes in all legal ways; therefore, they must be continually aware of any relevant changes in U.S. tax laws.

Import/Export Regulations

At one time, up until the early part of this century, the primary source of income for the various governments was from tariffs on imports. The regulations covering the tariffs are lengthy and complex. They represent an accumulation of many years of continual tinkering with the rules and laws. It is therefore of real importance that the controller have an understanding of these regulations so that he can organize and operate in the most effective manner and in the best interest of the company. Very often the import/export department does not report to the controller, but the controller must be knowledgeable about the operation and be involved in negotiations, procedural controls, and so on.

Duties are usually assessed on imports not on exports. However, it is the exporter who must prepare documentation in accordance with the regulations of the country of import so that the goods delivered into the country are clearly labeled and identified. This facilitates customs clearance and should result in earlier delivery of products or services to customers and earlier receipt of payment by the exporter.

There are many import/export brokers who are invaluable in helping firms find their way through this most complex operation, worldwide. Their services should be utilized. The parent company working with subsidiary company management should identify and engage the broker best qualified to handle the kind of business in which the company is engaged.

Managing Currency Risk

A controller can take some steps to lessen the impact of wildly fluctuating currency on the operation of the business, insofar as imports and exports are concerned. If, for example, the parent currency is stable and strong, then billing and requiring payment in the parent's currency will eliminate losses due to the decline in value of a foreign currency. Assume the following wherein the foreign currency has an inflation rate of 10% with a corresponding loss in value of its currency.

	May 1	June 1
U.S. dollar	1	1
= Foreign currency	1	0.9

The U.S. company sells 1,000 units at $1.00 each on May 1 and bills the customer $1,000 to be paid in 30 days. On June 1, $1,000 is received from the customer and deposited in the bank. There is no gain or loss on the transaction.

However, what happens if the U.S. company sells 1,000 units at 1 foreign currency each on May 1 and bills the customer 1,000 foreign currency. On June 1, 1,000 foreign currency is received from the customer but when converted into dollars at the bank only $900 is deposited. There is a $100 loss due to changes in exchange rates (inflation).

What can the U.S. company do to protect itself against such a loss? There are several actions available.

• Do business only in the parent company's currency.

• Require cash payment on delivery if business is done in foreign currency.

• Buy a forward exchange contract if business is done in foreign currency and credit terms are offered.

Currency Hedging. The first two items need little elaboration. If the transaction is made in the seller's currency then all risk of loss is transferred to the buyer. If cash is paid on delivery there is no risk of exchange loss.

However, in many instances, those two options are not available and the seller must do business in foreign currency and offer credit terms. In these instances, in order to mitigate the exchange loss the seller can buy a contract from a bank to sell foreign currency 30 days after the transaction. In the example, the contract would be bought on May 1 to deliver 1,000 foreign currency on June 1. The price is established by the bank (which is also entering contracts to deliver foreign currency to other customers) and might be for $950 for each 1,000 foreign currency delivered. The amount of loss is therefore known at the time the contract is entered into. This is called hedging and while it takes uncertainty out of the transaction, it will still produce some loss to the company, since the bank will charge a fee for handling the exchange contract in addition to reflecting an estimate in the movement of the currency.

If the company is purchasing from a foreign business, similar dynamics are at work. If you buy in foreign currency you stand the risk of inflation impacts. If the foreign currency declines faster than the buyer's currency there will be a gain; if slower, there will be a loss. The loss can be hedged by buying a contract to purchase foreign currency at a set price at some time in the future. Again, this will not usually eliminate the exchange loss, but it will eliminate uncertainty as to how much it will be.

Hedging can be used in connection with the payment of dividends, interest, and royalties, and can also be extended further into the future to cover probable purchases (e.g., where there is a single foreign supplier) and sales in an ongoing operation.

CENTRALIZE CURRENCY RISK MANAGEMENT
If there are many corporate locations in multiple countries, it is best to centralize currency risk management in one place. Otherwise, single locations may take steps to reduce currency risk that are unnecessary when viewed in relation to cash flows originating in other divisions.

Foreign Corrupt Practices Act

No discussion of the controller's role in international operations would be complete without addressing the FCPA. In the 1960s and 1970s, some multinationals had been involved in bribing foreign officials in order to get or keep business in their countries. It was a serious problem that had to be resolved. In December 1977, the U.S. Congress passed an act making it illegal for an issuer of securities in the United States to make certain payments to foreign officials. It also required such issuers to maintain accurate records. Following is a summary of the Act's key requirements:

1. *Payments to officials.* The act made it unlawful for American companies to offer money or gifts to any foreign official, political party, or political candidate in order to influence that person in his official capacity. Influence meant having the person fail to perform his official duties or having the person use his influence with others in order for the company to obtain or retain business in the foreign country.

    The penalties for violation of this act are fines of up to $1,000,000 for any concern convicted of the violation. In addition, individuals involved in such illegal payoffs are subject personally to fines up to $10,000 and prison for up to five years.

2. *Accounting and control requirements.* The act also requires that issuers of securities make and keep books, records and accounts in reasonable detail, that accurately and fairly reflect the transactions and dispositions of assets.

    Devise and maintain a system of internal accounting controls that is sufficient to provide reasonable assurances that:

    (a) The transactions are executed in accordance with management's general or specific authorization.

    (b) Transactions are recorded as necessary to permit preparation of financial statements in conformity with GAAP.

    (c) Transactions are recorded to maintain accountability for assets.

    (d) Access to assets is permitted only in accordance with management's authorization.

    (e) Asset records are verified with physical assets periodically and appropriate action taken with respect to any differences.

The controller has a basic responsibility to comply with the requirements of the FCPA and any related legislation and amendments which pertain to maintaining an adequate system of internal control. (See Chapter 8.)

10

RECRUITING, TRAINING, AND SUPERVISION

IMPORTANCE OF THIS CHAPTER

The new employer must rely to a great extent on the knowledge base of other accounting staff who have been with the company for some time. In order to maintain a reasonably functional department, she must ensure that key staff stay in the department and new staff of sufficient quality are hired. Consequently, this chapter is extremely important as a source of tips for recruiting, promoting, and retaining accounting staff.

A prospective controller is well advised to peruse this chapter several times, for it contains information that is vital to the controller's career. If the accounting staff is carefully selected, properly trained, and motivated, the controller will enjoy a huge productivity advantage over a controller who does not pay attention to these factors. The inevitable results of not doing so are slipshod work, high employee turnover, and massive inefficiency due to the time needed to constantly recruit and train new employees. Consequently, the recruiting, training, and supervision functions are crucial to the success of a controller.

It is unfortunate, but business schools rarely give any formal training in this most important area, so controllers must pick up the requisite knowledge through either hands-on experience, a mentor, or additional training. This chapter is also a valuable source of information on the topic, but should be used as an overview. More detailed information can be obtained from books that deal entirely with business management.

RECRUITING SOURCES

This section describes a number of sources a controller should consider when searching for candidates for accounting positions. There are three key factors involved in selecting a recruiting source, and these factors are discussed for each of the possible recruiting sources:

1. *Recruiting cost.* The cost of recruiting an accounting person can range from $100 for an advertisement in the local newspaper to one third of the hired person's salary, which is a typical charge if the person is hired through a search firm. The recruiting cost tends to have a low level of importance if the recruiting task must be completed at once and a higher one if there is a long time line involved. Also, the lower-cost approaches tend to involve extra time by the controller to screen recruits, whereas more expensive approaches, such as using a search firm, tend to require less screening time, because this task is completed by the intermediary. In short, a cheap recruiting method takes longer and requires more effort than an expensive approach.

2. *Recruiting quality.* The quality of the person hired tends to go up if there is a long time interval for the recruiting process. This is because a controller can take the time to obtain a large pool of candidates, interview them at his or her leisure, and spend the extra time needed to review their references. The reverse is generally true if there is a time crunch involved. However, these assumptions are generalizations, for it is also possible to run into a perfect candidate on the first day of a search.

3. *Recruiting time.* As noted in the first two factors, the time allowed to conduct a recruiting campaign will usually result in higher costs if there is little time available, because a controller must resort to expensive sources. Also, there is a chance that the quality of candidate recruited will be lower if the recruiting period is short, because there is only enough time to meet with and evaluate a limited pool of candidates.

Once a controller has determined which of these three factors (or a combination thereof) are paramount in the search for a specific candidate, it then becomes an easier matter to select the correct recruiting source. For example, if a controller needs a new payroll clerk immediately, even if there is a high cost involved, it is best to go straight to a search firm, which will charge an inordinately high price but will present a set of qualified candidates in as little as a day. However, if there is no rush to fill a position, the search firm may be the last source consulted. The recruiting sources are:

- *Audit and consulting firms.* It is common for a controller to hire from the ranks of the auditing and consulting firms that work for the company. This approach is very inexpensive, because the controller probably already knows the best performers within these firms and just calls them to see if they are interested in a position. This can also result in a fast hire, so there is a very short time line involved. The quality of the person hired also tends to be high, because the audit or consulting firms have already done the prescreening when *they* hired these people. In short, this is an excellent way to bring in top-notch personnel quickly and at low cost.

- *Authors.* A rarely used recruiting technique is to hire the authors of published accounting works. This approach ensures specific knowledge by the candidate of the subject matter for specific jobs. However, there is no assurance that this knowledge equates to good job performance. Also, there are very few published authors within the geographic range of most companies, so the volume of candidates acquired through this approach is slim. The cost and time needed to hire through this approach are minimal, because the controller already knows the name of the person to hire—it is simply a matter of making contact and arranging an interview.

- *Campus recruiting.* A good recruiting source for lower-level positions is the college campus. However, it is difficult to determine the quality of the people hired, because they have never worked before. Also, this tends to require a very long lead time, since candidates must be recruited months in advance; thus, this approach is useful only for filling positions that are constantly needed and for which accurate hiring projections can be made. It is also expensive to send personnel to colleges for recruiting and costly to bring in candidates for additional interviews.

- *Employees.* One of the best sources of recruits is current employees. This approach works best when a company offers recruiting bonuses to employees. This incentive turns the entire employee group into an enthusiastic horde of recruiters. They have the additional advantage of recruiting their own friends, which typically results in a great deal of prescreening by the employees, resulting in a high quality of recruit. This also tends to be a fast way to gain recruits. The only problem is that the recruiting bonuses paid to employees can be rather large, usually exceeding $1,000 and sometimes going higher than $5,000 for each person hired.

- *Former employees.* A controller should go to great lengths to maintain contact with quality employees who have left the company. Sometimes, the reasons why they left (higher pay, better positions, etc.) are not good enough, and they may be willing to return to the company. This approach is not only quick and inexpensive, but best of all, it results in highly qualified candidates who require minimal interviewing before being hired back. This is one of the best recruiting methods, though it typically results in only a very small proportion of the people hired into the accounting department.

- *Internet postings and advertisements.* A new recruiting method is to use the Internet. This can involve either posting a job or reviewing posted resumes. Either alternative is inexpensive but requires screening an inordinate number of potential recruits. It is a quick recruiting method that even beats the speed of newspapers, because one can access an Internet site and immediately review resumes or post a job opening, with no transactional delay. However, this approach is similar to newspapers (see below) in that the quality of recruit tends to be low.

- *Newspaper advertisements.* This approach involves placing ads in newspapers to attract candidates. This is the most common recruiting method, but it has a major problem: It typically results in a vast number of applications, which requires a great deal of screening to arrive at a small group of qualified candidates (or none at all!). However, advertisements are inexpensive and can be placed in newspapers on very short notice. For the more senior accounting positions, this approach tends not to result in a very large pool of qualified candidates. The biggest reason for the low quality is that only those people who are actively looking for work are reviewing the advertisements; this ignores the most qualified people, who are currently working elsewhere.

- *Professional organizations.* This approach involves meeting qualified candidates through the meetings of professional organizations. It requires a great deal of "face time" by a controller or other members of the accounting staff, who must attend many organizational functions to meet with potential recruits. Though there is a minimal direct cost, the amount of labor by the accounting staff can be excessive. Also, it takes many months of attending meetings to build up a lengthy list of potential recruits. However, this can result in high-quality candidates who have been prescreened through the organizational meetings. Due to the time involved, this tends to be a little-used recruiting method.

- *Professional publications.* This involves advertising in a professional publication to which an accounting person subscribes, such as the *Journal of Accountancy.* The advantage of this approach is that only a select group of trained accountants will see the advertisement, which thereby reduces the pool of recruits to a select group, thereby increasing the quality of applicant. This tends to be a slow recruiting method, due to the lead time needed to advertise, so it works best if there are many accounting positions that must be continuously filled.

- *Search firms.* This is the most expensive recruiting approach, for search firms typically charge between one quarter and one third of a hired person's first year's salary as their fee. However, there are good reasons for using this method. One is that the search firms conduct their own screening of candidates, which results in a higher quality of applicant. Also, most search firms maintain a lengthy backlog of resumes, and so can bring in many candidates on short notice. Thus, the quality of recruits and the speed with which they can be brought to the controller may offset the high cost of this alternative.

- *Unsolicited applications.* The lowest-cost recruiting method is to receive an unsolicited application, because there is no advertising cost at all. Also, if a company stores these applications, there is no wait time needed to collect resumes, since they are all kept on file. However, despite these favorable points, unsolicited applications tend to result in the lowest possible quality of candidate. This is because there is no screening mechanism built into the process, which results in lots of interviews by the controller to separate the chaff from the wheat. On the whole, the extremely low quality of candidates results in very few companies relying on this recruiting approach.

There are a variety of ways to recruit qualified accounting candidates, based on the key factors of time, cost, and quality of recruit. A controller can pick a selection of recruiting methods from this list to create a mix of methods that will greatly enhance the chance of bringing in the right recruits within the required time frame and at the right cost.

FACTORS TO CONSIDER WHEN RECRUITING

There are a number of applicant attributes to consider when recruiting. An applicant should possess as many of them as possible to a high degree, for any lack may lead to an excessive degree of turnover, poor job performance, or complaints by other people who work with the recruit. The key attributes fall into the categories of technical ability, communication skill, and stability. In more detail, they are:

- *Integrity.* The accounting department has some control or influence over the disposition of assets, the reporting of financial information, and the use of controls. If a person lacks integrity, a controller may find that assets go astray, financial information is incorrectly reported, or controls are not enforced. The resulting havoc occurs because accounting personnel were not concerned about doing the right thing. Instead, accounting employees must care about their reputation for honesty and objectivity, which causes them to point out unethical considerations or actions to higher management even if such things are not illegal but perhaps only misleading or unfair. Due to the extreme importance of this factor, any hint of minimal integrity on the part of a candidate should immediately disqualify that person from receiving a job offer.

- *Process knowledge.* The accounting function is similar to manufacturing in that it involves highly predictable process flows that must be carefully organized in order to reach peak levels of efficiency. Clearly, it is of great use if new employees already have these skills, so it is useful to include process flow questions in an interview. To determine whether an applicant has these skills, interview questions should cover an applicant's knowledge of and experience in implementing and using accounting best practices. Applicants with this kind of background are most likely to create an efficient and effective accounting department.

THE IMPORTANCE OF INTEGRITY

It is not a long stretch of the integrity concept to view the accounting department as the one department where the level of ethics needs to match that of a minister or priest. The reason is that a lack of ethics can lead to wildly inaccurate reported financial information (just look at Enron), which in turn tends to color the operations of the entire company. Consequently, any hint of ethical impropriety is an excellent reason *not* to hire someone.

- *Certification review.* If an applicant holds one of the major accounting certifications (e.g., certified public accountant, certified management accountant, or certified internal auditor), the company should contact these certifying organizations. There are two reasons for doing so. First, the company should verify that the applicant actually has earned the certification and that it has not lapsed. Second, the company should ask if there have been any warnings (of which there are various levels, such as license suspensions or revocations) issued by the certifying organization to the applicant for misconduct in the past. Any such occurrences should be grounds for considerable additional investigation prior to issuing a job offer. Usually, given the level of trust required in an accounting position, it is not a good risk to hire someone to whom a warning has been issued.

- *Communication skills.* An invaluable attribute is excellent communication skills. In order to succeed, a candidate should be able to actively participate in meetings with other employees, clearly summarize and present information, and create understandable written reports. It ultimately means having others understand what you want to tell them. This can be difficult when financial people communicate with nonfinancial people, because the complexity and jargon of the profession must be replaced with simple business language.

- *Drive.* Though a candidate may have an overwhelming impressive set of credentials, strong interpersonal skills, great integrity, and fine background experience, none of these factors will be of much use if the person lacks the drive to complete work in a timely manner and take the initiative in undertaking new projects. This is the key underlying factor impacting a person's ability to be promoted into new and more difficult positions. It is also one of the most difficult issues to fully understand when interviewing a candidate. To do so, a considerable portion of the interviewing time should cover a candidate's underlying goals and objectives—a strong goal orientation is a sure sign of a strong drive to succeed.

- *Technical capability.* An accounting recruit must have the basic accounting knowledge that can be imparted only through a regular course of training, which can include a bachelor's or MBA degree. Possessing such a degree from an accredited university should form the basis of a minimal technical qualification. If the person does not have such a degree, then further evaluation is necessary to ensure that the person can adequately complete any assigned work. Bringing an untrained person into a professional job, no matter how good the other qualifications, will probably result in that person's becoming dissatisfied and discouraged and eventually leaving the company or requiring unusual amounts of management attention.

- *Teamwork skills.* An applicant must be able to function with the rest of the group. It is easier to identify characteristics that will inhibit integration rather than those that will guarantee it. If a candidate, who should be on his or her best behavior, comes across as abrasive, it is reasonable to expect that this person will have a negative influence on the work group. This behavior will likely turn off fellow workers and require an excessive proportion of the controller's management attention. Both results will detract from the quality of performance of the work group as a whole. For evidence of teamwork skills, the interviewer can question the candidate about leadership roles. This can be leadership in school activities if the person is coming from college, or civic or work-related activities if the person has some experience outside of college.

- *Turnover likelihood.* Because it is a time-consuming and expensive process to hire a professional, it follows that the people who are hired should have a high probability of staying with the company. There are many considerations in trying to assess a candidate's staying potential. From the candidate's perspective, some of the considerations are the likelihood of being satisfied with his or her professional responsibilities, prospects for advancement, and degree of comfort with the culture of the organization. From the company's perspective, some of the considerations are the person's ability to handle changing environments, acceptance of retraining, and ability to relocate as necessary. Evaluating these considerations may be the most difficult assessment of all for a recruiter to make. Each of the above subjects should be discussed in depth and the candidate's views and preferences carefully considered.

There are a variety of factors to consider when evaluating a potential job candidate. It is useful for a controller to review this list of factors prior to extending a job offer.

FACTORS TO CONSIDER WHEN PROMOTING

A controller can do a wonderful job of recruiting the best possible staff and still experience high staff turnover due to a poor promotion policy. This section discusses two kinds of promotion, as well as the reasons for engaging in one type versus the other.

The most common kind of promotion is one that shifts a staff person sideways through the hierarchy of the accounting department. This type of promotion is intended to expand a person's skill base. For example, a person who is fully experienced in the billing area can be shifted to accounts payable in order to gain experience in how that functional area operates. The same approach can be used to add to the experience of the staff in other areas, such as collections, fixed assets, taxes, or producing the financial statements. This type of promotion can be given to the entire accounting staff, which rotates among the various functional areas. Generally, it reduces turnover, because the controller is giving all employees a chance to acquire new skills. However, the reverse can also happen if a staff person does not want to shift to a new skill area, and may even quit if the change is effected. A controller must watch out for this problem by carefully interviewing the staff about prospective switches to new areas. If it is clear that a person has "maxed out" and no longer desires to learn new tasks, then it is best to leave that employee alone in order to avoid any turnover.

A less common type of promotion is of the vertical variety, in which someone is shifted upward in the corporate hierarchy. This will always be less common, for there are far fewer positions available at the management level than at the clerical level. Promotion to a management position is based on the presence of an entirely different set of skills than are used as the basis for a sideways promotion. A controller must be extremely careful in evaluating employees for promotion to a management spot, for any missing skills may not only result in the departure of the person being promoted (who was probably an excellent performer at the lower, clerical level), but also of the staff reporting to that person, and will likely result in a great increase in the time required by the controller to handle the situation.

What are the key skills needed by someone being promoted to management? Certainly, it is necessary to have a reasonable knowledge of accounting theory and practice, but the primary emphasis is no longer in these areas, especially as a person is promoted to higher levels of the organization. Instead, the main focus is on people skills: communication, team building, reviews, and interviews, as well as planning and control. The mindset of anyone in this position is to effectively coordinate the activities of the underlying personnel, *not* to continue doing the work that took place prior to promotion. This is an extremely difficult transition for many people in the accounting profession, for it is filled with a large proportion of people who are introverted and process oriented, which results in a good clerk but a poor manager. The best approach for a controller who has just promoted someone to management is to realize the most likely traps into which the former clerk can fall, and to provide constant monitoring and advice. This should be intensive during the first few days of the promotion, thereby giving the promotee the best possible chance of succeeding in the new position.

IMPORTANCE OF REDUCED TURNOVER

The bane of many accounting departments is the turnover of the accounting staff. It results in staff turmoil, inefficient transaction processing, and lots of wasted time on the part of the controller. This section describes the impact of turnover, and how to prevent it from happening.

Some company departments assume that high employee turnover is a common fact of life, and that they must continually deal with bringing in a high percentage of new employees every year. This is true for many low-skill areas, such as assembly, where the entire workforce can turn over in one year. Alternatively, a highly skilled profession with lots of stress, the consulting industry, also has very high turnover, typically in the range of 25 percent to 33 percent per year. However, the accounting area should not be an excessively high-stress area, so it should not have the turnover rates common in consulting. It also requires a significant level of skill, so its turnover rates should not match those of an assembly operation. Instead, a controller should target a turnover rate well below 20 percent, and preferably only half that amount. This means that the average accountant should stay in the controller's department a minimum of five years, and preferably ten.

By keeping the staff turnover rate as low as possible, a controller can avoid many problems that result in gross inefficiencies, poor customer service, high error rates, and increased costs. These problems are:

- *Add poorer methods.* A new recruit may have his or her own ways of dealing with transactions, which may not be as efficient as the ones developed during the tenure of the person being replaced. When this happens, the efficiency level of the position drops for some time, until the new person has reviewed and evaluated how work is completed and improved operations based on that experience.

- *Increased costs.* Not only must a controller pay for recruiting costs to replace someone (e.g., newspaper advertisements, search firm fees, and travel expenses), but there are the added and less clearly defined costs of training new employees and correcting the inevitable mistakes that they will make as they learn their jobs. In addition, the controller must pay for replacement staff to fill in during the period when the old employee has already left the company and the new one has not yet started.

- *Increased inefficiency.* The typical new hire, unless vastly experienced, will not reach the efficiency levels of the person being replaced for at least six months. This inefficiency will appear in several ways: the extra time required to complete tasks, the extra temporary help needed to support the person, and the time of other staff people needed for training. For some recruits, performance never reaches the level attained by the previous employee, in which case the controller may be forced to move the new hire to another position, or else let the person go and then spend even more time looking for *another* replacement.

- *Increased time by the controller.* The recruiting process is a very time-consuming one, and the time a controller puts into it takes away from other tasks, such as preparing and evaluating financial statements, undertaking new cost-reduction projects, or analyzing various accounting-related proposals from around the company. In short, recruiting reduces the time available for completing other aspects of the job.

- *Loss of specialized knowledge.* Every company has a unique set of processes. When a company loses an employee, it also loses that person's knowledge of the processes. When a new person arrives to replace the outgoing person, some of that specialized knowledge may be lost, or at least take many months before it is assimilated from the other members of the accounting department. If turnover is extremely high, there may so few "old timers" left in the department that this specialized knowledge is permanently lost.

- *Risk of an inappropriate hire.* Bringing in a new person carries with it the risk of hiring someone who is hiding a past of improper behavior, who may attempt to take company assets once in a position to exercise control over assets (a common enough position in the accounting department). Another risk is that a controller may find that the person hired is so inappropriate for the position that termination is the only answer, and then find that the new employee has sued the company for wrongful termination. No matter how correct the controller's actions may be in getting rid of the employee, the company must still expend a large amount of money to defend itself against litigation.

Obviously, there are many reasons to avoid turnover. However, in today's environment of highly mobile employees who can find work elsewhere in little time, and who feel little association with a single company, how is it possible to drive turnover down to such low levels that a controller no longer has to deal with its effects?

The answer is to meet the needs of employees. They may not feel any closer association with the company (a difficult proposition), but they will react well to an enlightened style of management that is revealed by the factors noted in the following list, such as flex hours, slightly higher rates of pay, and recognition programs. A controller will find that these factors will vastly reduce turnover by giving employees no possible reason to leave the company. The ways to reduce turnover are:

- *Clarify jobs and related procedures.* There is nothing more irritating for a new employee than to be unceremoniously dumped into a new job without any clue regarding what the job entails or how to perform tasks. This lack of information causes a great deal of stress for a new employee, who must essentially build a job description from scratch, probably making mistakes along the way. It is also difficult to get a good performance review if there is no baseline job description against which to be measured. A controller can avoid this degree of uncertainty by supplying each new employee with an accurate job description that is supplemented by detailed procedures that clearly describe how each required job element can be completed. An example of such a job description is shown in Exhibit 10.1.

Position: Assistant Controller

Report To: Controller

Review Dates:
  1. 01/20 Quarterly Review
  2. 04/20 Quarterly Review
  3. 07/20 Quarterly Review
  4. 10/20 Annual Review

Pay Change Criteria:
  1. If issue financial statements within 5 days of month-end.
    • OK performance: ____% if reach 5 day close by end of 20XX.
    • Good performance: ____% if reach 5 day close by September 20XX.
    • Great performance: ____% if reach 5 day close by July 20XX.
  2. If achieve accounts receivable turns of 9.0.
    • OK performance: ____% if reach 9 turns by end of 20XX.
    • Good performance: ____% if reach 9 turns by the end of September 20XX.
    • Great performance: ____% if reach 9 turns by the end of July 20XX.

Overview of Tasks:

Timing	Description
Daily	Collect accounts receivable
Daily	Maintain general ledger accounts
Daily	Receive and apply cash receipts
Daily	Run batch jobs and backups
Daily	Clear checks for accounts payable and accounts receivable
Daily	Reconcile invoices with customers
Daily	Take deposits to bank
Monthly	Calculate monthly quality bonus
Monthly	Complete bank reconciliations
Monthly	Conduct internal audit tasks
Monthly	Create variance report
Monthly	Prepare borrowing base reports
Monthly	Prepare financial statements
Monthly	Prepare tax returns
Monthly	Prepare workers' compensation insurance reports
Monthly	Track fixed assets
Monthly	Track mold shop expenses
Yearly	Create documents for annual audit
Yearly	Update archives

Development Areas:
  1. Financial statement preparation
  2. Activity-based costing
  3. Report writer training

EXHIBIT 10.1 SAMPLE JOB DESCRIPTION

- *Improve communications.* Employees want to know what is going on. For example, a controller can sit down with the accounting staff every month, after financial statements are published, and go over the company's results with them. This gives the staff a good feel for how the company is doing, what they can do to improve the situation, and (above all) it tells the staff that the controller is not trying to hide anything from them. This sets the tone for an open and constructive dialogue between the controller and the staff; if the controller is willing to impart information to them, they will be more comfortable with bringing information to the controller.

MONEY CAN BUY HAPPINESS

One of the first things a new controller should do is review the condition of all computer and office equipment in the department, as well as the version number of the software being used. Then gain approval of a replacement budget, and become involved in upgrading the most archaic items. The staff will be especially appreciative if the controller personally shows up with a new flat-panel monitor, computer, and so on.

- *Increase pay.* Many companies have a policy of paying employees the median pay rate for their job classifications. Though this ensures that a company is not paying too much for its staff, this policy does not take into account the total cost of employment. If a company loses employees to competitors who are willing to pay somewhat more than the median pay rate, it must then incur substantial additional costs to recruit and train a replacement. When this recruitment cost is added to an employee's median pay rate, it becomes apparent that a company should actually pay somewhat *more* than the median rate in order to avoid the costs of turnover.
- *Look for a history of job longevity.* A controller can avoid turnover up front by hiring only recruits with a history of staying with their previous companies for long periods. This avoids potential employees who are more likely to walk out for minor reasons over which a controller may have little control.
- *Meet special employee needs.* Employees may have special needs, such as flex time, so that they can handle various aspects of their personal lives that might otherwise interfere with company business. A controller should consider these needs and modify employee work routines (within reason) so that employees can continue to work for the company. It is important not to allow too many exemptions to specific employees, because this may engender ill will among other employees who do not appreciate the special favors being extended to a minority of them.
- *Recognize employee efforts.* Some employees make exceptional efforts on behalf of the companies where they work, yet receive no recognition for these efforts. After going to extra lengths to help the company, an employee should receive some special recognition, which makes that person want to stay with the company—not because they are making more money or have a fancy title, but because they feel appreciated. This type of recognition can take a variety of forms, such as tickets to sports events, plaques, public recognition, or an employee-of-the-month parking spot.
- *Review employees frequently.* Employees want to know where they stand in terms of performance, potential advancement, and the impression given to coworkers. It is difficult for an employee to make meaningful changes to work habits in a timely manner if this information is communicated only once a year, during the annual review. Instead, a

---

KEEP A STASH OF GIFT CERTIFICATES

The author has had considerable success for years by rewarding excellent performance with gift certificates. Whenever an employee does something especially well, they receive one on the spot. I usually have a variety of gift certificates on hand, so I can most closely match the certificate to the recipient. Representative stores for which I keep certificates on hand include a restaurant, home furnishings, sports equipment, and building supplies.

---

controller should schedule informal quarterly reviews to supplement the annual review, plus more frequent feedback if there are issues that require immediate corrective action. By giving frequent reviews, a controller not only ensures improved behavior by employees, but also a better sense by staff of how they are doing, which reduces their level of uncertainty.

There are a number of techniques for avoiding turnover, which tend to emphasize clear job descriptions for employees, frequent communications, and paying attention to special employee needs. By taking these steps, a controller can greatly reduce the costs of turnover and increase the productivity of the accounting department.

IMPORTANCE OF DEVELOPING CAREER PLANS FOR EMPLOYEES

Even though accountants are known to be a thoroughgoing and detail-oriented group, most do not engage in a sufficient degree of career planning. This results in a considerable amount of movement between jobs, as they go in search of perceived incremental improvements to their positions, presumably resulting in better titles, greater responsibilities, and more pay. This behavior also results in a great deal of turnover, which, as noted throughout this chapter, is anathema to any controller. This section describes how to lock in employees for long periods of time by assisting them in developing career plans.

For the typical accountant, there is no specific career plan, and for only the rare few is it even committed to paper. A more common career plan is to acquire some sort of certification or college degree early in the career and then use these credentials to gradually work up through the ranks at a corporation until reaching the pinnacle of success, the chief financial officer (CFO) position. Because only a small proportion of accountants can reach this position (after all, there are not many CFO positions available), every accountant needs a great deal of preplanning to assist in achieving this goal, or to aim for goals culminating in different positions. The controller can assist with this difficulty by meeting each staff person and comparing the aspirations to the existing set of experience and skills, and determining where there must be improvements for that person to reach whatever the goal may be. This plan should clearly define required skills, a time line for achieving them, and specific action steps by the staff person as well as the controller to ensure that those steps are reached. For example, an accounts payable staff person may have no experience with payroll. To acquire it, the controller can commit to assigning the staff person as a backup to the regular payroll person for the next year. In exchange, the payroll person will become the backup for the accounts payable person for the same period. This ensures that both employees acquire more knowledge and experience.

Why would a controller go to some lengths to ensure that the entire accounting staff will eventually be in a position to replace the controller? There are several reasons. First, putting every staff person on a solid career path will lock them into working for the company for a long time. For example, encouraging employees to take reimbursed college courses will keep them with the company until a degree is acquired, which can easily take six years. Also, rotating a staff person through all possible accounting areas takes a number of years, especially if the company is a large one. In both cases, a controller can effectively reduce (if not eliminate) turnover by keeping the entire staff busy with various kinds of training programs. The second reason is that very few accounting employees really have the wherewithal to become a CFO; instead, they will be promoted to the point where the job responsibilities match their abilities, and they will stop. By using career planning and reviewing progress, it will become obvious to both the staff person and the controller when this point is reached, and the controller can then shift the motivational focus to retaining that person in the same position for as long as possible. Third, a mature controller will realize that an accountant who has the ability to eventually become a controller or CFO should be allowed to do so. Rather than getting mad at an employee who has been thoroughly trained by the controller, it is best to throw a farewell party for the person and maintain relations when the person moves on to other organizations. This not only maintains goodwill between the controller and the former staff person, but also makes it easy for the person to return someday, or to refer other people to the controller for various positions. Finally, a controller can use career planning to determine the timing of changes in the department. For example, if it is obvious that a qualified subordinate should go outside the company to take a controller position elsewhere, the controller can use the career plan to make a rough estimate of when this might occur (or even discuss the issue with the subordinate), and then make plans to promote other people in an orderly fashion to fill in the post that is about to be vacated. In short, career planning reduces turnover while promoting employees to the maximum level and allowing the controller to plan for employee advancement in an orderly manner.

Some controllers include career planning in an employee's annual review. This is a mistake, because the annual review is supposed to cover issues that the employee is *required* to do, whereas a career planning session discusses items that are *optional*—an employee may take additional steps to advance his or her career, but those steps can be taken at the discretion of the employee. For example, a goal that might be discussed during an annual review is the ability of an employee to issue financial statements within a specified time period and to determine a course of remedial action if that goal has not been met. A career planning session discusses any steps an employee has taken along his or her career path, and what assistance the controller can give in furthering that person's aspirations. In short, a controller adopts the role of a supervisor when using an annual review to cover immediate performance issues, but must switch roles to be a mentor and coach when covering career planning issues. Due to the different roles of the controller and the differing types of discussions, these two meetings should not be merged.

A key part of career planning is sharing the salary ranges of targeted positions with the accounting staff. There is a considerable motivation in knowing that there is a large increase in pay associated with gaining a higher-level accounting position. Telling employees about market rates for desired positions can also keep them from making a mistake in pursuing a position that does not yield a significant pay increase in proportion to the amount of work required to attain the position. One may think that there is some risk in appearing to promise specific pay rates to employees well in advance of their being placed in those positions, so it is important to tell employees up front that prospective pay rates fall within fairly wide pay ranges, and that they can expect to begin at the lowest levels of the pay rates and gradually gain additional compensation as they gain experience and skill. Informing employees of the pay rates for future positions is a key part of the career planning process.

A controller should encourage the accounting staff to earn certifications. There are many accounting certifications, all of which require a considerable amount of training before one can pass the required examinations. By taking the training, an employee can improve his or her skill set, which directly benefits a company by bringing more expertise to its accounting operations. To encourage the acquisition of certifications, a controller should actively pursue the purchase and distribution of study materials, as well as pay employees for the time off needed to take the tests. To really encourage acquiring certifications, a controller can even offer one-time bonuses or pay raises to those who have successfully completed their examinations. The most common certifications for an accounting person to earn are:

- *Certified Public Accountant (CPA).* The examination is standardized, but additional certification requirements vary by state. Contact your state's Department of Regulatory Agencies (or such similar organization) for more details. The examination requires three days of testing.

- *Certified Management Accountant (CMA).* The examination is standardized and requires 90 hours of CPE every three years to renew. The examination requires three days of testing.

  o *Address:* Institute of Certified Management Accountants, 10 Paragon Drive, Montvale, NJ 07645. Phone: 201-573-6300

- *Certified Internal Auditor.* The examination is standardized and requires 100 hours of CPE every three years to renew. The examination requires two days of testing.

  o *Address:* Institute of Internal Auditors, 249 Maitland Avenue, Altamonte Springs, FL 32701. Phone: 407-830-7600

- *Certified Production and Inventory Manager.* The examination is standardized and requires no continuing education. There is no required renewal. The examination requires the completion of six tests, which can be completed at different times.

  o *Address:* American Production and Inventory Control Society, 500 West Annandale Road, Falls Church, VA 22046. Phone: 800-444-2742

- *Certified Production Manager.* The examination is standardized and requires 120 hours of CPE every five years to renew. The examination requires one day of testing.

  o *Address:* National Association of Purchasing Management, P.O. Box 22160, Tempe, AZ 85285. Phone: 602-752-6276

Some of the certifications listed do not directly cover accounting topics. Instead, they address such areas as production, logistics, and purchasing. It is useful for an accounting person to acquire these extra certifications, because there is great value in having a broad knowledge of how a wide array of processes function throughout a company.

IMPORTANCE OF COMMUNICATIONS WITH EMPLOYEES

The title of this chapter includes the words "training" and "supervision." Communicating with employees comprises a key element of both activities. A controller should include a variety of modes of communication with the accounting staff, which can vary in frequency based on the type of communication. This section notes the different types of communication, as well as the offsetting risks of losing some confidential information to competitors.

There are several distinct types of communications that a controller should use. One consists of *operational information*. This type of information describes company performance, and that of the accounting area in particular. It can include such performance information as the number of days to issue financial statements, accounts receivable turnover, and the dollar amount of accounts payable discounts that were not taken. It is crucial to impart this information regularly, because the accounting staff needs it to determine its own performance, as well as to form a basis for requesting additional improvements in the future. The information is best presented in a historical context, so that there are a string of performance figures that clearly show a trend line of performance; this is best presented in a chart or white board, so that the information is presented visually, not verbally.

Another type of communication consists of *financial information*. Since one of the primary functions of the accounting staff is to generate information that is summarized in the financial statements, it makes sense to show them the result of all that work—the financial statements. Many company managers shy away from the prospect of revealing company performance to employees, especially if performance is poor, but one of the best ways to motivate employees is to give them this information; then they are more likely to pitch in and suggest ways to improve performance. The only type of financial information that one can legitimately withhold from employees is salary data, because this is considered confidential by most managers, not to mention most employees. Financial information can also include the budget, which can be shared with the staff without divulging payroll information. The financial statements and accompanying budget yield much greater employee understanding of a company's overall situation.

An additional type of communication is of *personal performance information*. This is a form of communication that many controllers do not perform well. The worst case is when controllers essentially ignore the accounting staff, never giving them any feedback on their performance. This tells the staff nothing about how they are doing, and in the absence of information, they tend to assume the worst. The next worst form of communication is going over performance only during an annual review. Though many controllers consider this to be a sufficient interval for giving feedback, it is actually far too infrequent. There may be a problem with performance early in the review period, which a controller notes for the annual review but does not mention to the employee until the actual review. This means that the staff person is performing improperly for nearly a year before getting any feedback! Many controllers delay in giving feedback because they do not relish the charged emotional atmosphere that frequently results. However, by waiting until the review and churning out a long list of faults, this tends to exacerbate the situation and results in a difficult review. By far the best way to issue personal performance information is by wandering through the accounting area on a daily basis and giving feedback in small doses to everyone. This gets the staff used to continual feedback and results in a vastly more relaxed working environment. In short, the frequency of feedback is very important when relaying personal performance information.

A final type of communication is of *general information*. This can be directives issued by senior management (such as news about a company merger), notes about the work schedule (such as when the company will observe holidays), or similar information. Though the most minor forms of general information can be communicated by such media as voice mail, e-mail, or the venerable memo, more important information, for which employees may have questions, is best communicated in person. The timing of the information may also have a bearing on the form of communication used. For example, a notice regarding when an official holiday will be taken is easily communicated by memo if done a month in advance, but may require an in-person discussion if it is being communicated one day in advance, because this may interrupt work schedules and require some negotiation with the staff regarding taking alternate holiday time. Thus, the form of communication used to impart general information depends on the lead time used, as well as the likelihood of answering questions from the staff.

LEARN THROUGH LUNCH

The author has made a point of taking a mix of different staff out to lunch at least once a week for years. This tends to be the best place to learn about what is really going on all over the company. Employees are more likely to unwind and talk about a wide range of topics in this setting, where they would be less inclined to do so in the more formal office environment. This is also a good chance to be with junior staff people who would otherwise have little face time with "the boss."

This section has focused on feeding as much information as possible to the accounting staff, on the assumption that a well-informed staff is a satisfied one. However, the response of senior management to this approach is frequently that of the risk to the company—what if a dissatisfied employee takes the information to a competitor or issues it to the press? Of course this can happen, but usually only when relations with the staff are so bad (perhaps due to a lack of information) that employees are actively looking for a way to harm the company. In this case, the controller is well advised to look for employment elsewhere, since the working environment is exceptionally difficult. When staff relations are good, the risk of disseminating information outside the company is much lower. To provide additional coverage to the company, all financial information can be marked as classified, which gives the company some recourse to legal action if it finds that information has left the company. Usually, it is much more beneficial to issue information to the staff than to worry about the much smaller risk that the information will get out to the general public or to competing firms.

The recurring recommendations in this section have been to give lots of information to the accounting staff, and to do so as frequently as possible. This is very important for maintaining good staff morale and usually results in better performance. Many old-time controllers who were brought up in an environment of "closed books" will have a hard time with this approach, especially if it requires lots of face time with employees. Nonetheless, the controller who invests time in his or her staff will reap considerable rewards in terms of a happy, well-informed, and productive department.

HOW TO MOTIVATE EMPLOYEES

Motivating employees clearly improves employee morale as well as department performance, but motivation should be based on a multilayered motivation scheme that covers the long, medium, and short term. By using this multilayered approach, employees are presented with a richer environment in which to work, which is more satisfying for them, and gives them many good reasons for staying with the company. This section discusses multilayered motivational systems.

A long-term motivational system is based on the career plan. As noted earlier, in the "Developing Career Plans" section, the controller should discuss career options with all accounting employees, and devise a progression of steps that will last for a number of years, culminating in greatly increased levels of experience and expertise for them. This is an excellent long-term motivator, but does not grab the attention of the typical employee on a day-to-day basis, because it is typically comprised of course work that happens only after working hours or involves occasional seminars or job switches. Something more is required that will make motivation a more immediate issue.

A midrange motivational system is the annual performance goal. Many controllers set up goals for each employee to reach, which are used in determining pay raises or bonuses at the end of the year. Examples of these goals are increasing accounts receivable turnover through greater attention to collections, taking all purchase discounts, and issuing financial statements by a specified date. These can even be tied to a specific pay raise. For example, accounts receivable turnover of 8.0 can be awarded with a 2 percent raise, while a turnover rate of 10.0 will result in a 3 percent raise. This type of motivational system is an excellent way to focus the attention of the staff on key improvement goals, while rewarding them as well. Though this is a good motivator, especially when used in concert with the longer-range career plans, it still does not focus day-to-day attention on the tasks at hand. That requires a short-range motivation system.

A short-range motivation system is one that grabs and holds the attention of the accounting staff every day. This system is much more difficult to arrange than the long-term and midrange motivational systems, and also requires much more work by the controller to keep it operational and meaningful. The reason for the excessive level of attention is that the motivational targets must be changed from time to time to avoid boredom, while the types of awards must also be changed for the same reason. When constructing short-term goals, a controller can devise an enormous array of potential targets, such as the cleanest desk or the fastest response to an e-mail. However, it is best to create group goals so that the entire team wins, rather than just one person. The targets are not necessarily intended to cause any long-term change. Instead, they should be fun and make employees feel better about coming to work. For example, a clean desk week may leave no lasting impression or enhance company performance, but it will give the staff something to focus their attention on in the very short term. Also, the rewards for reaching such goals should involve the group, such as a free team lunch or a block of tickets to a sporting event. The reward should always act to bring the group together by treating them as a unit, not split them apart by giving different awards to different people. A short-range motivational system is targeted at employee morale, not at reaching any quantifiable goals.

In summary, employees can be motivated with three types of motivation systems. The first is the long-range career plan, which requires minimal attention by the controller to maintain. The second is annual performance goals; this is the most common motivational system employed by controllers and also requires minimal work to maintain. Finally, there should also be brief, team-based contests or targets in the very short term (e.g., weekly) to grab the attention of the accounting staff and add some spice to the work experience. This short-term system requires the most work by the controller but also greatly contributes to a more pleasant work environment, which is a prime factor in motivating employees.

11

CONTROLLER'S ROLE IN INVESTOR RELATIONS

IMPORTANCE OF THIS CHAPTER

If there is no CFO, the controller is likely to be in charge of investor relations. This group can include directors, senior managers, and a variety of outside interests, all of whom can variously sue the company or be ready sources of more funds, so it calls for a considerable amount of circumspection and skill in dealing with them. This chapter covers a number of key areas in determining the information needs of various constituencies as well as how to disclose information to them.

Very little has been written about the controller's role in investor relations (IR). This is partially because many controllers, by all outward signs, are not actively engaged in this function—at least as far as the public is concerned. In Chapter 2 of this text, investor relations activities of the controller are included in the category of "Additional Controller Functions." To many outsiders with an interest in investments, the controller is variously regarded as the "inside man," the number cruncher, the figure man, or the introverted accountant. To be sure, many of these same representatives do not have a real understanding of what the controller should do or can do.

In contrast to this view of the controller, in discussions with security analysts, they have expressed opinions to the authors concerning a preference for talking about financial matters with the controller because "he has the facts" (while many of the nonaccounting-trained public relations persons do not). Certainly, if the chief accounting officer wishes to climb the financial ladder or aspire to a broader executive career, experience in the IR arena may be very useful.

In reaching some conclusion concerning those duties the controller might perform in this interesting IR function, a review of the following facets may help in ferreting out those activities for which the controller might be suited, and which he or she might enjoy:

- The objectives or purpose of the IR function
- The nature of the function
- The principal vehicles used to convey financial information
- The nature of the "customer"
- What type of information is desired and limits on its disclosure
- Some brief observations about organization structure in this field

OBJECTIVES OF THE INVESTOR RELATIONS FUNCTION

In a general sense, it may be said that the principal purpose of the IR function, regardless of who performs it, is the enhancement of shareholder value. Isn't this a familiar term? The stated purpose by the perpetrators of some hostile takeovers is "to enhance shareholder value"; the defense against such actions, as voiced by some chief financial officers (CFOs) of the targets, is an effort "to enhance shareholder values by increasing the price of the common stock." As a matter of fact, one of the purposes of sound financial policy is to enable the company to raise funds, on an acceptable basis, to meet its needs, so as to enhance the long-term interests of the shareholder; and a related corollary is to cause the entity to be so well regarded in the financial marketplace that its stock will command an acceptable price/earnings ratio.

Some chief executive officers (CEOs) might still regard the IR function as a simple financial reporting activity, with no intent to affect the stock price. But many CFOs will bluntly state that the objective is to maximize the market price so as to minimize the cost of equity capital. Executives of brokerage houses will acknowledge that a continuing IR program helps prepare the market for a public offering, and influences the credit ratings of fixed-income securities. Certainly, the importance of the stock price is not lost on those CEOs engaged in sell-offs, acquisitions, or other restructuring. In the view of the authors, these enumerated purposes, however described, translate into an objective of enhancing shareholder value.

In today's environment, companies must compete for investment capital—whether in the bond market or the equity market. But to secure recognition, the story of the enterprise must be told. Just as the advantages and uses of a company's service or product must be described and marketed, so also information about the value of an entity's securities and its financial prospects must be disseminated, understood, and accepted.

EVOLVING NATURE OF THE FUNCTION

Investor relations has been, and probably still is, an evolving activity. About 30 years ago, it often was a part of the public relations department, perhaps viewed as a somewhat specialized communication function. In the 1950s through the 1960s and into the early 1970s, with the rapid growth of employee retirement funds, many blue-chip companies, including General Electric, used skilled communicators to "educate" portfolio managers and brokerage intermediaries about the investment merits of the company's stock. By the mid-1970s, when many individual investors abandoned the stock market, when the market was dominated by large institutions, when many less-than-blue- chip companies felt they were neglected by the brokers and investing institutions, and when the need for more capital intensified, many managements became more aggressive, and began directly contacting potential investors, both institutional and individual, who were willing to take more risks and were often receptive to growth situations and better-than-average returns. The individuals representing these companies were variously communication specialists and security analysts. In this time frame, with the growth of dividend reinvestment plans, self registration, and an increased recognition of the need to plan and sell new security issues, the IR function became more marketing oriented.

These changes also induced changes in the nature of the IR specialist. While communicators (public relations) and security analysts had predominated, gradually more and more individuals well acquainted with finance assumed a greater role. The customers became far more sophisticated about what they needed. So the IR function evolved into a combination of two disciplines—communications and finance.

Accordingly, in this century, the IR function must not only communicate effectively about past performance, but it must more closely align itself with the strategic plans of management and tell its customers more about corporate goals and the entity's strengths and weaknesses.

COMMUNICATION VEHICLES FOR INVESTOR RELATIONS

At this point, perhaps a recap of the several vehicles now commonly used to communicate with "investor relations customers" may be helpful. Each is directed to a somewhat different audience, and each typically conveys a disparate or varied message—but always with an investor-related aspect. They are distinct in words and tone from the typical product or service advertising originating with the advertising or marketing department. The methods used to communicate investor-related messages, in no special order, include:

- Annual report to shareholders
- Quarterly reports to shareholders (and the financial community)
- Annual meeting with shareholders
- Reports to the Securities and Exchange Commission (SEC)
  - Annual Report Form 10-K
  - Quarterly Report Form 10-Q
  - Current Report Form 8-K
- Regular or special meetings with security analysts, institutional investors, brokers, and large individual investors—often arranged in cooperation with one of the several associations or societies for analysts
- Institutional advertising in newspapers or periodicals (financial or general interest)
- Dividend stuffers
- Corporate announcements of special interest to investors or potential investors:
  - New products or services
  - Management changes
  - Acquisitions and/or divestments
  - Reorganization attempts, etc.: restructuring, unfriendly takeovers
- Videocassettes dealing with financial matters
- Use of toll-free telephone numbers
- Individual meetings with government representatives and the stock exchanges concerned with financial matters (Internal Revenue Service, SEC, etc.)

> ### ELECTRONIC INVESTOR COMMUNICATIONS
>
> A simple and essentially free form of communication with investors is to issue them an electronic version of the company newsletter. Many organizations already convert their newsletters into electronic format and e-mail them to a variety of suppliers and customers, so adding investors to the e-mail list is all the work that is needed.

INVESTOR RELATIONS MESSAGE RECIPIENTS

Broadly and technically speaking, the IR function must service an unusually complex and diverse audience. For example, here is a typical listing (with some overlapping) of the vast potential "customers":

- Investors and potential stock investors (small)
- Large institutional stock investors and potential investors
- Security analysts
- Credit-rating agencies
- Financial advisory services
- Brokerage firms
- Bond-rating agencies
- Bank loan officers
- Bondholders
- Financial press
- Portfolio managers
- European/Japanese investors
- Acquisition candidates
- Government agencies dealing with financial matters (federal, state, and local)
- Employees

Having said this, it should be realized that three broad groups with which the IR activity is *primarily* and continuously directed are (1) security analysts, (2) stockbrokers, and (3) large institutional investors. Practically speaking, and as discussed later, some of these information-seeking persons would deal directly with the CFO—that is, the bank loan officer handling most of the company's current bank borrowings, the bond-rating agency, or credit-rating agency—in some kind of one-on-one desired meeting that is heavily and technically financial in nature.

Many of the members of the three principal groups mentioned—security analysts, stockbrokers, or institutional or other large investors (or their representatives)—are quite sophisticated financially. Each of the three groups may, and usually does, have different information needs; and each may be motivated, for different reasons, to discuss the financial affairs of the entity.

INFORMATION NEEDS OF THE FINANCIAL ANALYST

The management of a company usually desires that it be perceived in its most favorable light—hopefully without exaggeration, and as objectively determined. While communication with all segments of the IR audience on this matter is important, perhaps the key person is the financial analyst, also called the security analyst. He is in a position to influence a large cross-section of investors. It therefore especially behooves the IR executives to know what information the analyst needs and how he will probably use it. It is imperative that the financial executive involved (CFO or controller) properly interpret the information for this analyst and not merely infer certain conclusions. In most instances, the analyst desires information so that he can reasonably predict earnings (and hence market price, potential of the stock dividend rate, etc.).

A most important source of information for the security analyst is management presentations generally made to large institutional investors, and brokers, or investment bankers, as well as the analysts themselves. The information gained from such meetings, plus that distilled from annual and quarterly reports, or Form 10-Ks and the like, together with discussions among other analysts, and other articles about the company and the industry, enable the analyst to reach certain conclusions about the entity and aid in helping him predict financial performance.

These analyst meetings present an unusual opportunity for the company to portray itself in its best light. They not only permit the company to make *factual* presentations, but also to subjectively influence the analyst about the depth of management and long-term objectives of the company. Moreover, they enable management to directly answer the questions of the group and fully explain troublesome events, such as complicated footnotes to the annual report and so forth.

Each industry and each company has certain factors that are important to its well-being and growth. For example, in the aerospace business, the order backlog is of significance, as well as the status of various contracts or programs. In other companies, product development might be of major interest. Facts and opinions should be divulged within the limits of prudent disclosure. Such meetings with analysts are not just public relations events. Solid and specific information is needed.

While each entity has its own requirements, here is an outline of suggestions about presentation content to analysts for a well-established, reputable company.

1. To give a sense of an experienced, in-depth, and well-qualified management:

   (a) The CEO should be present and give the principal talk—about prospects, style of management, management development programs, market position, etc.

   (b) The key executives should be introduced, and usually should make some short comments about their areas of responsibility.

   (c) Perhaps the organizational structure and incentive system and the like should be discussed.

2. To provide an insight into the long-term prospects of the entity, the following subjects might be covered by a knowledgeable executive (CEO, executive vice-president, senior vice president of finance or controller):

   (a) The system or method of strategic planning

   (b) The short-term or annual plan process, and the related control system

   (c) Some examples of long-range objectives that have been achieved (and perhaps some that were not)

   (d) The long-range outlook for the industry or selected products or markets

   (e) The status of market penetration or dominance for some key products

(f) Important research and development programs underway (Whether specific quantified projections or plans should be divulged may depend on the individual circumstances.)

3. To provide a broad financial picture, including the financial strength of the company, perhaps a slide presentation (graphs and charts) could be given that would identify:

   (a) Status of orders on hand

   (b) Trend of sales, by product line

   (c) Margins by product line, or organizational units, and trends thereof

   (d) Financial position through comments about a condensed balance sheet, with emphasis on key ratios or relationships

   (e) The trend of long-term indebtedness, times debt service is covered, debt capacity, and so on

   (f) The trend of cash flow by important segments: from operations, investing activities, and financing activities, and perhaps cash flow per share from operations

   (g) Trends on equity and earnings:

   ○ Growth in equity

   ○ Equity relationships (ROE)

   ○ Earnings per share

   ○ Return on assets

   (h) By simple explanation and illustration, any aspect of the financial statements that often causes confusion (inventory, valuation method, tax accruals, reserves, etc.)

   (i) Perhaps some comparative ratios with industry or selected competitors

   (j) Company posture regarding acquisitions or diversification

4. The chief marketing executive probably should make a presentation that would describe and illustrate major new products, or major revenue procedures, and the sales prospects for the next year or two

5. Other executives, as appropriate, might discuss any timely topics, such as:

   (a) Employee relations

   (b) Cost reduction programs

   (c) Process improvements, including use of computers

   (d) Information resource management

   (e) Quality control changes

   (f) Any major troublesome contracts or publicity items and the like

The objective should include a demonstration of financial conservatism, stability, and ability to raise capital when needed. Interpretation of what the figures mean should be given; it should not be left to the unaided judgment of the analyst.

In fact, the executives deeply involved in the process should know their audiences and determine what they need to know, so that the analysts (and others) may make a proper evaluation of the entity.

These are some key points that should be covered. Experience at meetings with analysts, including their questions, will provide guidance as to other subjects of interest.

The data presented to the analysts might serve as a point of departure for responding to the information needs of other groups.

Above all, the presentations by management, and the responses to questions raised by the analysts, must be open, frank, and responsive to the information needs. Any sense that management is not forthright and will not truthfully answer reasonable questions will cause analysts to choose not to follow the company's progress.

INFORMATION NEEDS OF OTHER GROUPS

The financial analysts and large investors of all groups, as might be expected, do the most probing. Their approach is highly analytical. Usually, when a company can adequately communicate with this group, it can deal effectively with most others.

These other players have varying interests, some of which involve answers to the items raised in the preceding sections. Perhaps the typical individual shareholder is most concerned with the general progress of the company and the prospect of continued and increasing dividend payments. A highly skilled financial background is not required to meet her inquiries. At the other extreme, a bank loan officer will be interested in the prospects of repaying the loan on time; and it might be proper to make available to him the annual plan or budget for the next year or two, and perhaps the long-range financial plan. His relationship is more confidential than the general public, and he is entitled to such knowledge. Bond-rating agencies may be exposed to past and prospective debt service coverage and related matters. Credit agencies, who have the published annual report available, may direct their questions to the content of the balance sheet items, and prospective earnings. Many other investors may be interested in the significance of certain litigation, or product development. The required financial knowledge of the IR interface person will depend on the types of questions and the inquisitor's knowledge and interest.

DISCLOSURE POLICY

In providing information to or communicating with analysts, brokers, investors, or others, a matter to be resolved is: What constitutes proper and adequate disclosure? Typically, management is concerned about excessive disclosure that may harm the company. On the other side of the question, there should be sufficient disclosure to enable the analysts and others to discern shareholder value. Hence, the problem is one of weighing the benefits versus the costs.

On the one hand, the dangers of excessive disclosure include:

- Loss of competitive advantage through early disclosure of new products or marketing strategy or other strategic information
- Exposing the entity to litigation by reason of allegedly providing insider information, or attempting to foreclose competition or otherwise violate antitrust laws
- Generating earlier competitive reaction, or even new competitors, than would otherwise be the case
- Revealing strengths or weaknesses that might invite an unfriendly takeover attempt

Most analysts would prefer to get information first, or early, but normally there is no benefit to them in causing long-term share decline. And most appreciate the need to protect competitive information.

While there is a danger in excessive disclosure, there are sometimes unrecognized costs of insufficient disclosure. Some of these are the following, resulting in a share price lower than normally might be the case:

- Failure to provide adequate data may encourage analysts and others to avoid the company and fail to follow its progress.

- Lack of information may cause unpleasant or unexpected surprises—something the financial community abhors.

- If the management does not maintain good relations with analysts and investors, it usually takes much longer for positive developments to become known and reflected in the stock price.

- Most importantly, lack of firsthand knowledge, such as that secured through personal contact, prevents analysts and other interested parties from "kicking the tires"—from assessing the depth and quality of management, the adequacy of the company's controls, its ability to cope with change, as well as the quality of the product and services.

IMPACT OF REGULATION FD

The Securities and Exchange Commission recently issued Regulation FD, stating that a company cannot issue information to a small subset of the investment community, thereby potentially giving those people an investment advantage over the general public. Some companies have reacted to this regulation by halting all contact with financial analysts and issuing a flood of general press releases, while others have elected to issue the minimal amount of required information to the investment community. So far, it appears that the issuance of more information is winning out.

The IR group and management must thoroughly weigh what constitutes a proper balance in its disclosure policy.

ORGANIZATION STRUCTURE FOR INVESTOR RELATIONS

A successful IR program must, as previously mentioned, permit the exercise of two skills by company executives: the ability to (1) communicate effectively and (2) ferret out and comprehend the financial significance of operating trends and relationships, together with the composition of the various elements in the financial statements and their significance or impact. Company representatives must clearly, and often in sophisticated or knowledgeable financial terms, discuss highly technical financial issues with a great many types of investors or potential investors. What organizational structure best fills or facilitates this execution?

Several structures may be observed in operation, but one truth is paramount: There must be a coordinated approach; the company must speak with one voice. Thus, confusion is created if the vice president of sales discusses the potential financial impact of a new product to a group of distributors as having certain results, and the financial vice president describes a quite different financial impact with a group of financial analysts.

Assuming adequate and effective coordination among the company's spokespersons, as to the presentation of financial data, what organizational structure is desirable? One answer is, "The one that is effective."

The external or investing public of a company is viewed by many top executives as consisting of several parts of the whole. The result is a dichotomy of views about proper organization:

- In some companies there is no single executive who is responsible for the external investor relations (as distinguished from employee relations). Basically, each major executive meets with his audience, e.g., a research audience, a marketing audience, a manufacturing group, a financial group. However, whenever financial content is involved, it would be cleared with the proper financial executive.
- In other entities, a single executive is held accountable for the IR function. Under this latter scenario, the IR activities might be a segment of the public relations department (renamed an investor relations department). Also, under such a plan the finance department, including the controller, would be considered an internal function—a resource to be made available to those responsible for the IR activities.
- Some other organizational structures divide the responsibility into two segments: (1) The activity relating to preparation of the annual and quarterly reports to shareholders, institutional or financial advertisement, small shareholder inquiries, and the like, is handled by the public relations department (and coordinated with finance)—the so-called mass media facet; (2) the unit relating principally to contacts with security analysts, large institutional or individual investors, investment bankers, rating agencies, and so forth—that audience assumed to possess considerable financial know-how— is handled by an investor relations unit reporting to the CFO or a financial officer. Presumably the members of this unit have a financial background (CPAs, accounting, investment banking) but have also been trained in communication skills.

The type of "customer" determines the unit most likely assigned the task. There must be coordination with the public relations segment or unit.

Finally, one other factor should be mentioned as a possible participant in the IR activity, and that is a professional IR agency. While such a firm often may be used by small companies, sometimes they can also be helpful consultants to medium-sized and larger entities in properly organizing the IR function. The authors should point out, however, that most investor/analyst types prefer to deal with a member of management, and not an outsider, in seeking financial information about a company.

The proper organizational structure for a specific company will depend, again, on the interests, ability, and personality (and perhaps financial interest) of the officers and executives who are actual or potential participants—consistent with management philosophy, style of management, available time, and so forth.

ROLE OF THE CONTROLLER AND OTHER PRINCIPALS

Having provided only a very general background on the sources of financial information about the company, the type of inquirers, and suggestions about management presentations to the security analysts in particular, the basic question is, "What should be the role of the controller?"

As is often true, what functions an officer performs depends on several factors, including his or her ability, personality, and interests, along with the interest and capabilities of the other officers, as well as the size of the company, management organization structure, management style, and so forth. If there is a CFO as well as a controller, the duties will be shared. And in those instances where the CEO feels he himself should play a major role in IR, that will further divide the effort. If the controller is a good financial analyst, certain activities will tend to be assigned to this position; and if the chief accounting officer is, in addition, a good presenter or communicator, then still other duties are likely to fall in this direction.

For the typical medium-sized to large company, where the CEO is somewhat active in IR, and where the CFO tends to spend some time with IR activities, a likely split of functions might be listed as:

Controller

1. An *information resource* or source for any *financial* data, for those officers and executives who need it for IR purposes including:

   (a) Financial statements reflecting actual results and/or condition of the entity and/or any segments, such as

      (i) Statement of income and expense

      (ii) Statement of cash flows

      (iii) Statement of financial condition

   (b) Relevant financial *analyses* of actual data and trends of these statements, as required for IR purposes, such as

      (i) Inventories

      (ii) Accounts receivable

      (iii) Long-term debt, by category of debt

      (iv) Plant and equipment, by location

      (v) Relevant ratios, including comparisons with industry and competitors

      (vi) Detail and type of revenue and expenses by appropriate segment

   (c) Financial statements and related analyses representing *planned* or *forecasted* results or condition, both the annual plan and long-range plan, for the consolidated entity and any segment. (This data should be available, but often should not be disclosed to the analyst groups, etc.)

   (d) Relevant *graphs* and tabulations, showing financial trends and relationships, actual and projected. Basically, all financial data (whether to be presented to outsiders, or simply used as background or a reference source) should be prepared under the supervision of, or by, the controller, subject to appropriate suggestions or constraints by the CFO or CEO.

2. As required, an *interpreter* of the financial data, when asked to do so by other major officers or executives present, to the appropriate IR audience (groups, individuals [analysts, investors], financial information sources such as Dun & Bradstreet, TRW, bank loan officers, etc.)

3. A *communicator* of financial information to individuals and groups entitled to receive it, under the applicable working rules. This would include presentations to groups or individual analysts, investors, or brokers, and so forth, as well as the answering of their questions. It might be that the controller would (1) make presentations in the absence of the CFO, and (2) give talks to small groups regularly, with the CFO (or even the CEO) handling the larger or more important meetings. Certainly, if the controller is a good communicator he or she should be trained to be the alter ego of the CFO.

4. Either prepares, or reviews for accuracy and completeness, any financial commentary in such financial documents as the annual report to shareholders, quarterly report to shareholders, Form 10-K, or 10-Q, etc.

5. A *reviewer* for content and accuracy all news releases, special announcements, and publications of the investor relations activity (and those of other executives) dealing with *financial/accounting* matters. As applicable, the controller would make his or her recommendations or comments to the CFO, unless she is authorized to make the final decision in the event of disagreement or needed major changes.

When the controller is de facto the CFO, he or she would exercise the duties listed previously, plus those of the CFO enumerated next.

PUT YOUR ROLE IN WRITING!

There are few areas in which a new controller can get into more trouble with senior management than in the area of investor relations. Knowing that he is new, an investor may contact the controller and attempt to extract information about the company. The fallout from this situation can require a great deal of time by senior managers to fix. To avoid the problem, sit down with the CFO or president as soon as possible and define exactly what the controller is or is not allowed to do with investors. Write down the results and send back a copy, so there is evidence of what was agreed upon.

Chief Financial Officer

1. Should be the principal communicator of financial policy, and the reasons therefor, financial status and operating trends and relationships to major groups, including the leading security analysts of the industry, major brokerage houses, and large investors— actual or potential—whether institutional or individual.

2. Should be the principal spokesman or negotiator, subject to approval of the CEO and/ or board of directors, as may be applicable, in connection with the actual and imminent raising of capital—whether equity or indebtedness. Thus, he or she would be the principal contact with investment bankers, large commercial bankers, lessors, and institutions, using such advice and assistance deemed necessary.

3. Should delegate to the controller any of the above duties, and any lesser ones, relative to investor relations when deemed to be in the interest of the company, and assuming the controller is experienced and capable.

4. Should review all major published financial documents (annual report to shareholders, quarterly reports, financial news releases), and receive comments from controller, for accuracy, completeness, adequate disclosure, and the like.

5. If the IR department is a part of the financial organization, should direct its activities, establish appropriate disclosure policies, and develop a competent and professional IR staff to handle those functions not assigned to the CEO or the controller or himself.

   If the IR activities are under the cognizance of the CEO or the public relations officer, the CFO should make appropriate recommendations on suggested improvements.

Chief Executive Officer

1. Preside over major meetings with security analysts, large investors, and the like and present the background and related information on such important matters as:

    (a) Company mission, purpose, goals and objectives, and so forth

    (b) Competitive position of the company

    (c) Major operating accomplishments in recent periods

    (d) Direction company is headed

    (e) Any forthcoming major events that can be announced (management changes, acquisitions, divestments, etc.)

    Additionally, he should answer the questions of the audience on major public matters and the like. By bearing and knowledge he should demonstrate that he is, indeed, the CEO.

2. Meet, on a one-to-one basis or with a few individuals only, any major investor, opinion maker, banker, and so on, who wishes to see him. Discuss major points as in 1 above.

3. As appropriate in IR meetings, refer financial questions to the vice president of finance or controller, and certain operating questions to the operating executive present.

4. As to important financing matters, meet with other major players, as deemed proper: commercial bankers, investment bankers, rating agencies, institutional investors, etc. He should lend support to the proposed transactions, provide relevant background about the company, and answer questions directed to him.

5. Ascertain that the messages in any important public statements (e.g., the annual report, quarterly financial reports, financial-type news releases) are as he thinks they should be, or understand why not.

6. Address important company matters and the annual meeting of shareholders.

CHANGES IN THE CAPITAL MARKETS

Among other objectives, a purpose of the IR function is to enable the company to raise funds to meet its needs, on an acceptable economic basis, so as to enhance the long-term interests of the shareholders. But the financial environment changes, among other things, as the business cycle changes, or the perceived relative status of the company or industry changes, or, indeed, as the moods of the investor vacillates. Some recent developments include demands by some pension funds that they have a greater voice in certain company policy decisions; increased agitation by unhappy shareholders about exorbitant levels of executive compensation or perquisites; pressures by some institutional investors to make the board of directors more independent of the CEO; proposals by company management for the "protection of shareholders" in the event of an unsolicited bid for the corporation; and vastly increased volatility in the stock market. While circumstances will differ company by company, there will be instances wherein the CFO, probably assisted by the controller, will find it necessary to become more aggressive in cultivating the financial market, and take these actions: (1) Establish *specific* financial market related objectives, which will be in the shareholders' interest; and (2) develop some methods of helping to reach these (new) objectives. All of this is to say that the IR function is not merely a passive communication caper.

Some Suggested Financial Market Objectives

The objectives of the company, with respect to financial markets will depend on what condition appears to need improvement or change. In the experience of the authors, here are some typical objectives, one or more of which might apply to a particular entity:

- Increase the P/E ratio to X, or to the Standard and Poor's (S&P) 500 level, or to the best in the industry.
- Lengthen the average stock holding period by attracting more long-term investors.
- Reacquire 25% of the present outstanding shares through stock repurchase programs.
- Increase the average daily share sales volume—to, say, 100,000 (so that institutions can buy or sell in a given day without significantly moving the stock price).
- Reduce volatility by expanding the shareholder base.
- Build shareholder demand (by diversifying the shareholder base).
- Create a greater demand for company bonds or other debt securities.
- Reduce the proportion of shares held by institutional investors.

BUY BACK SHARES FROM SMALL INVESTORS

An emerging best practice for investor relations is to buy back shares from investors owning only a few shares of stock. By doing so, the company can save money tracking fewer investors and mailing out fewer annual reports. The savings can be considerable if there are many thousands of small investors.

While consistent earnings growth, based on good products and capable marketing, and a sound financial position, are fundamental in attaining and maintaining many of these objectives, another aid is to target particular markets and properly communicate relevant financial information. Which targets need to be reached will require an analysis of the present shareholder types, and so forth. A few comments on this phase follow.

Some Suggested Methods

A successful IR program involves providing reliable, consistent, timely, and truthful information about the company on such matters as depth of management, developments as to products and markets, probable trend of sales and earnings, and some guidance on company financial objectives—not only to the usual array of stock brokers, security analysts, and individuals, but more especially to carefully selected institutions that probably would be a desirable type of shareholder—who could aid in meeting the objectives set out in the investor relations agenda. Some suggestions include:

1. *Maintain a current, well-documented background book which is available to all key executives, and for all key contacts with the investing groups.*
   Such an information source would provide these benefits:
   (a) The reader will have a better idea of what subjects are matters of concern to an investor or potential investor.
   (b) The executives will have a consistent and uniform response to the queries.

(c) The reader will be updated on the current developments in his company which should be communicated to the investing public.

In terms of content, aside from the financially relevant information on the company itself, the data book might contain information about potential investor contacts: location, position, investment patterns, availability for conference calls, and so on.

2. *Be certain that all key internal officers are current on new and important developments and that the investor significance is understood.*

With such a background, the likelihood is reduced of making offhand comments which can be misinterpreted.

3. *Establish close one-on-one relationships with selected institutional investors where particular investor relations objectives can be furthered.*

It already has been mentioned that increasing the investor base by the addition of long-term investors will lengthen the average holding period. Creating closer relations with institutional investors also may reduce volatility. Volatility occurs or increases because large segments of the shareholder population decide to take the same action at the same time, for example, sell the shares. If large shareholders are kept informed about the company, this may decrease the tendency to follow the actions of other investors. These long-term investors may buy more shares while the short-horizon investors may be selling—thus creating a balance in the marketplace, and maintaining the price.

The program for contacting large institutional investors or potential investors can include periodically scheduled visits (once or twice a year) to the financial centers (New York, Boston, Chicago, San Francisco, etc.) to meet particular institutional investors and security analysts.

4. *Consider the possibility of conference calls to selected investors or security analysts.*

This has the advantages of (a) making one call instead of numerous ones, (b) releasing the data to many sources at the same time, and (c) keeping the message more consistent. A disadvantage arises of making it more difficult to answer all the questions of every analyst, and so on.

5. *In some circumstances, increase the contacts with noninstitutional investors.*

Some corporate financial executives have felt their company might be vulnerable to extend pressures when too large a portion—say 75 percent to 80 percent—of the shares were in the hands of institutional investors. For example, the entity might become a target for a hostile takeover. Hence, there could be merit in expanding the ownership base through appropriate and frequent contacts with buy-side security analysts, brokers, and so on.

So there is much to be said for considering certain *specific* investor relations objectives and developing a specific program to meet them.

12*

TAXATION STRATEGY

IMPORTANCE OF THIS CHAPTER

Taxation is an area cluttered with land mines for the new controller, usually involving tax late fees and penalties. However, there are also opportunities to save a considerable amount of money through the use of such tax tools as net operating loss carryforwards and inventory valuation techniques, and the use of transfer pricing. This chapter makes the new controller aware of both types of issues.

The obvious objective of tax strategy is to minimize the amount of cash paid out for taxes. However, this directly conflicts with the general desire to report as much income as possible to shareholders, since more reported income results in more taxes. Only in the case of privately owned firms do these conflicting problems go away, since the owners have no need to impress anyone with their reported level of earnings, and would simply prefer to retain as much cash in the company as possible by avoiding the payment of taxes.

For those controllers who are intent on reducing their corporation's tax burdens, there are five primary goals to include in their tax strategies, all of which involve increasing the number of differences between the book and tax records, so that reportable income for tax purposes is reduced. The five items are:

1. *Accelerate deductions.* By recognizing expenses sooner, one can force expenses into the current reporting year that would otherwise be deferred. The primary deduction acceleration involves depreciation, for which a company typically uses MACRS (an

---

*Portions of this chapter were adapted with permission from Chapter 3 of Steven M. Bragg, *The New CFO Financial Leadership Manual* (Hoboken: Wiley, 2003); and pages 528–529 of Steven M. Bragg, *Accounting Reference Desktop* (Hoboken: Wiley, 2002).

accelerated depreciation methodology acceptable for tax reporting purposes), and straight-line depreciation, which results in a higher level of reported earnings for other purposes.

2. *Take all available tax credits.* A credit results in a permanent reduction in taxes, and so is highly desirable. Unfortunately, credits are increasingly difficult to find, though one might qualify for the research and experimental tax credit, which is available to those companies that have increased their research activities over the previous year. The only type of expense that qualifies for this credit is that which is undertaken to discover information that is technical in nature, and its application must be intended for use in developing a new or improved business component for the taxpayer. Also, all of the research activities must be elements of a process of experimentation relating to a new or improved function, or that enhances the current level of performance, reliability, or quality. A credit cannot be taken for research conducted after the beginning of commercial production, for the customization of a product for a specific customer, for the duplication of an existing process or product, or for research required for some types of software to be used internally.

There are more tax credits available at the local level, where they are offered to those businesses willing to operate in economic development zones, or as part of specialized relocation deals (normally available only to larger companies).

3. *Avoid nonallowable expenses.* There are a few expenses, most notably meals and entertainment, that are completely or at least partially not allowed for purposes of computing taxable income. A key company strategy is to reduce these types of expenses to the bare minimum, thereby avoiding any lost benefits from nonallowable expenses.

4. *Increase tax deferrals.* There are a number of situations in which taxes can be shifted into the future, such as payments in stock for acquisitions, or the deferral of revenue received until all related services have been performed. This can shift a large part of the tax liability into the future, where the time value of money results in a smaller present value of the tax liability than otherwise would be the case.

5. *Obtain tax-exempt income.* The controller should consider investing excess funds in municipal bonds, which are exempt from both federal income taxes and the income taxes of the state in which they were issued. The downside of this approach is that the return on municipal bonds is less than the return on other forms of investment, due to their inherent tax savings.

There is no single tax strategy that will be applicable to every company, since the tax laws are so complex that the controller must construct a strategy that is tailored to the specific circumstances in which her company finds itself. Nonetheless, there are a number of taxation areas that a controller must be aware of when creating a tax strategy using the preceding five goals. Those areas are listed in alphabetical order through the remainder of this chapter, ranging from the accumulated earnings tax to unemployment taxes. The controller should carefully peruse these topics to see if they should be incorporated into her overall tax strategy.

ACCUMULATED EARNINGS TAX

There is a double tax associated with a company's payment of dividends to investors, because it first must pay an income tax from which dividends *cannot* be deducted as an expense, and then investors must pay income tax on the dividends received. Understandably, closely held companies prefer not to issue dividends in order to avoid the double taxation issue. However, this can result in a large amount of capital accumulating within a company. The IRS addresses this issue by imposing an accumulated earnings tax on what it considers to be an excessive amount of earnings that have not been distributed to shareholders.

The IRS considers accumulated earnings of less than $150,000 to be sufficient for the working needs of service businesses, such as accounting, engineering, architecture, and consulting firms. It considers accumulations of anything under $250,000 to be sufficient for most other types of businesses. A company can argue that it needs a substantially larger amount of accumulated earnings if it can prove that it has specific, definite, and feasible plans that will require the use of the funds within the business. Another valid argument is that a company needs an amount of accumulated earnings sufficient to buy back the company's stock that is held by a deceased shareholder's estate.

If these conditions are not apparent, then the IRS will declare the accumulated earnings to be taxable at a rate of 39.6 percent. Also, interest payments to the IRS will be due from the date when the corporation's annual return was originally due. The severity of this tax is designed to encourage organizations to issue dividends on a regular basis to their shareholders, so that the IRS can tax the shareholders for this form of income.

CASH METHOD OF ACCOUNTING

The normal method for reporting a company's financial results is the accrual basis of accounting, under which expenses are matched to revenues within a reporting period. However, for tax purposes, it is sometimes possible to report income under the cash method of accounting. Under this approach, revenue is not recognized until payment for invoices is received, while expenses are not recognized until paid.

The cash basis of accounting can result in a great deal of manipulation from the perspective of the IRS, which discourages its use, but does not prohibit it. As an example of income manipulation, a company may realize that it will have a large amount of income to report in the current year, and will probably have less in the following year. Accordingly, it prepays a number of supplier invoices at the end of the year, so that it recognizes them at once under the cash method of accounting as expenses in the current year. The IRS prohibits this type of behavior under the rule that cash payments recognized in the current period can relate only to current-year expenses. Nonetheless, it is a difficult issue for the IRS to police. The same degree of manipulation can be applied to the recognition of revenue, simply by delaying billings to customers near the end of the tax year. Also, in situations where there is a sudden surge of business at the end of the tax year, possibly due to seasonality, the cash method of accounting will not reveal the sales until the following year, since payment on the invoices from customers will not arrive until the next year. Consequently, the cash method tends to underreport taxable income.

In order to limit the use of this method, the IRS prohibits it if a company has any inventories on hand at the end of the year. The reason for this is that expenditures for inventory can be so large and subject to manipulation at year-end that a company could theoretically alter its reported level of taxable income to an enormous extent. The cash basis is also not allowable for any C corporation, a partnership that has a C corporation for a partner, or a tax shelter. However, within these restrictions, it is allowable for an entity with average annual gross receipts of $5 million or less for the three tax years ending with the prior tax year, as well as for any personal service corporation that provides at least 95 percent of its activities in the services arena.

The IRS imposes some accrual accounting concepts on a cash-basis organization in order to avoid some of the more blatant forms of income avoidance. For example, if a cash-basis company receives a check at the end of its tax year, it may be tempted not to cash the check until the beginning of the next tax year, since this would push the revenue associated with that check into the next year. To avoid this problem, the IRS uses the concept of *constructive receipt*, which requires one to record the receipt when it is made available to one without restriction (whether or not it is actually recorded on the company's books at that time). Besides the just-noted example, this would also require a company to record the interest on a bond that comes due prior to the end of the tax year, even if the associated coupon is not sent to the issuer until the next year.

REMOVING THE CASH BASIS

Though the IRS allows companies to use the cash basis of accounting, it is certainly not GAAP, and so requires the new controller to adjust the accounting records for financial reporting purposes. Given the extra work involved, it is best to plan for a near-term conversion to the accrual basis of accounting.

INVENTORY VALUATION

It is allowable to value a company's inventory using one method for book purposes and another for tax purposes, except in the case of the LIFO inventory valuation method. In this case, the tax advantages to be gained from the use of LIFO are so significant that the IRS requires a user to employ it for both book and tax purposes. Furthermore, if LIFO is used in any one of a group of financially related companies, the entire group is assumed to be a single entity for tax reporting purposes, which means that they must all use the LIFO valuation approach for both book and tax reporting. This rule was engendered in order to stop the practice of having LIFO-valuation companies roll their results into a parent company that used some other method of reporting, thereby giving astute companies high levels of reportable income and lower levels of taxable income at the same time.

MERGERS AND ACQUISITIONS

A key factor to consider in corporate acquisitions is the determination of what size taxable gain will be incurred by the seller (if any), as well as how the buyer can reduce the tax impact of the transaction in the current and future years. In this section, we will briefly discuss the various types of transactions involved in an acquisition, the tax implications of each transaction, and whose interests are best served by the use of each one.

There are two ways in which an acquisition can be made, each with different tax implications. First, one can purchase the acquiree's stock, which may trigger a taxable gain to the seller. Second, one can purchase the acquiree's assets, which triggers a gain on sale of the assets, as well as another tax to the shareholders of the selling company, who must recognize a gain when the proceeds from liquidation of the business are distributed to them. Because of the additional taxation, a seller will generally want to sell a corporation's stock, rather than its assets.

When stock is sold to the buyer in exchange for cash or property, the buyer establishes a tax basis in the stock that equals the amount of the cash or fair market value of the property transferred to the seller. Meanwhile, the seller recognizes a gain or loss on the eventual sale of the stock that is based on its original tax basis in the stock, which is subtracted from the ultimate sale price of the stock.

It is also possible for the seller to recognize no taxable gain on sale of a business if it takes some of the acquiring company's stock as full compensation for the sale. However, there will be no tax only if *continuity of interest* in the business can be proven by giving the sellers a sufficient amount of the buyer's stock to prove that they have a continuing financial interest in the buying company. A variation on this approach is to make an acquisition over a period of months, using nothing but voting stock as compensation to the seller's shareholders, but for which a clear plan of ultimate control over the acquiree can be proven. Another variation is to purchase at least 80 percent of the fair market value of the acquiree's assets solely in exchange for stock.

When only the assets are sold to the buyer, the buyer can apportion the total price amongst the assets purchased, up to their fair market value (with any excess portion of the price being apportioned to goodwill). This is highly favorable from a taxation perspective, since the buyer has now adjusted its basis in the assets substantially higher; it can now claim a much larger accelerated depreciation expense in the upcoming years, thereby reducing its reported level of taxable income and reducing its tax burden. From the seller's perspective, the sale price is allocated to each asset sold for the purposes of determining a gain or loss; as much of this as possible should be characterized as a capital gain (since the related tax is lower) or as an ordinary loss (since it can offset ordinary income, which has a higher tax rate).

The structuring of an acquisition transaction so that no income taxes are paid must have a reasonable business purpose besides the avoidance of taxes. Otherwise, the IRS has been known to require tax payments on the grounds that the structure of the transaction has no reasonable business purpose besides tax avoidance. Its review of the substance of a transaction over its form leads the controller to consider such transactions in the same manner, and to restructure acquisition deals accordingly.

There is a specialized tax reduction available for the holders of stock in a small business, on which they experience a gain when the business is sold. Specifically, they are entitled to a 50 percent reduction in their reportable gain on sale of that stock, though it is limited to the greater of a $10 million gain or ten times the stockholder's basis in the stock. This exclusion is reserved for C corporations, and applies only to stock that was acquired at its original issuance. There are a number of other exclusions, such as its inapplicability to personal service corporations, real estate investment trusts, domestic international sales corporations, and mutual funds. This type of stock is called *qualified small business stock*. The unique set of conditions surrounding this stock make it clear that it is intended to be a tax break specifically for the owners of small businesses.

NET OPERATING LOSS CARRYFORWARDS

Since income taxes can be the largest single expense on the income statement, the controller should carefully track the use and applicability of net operating loss (NOL) carryforwards that were created as the result of reported losses in prior years. An NOL may be carried back and applied against profits recorded in the two preceding years, with any remaining amount being carried forward for the next 20 years, when it can be offset against any reported income. If there is still an NOL left after the 20 years have expired, then the remaining amount can no longer be used. One can also irrevocably choose to ignore the carryback option and use it only for carryforward purposes. The standard procedure is to apply all of the NOL against the income reported in the earliest year, with the remainder carrying forward to each subsequent year in succession until the remaining NOL has been exhausted. If an NOL has been incurred in each of multiple years, then these should be applied against reported income (in either prior or later years) in order of the first NOL incurred. This rule is used because of the 20-year limitation on an NOL, so that an NOL incurred in an earlier year can be used before it expires.

The NOL is a valuable asset, since it can be used for many years to offset future earnings. A company buying another entity that has an NOL will certainly place a high value on the NOL, and may even buy the entity strictly in order to use its NOL. To curtail this type of behavior, the IRS has created the Section 382 limitation, under which there is a limitation on its use if there is at least a 50 percent change in the ownership of an entity that has an unused NOL. The limitation is derived through a complex formula that essentially multiplies the acquired corporation's stock times the long-term tax-exempt bond rate. To avoid this problem, a company with an unused NOL that is seeking to expand its equity should consider issuing straight preferred stock (no voting rights, no conversion privileges, and no participation in future earnings) in order to avoid any chance that the extra equity will be construed as a change in ownership.

A GOOD TIME FOR TAX ADVICE

Because Section 382 can have such a severe impact on the amount of an acquiree's NOL that an acquirer can use, be sure to obtain qualified tax advice regarding this issue whenever a potential acquiree has an NOL. The resulting advice can alter the legal structure of the transaction and possibly allow the acquirer to still use some portion or all of the NOL.

If a company has incurred an NOL in a short tax year, it must deduct the NOL over a period of six years, starting with the first tax year after the short tax year. This limitation does not apply if the NOL is for $10,000 or less, or if the NOL is the result of a short tax year that is at least nine months long, and is less than the NOL for a full 12-month tax year beginning with the first day of the short tax year. This special NOL rule was designed to keep companies from deliberately changing their tax years in order to create an NOL within a short tax year. This situation is quite possible in a seasonal business where there are losses in all but a few months. Under such a scenario, a company would otherwise be able to declare an NOL during its short tax year, carry back the NOL to apply it against the previous two years of operations, and receive a rebate from the IRS.

NEXUS

A company may have to complete many more tax forms than it would like, as well as remit taxes to more government entities, if it can be established that it has nexus within a government's area of jurisdiction. Consequently, it is very important to understand how nexus is established.

The rules vary by state, but nexus is generally considered to have occurred if a company maintains a facility of any kind within a state, or if it pays the wages of someone within that state. In some locales, the definition is expanded to include the transport of goods to customers within the state on company-owned vehicles (though nexus is not considered to have occurred if the shipment is made by a third-party freight carrier). A more liberal interpretation of the nexus rule is that a company has nexus if it sends sales personnel into the state on sales calls or trains personnel there to educate customers, even though they are not permanently based there. To gain a precise understanding of how the nexus rules are interpreted by each state, it is best to contact the department of revenue at each state government.

A recent issue that is still being debated in the courts is that Internet sales may be considered to have occurred within a state if the server used to process orders or store data is kept within that state, even if the server is merely rented from an Internet hosting service.

If nexus has been established, a company must file to do business within the state, which requires a small fee and a re-filing once every few years. In addition, it must withhold sales taxes on all sales within the state. This is the most laborious issue related to nexus, since sales taxes may be different for every city and county within each state, necessitating a company to keep track of potentially thousands of different sales tax rates. Also, some states may require the remittance of sales taxes every month, though this can be reduced to as little as once a year if the company predicts that it will have minimal sales taxes to remit, as noted on its initial application for a sales tax license.

Some states or local governments will also subject a company to property or personal property taxes on all assets based within their jurisdictions, which necessitates even more paperwork.

Though the amount of additional taxes paid may not be that great, the key issue related to the nexus concept is that the additional time required to track tax liabilities and file forms with the various governments may very well require additional personnel in the accounting department. This can be a major problem for those organizations in multiple states, and should be a key planning issue when determining the capacity of the accounting department to process tax-related transactions. Some organizations with a number of subsidiaries will avoid a portion of the tax filing work by accepting the nexus concept only for those subsidiaries that are clearly established within each governmental jurisdiction, thereby avoiding the tax filing problems for all other legal entities controlled by the parent corporation.

PASSIVE ACTIVITY LOSSES

Many individuals and some businesses passively participate in business activities that result in income or losses. They can claim passive activity losses on their tax returns based on these financial results. Passive participation is defined as having a trade or business activity in which one does not materially participate during the tax year, or participating in a rental activity (even if there is evidence of a substantial level of activity in the venture). One is considered to be an active investor if any of the following tests are true:

- One annually expends more than 500 hours of participation in the activity.
- One's participation comprises essentially all of the activity for a business.
- There were more than 100 hours of annual participation, which was at least as much as any other participant in the business.
- One materially participated in the business in any five of the last ten tax years.
- One materially participated in a personal service business for any three previous tax years.

A limited partner is generally not considered to be materially involved in a business. A closely held corporation or a personal service corporation is considered to materially participate in a business if shareholders owning more than 50 percent of the corporation's shares materially engage in the business. Also, an investing entity is considered to be materially engaged in a business if it has an interest in an oil or gas well that is held directly or through an entity that does not reduce its liability.

Passive activity losses can be claimed only by individuals, estates, trusts, personal service corporations, and closely held C corporations. Conversely, passive activity losses cannot be claimed by grantor trusts, partnerships, and S corporations.

If passive activity losses have occurred, they can be offset only against passive activity gains. Activities that are defined by the IRS as *not* passive are gains on sale of property that has not been used in a passive activity, investment income, and personal services income. If there is an excess credit from a passive loss after all offsets have been made against passive income, then the credit can be carried forward to the next tax year for a later offset. However, all passive losses that are carried forward can be recognized at the time when the passive investor liquidates the investment.

The total amount of a passive loss will be limited to the total amount to which a passive investor is at risk. For example, if an entity invests $1,000 in a business venture, then it is only at risk for $1,000, and cannot deduct more than that amount under any circumstances as a passive loss.

PROJECT COSTING

A company that regularly develops large infrastructure systems such as enterprise resource planning (ERP) systems for its own use will usually cluster all costs related to that project into a single account and then capitalize its full cost, with amortization occurring over a number of years. Though this approach will certainly increase reported income over the short term, it also increases income taxes. If the avoidance of income taxes is a higher priority for the controller than reported profits, then it would be useful to separate the various components of each project into different accounts, and expense those that more closely relate to ongoing operational activities. For example, a strong case can be made for expensing all training associated with a major system installation, on the grounds that training is an ongoing activity.

Another approach is to charge subsidiaries for the cost of a development project, especially if the charging entity is located in a low-tax region and the subsidiaries are in high-tax regions. This transfer pricing approach would reduce the reported income in high-tax areas, effectively shifting that income to a location where the tax rate is lower. However, these cost-shifting strategies must be carefully documented with proof that the systems are really being used by subsidiaries, and that the fees charged are reasonable.

A variation on the last approach is to create a data center in a tax haven that stores and analyzes company data and then issues reports back to other corporate divisions for a substantial fee. This approach has to involve more than simply locating a file server in a low-tax location, since the IRS will claim that there is no business purpose for the arrangement. Instead, a small business must be set up around the data center that provides some added value to the information being collected and disseminated. This approach is especially attractive if a company acquires another entity with a data center in a low-tax location, and simply shifts its own facilities to the preestablished location.

PROPERTY TAXES

Local governments use property tax assessments as one of their primary forms of tax receipt. Personal property taxes are assessed based on a company's level of reported fixed assets in the preceding year, and typically paid once a year. In order to minimize this tax, the accounting department should regularly review the fixed asset list to see which items can be disposed of, thereby shrinking the taxable base of assets. Also, by increasing the capitalization limit, fewer items will be classified as assets, and so will also not be taxed.

AUDITS ARE FOR PROPERTY, TOO

Property taxes can be a considerable expense each year, and yet too many controllers simply accept the figures presented by the local government without argument. Instead, the new controller should conduct a fixed asset audit and eliminate from the property tax role any assets that are no longer on the premises, and then go a step further and schedule continuing annual fixed asset reviews on a fixed date. Also, if fixed assets are clearly not being used, dispose of them as soon as possible. The net result will be lower property taxes.

Local taxing authorities can also impose a tax based on any real property owned by a business. The buildings and land that fall into this category will be appraised by the local assessor, with the resulting assessment being multiplied by a tax rate that is determined by the local government. The assessment can be challenged. If a recent assessment change results in a significant boost in the reported value of a business's real property, it is certainly worthwhile to engage the services of a private assessor to see if the new valuation can be reduced.

If a business rents its property, the tax on real property can be either absorbed by the landlord or passed through to the business, depending upon the terms of the lease. If subleasing from another business, the property tax can be either absorbed by that entity or passed through to the business, again depending on the terms of the lease.

S CORPORATION

The S corporation is of considerable interest to the controller, because it generally does not pay taxes. Instead, it passes reported earnings through to its shareholders, who report the income on their tax returns. This avoids the double taxation that arises in a C corporation, where a company's income is taxed, and then the dividends it issues to its shareholders are taxed as income to them a second time. The amount of income is allocated to each shareholder on a simple per-share basis. If a shareholder has held stock in the corporation for less than a full year, then the allocation is on a per-share, per-day basis. The per-day part of this calculation assumes that a shareholder still holds the stock through and including the day when the stock is disposed of, while a deceased shareholder will be assumed to retain ownership through and including the day when he or she dies.

An S corporation has unique taxation and legal protection aspects that make it an ideal way to structure a business if there are a small number of shareholders. Specifically, it can be created only if there are no more than 75 shareholders, if only one class of stock is issued, and if all shareholders agree to the S corporation status. All of its shareholders must be either citizens or residents of the United States. Shareholders are also limited to individuals, estates, and some types of trusts and charities. Conversely, this means that C corporations and partnerships cannot be shareholders in an S corporation. The requirement for a single class of stock may prevent some organizations from organizing in this manner, for it does not allow for preferential returns or special voting rights by some shareholders.

There are a few cases where an S corporation can owe taxes. For example, it can be taxed if it has accumulated earnings and profits from an earlier existence as a C corporation and its passive income is more than 25 percent of total gross receipts. It also can be liable for taxes on a few types of capital gains, recapture of the old investment tax credit, and LIFO recapture. If any of these taxes apply, then the S corporation must make quarterly estimated income tax payments. On the other hand, an S corporation is not subject to the alternative minimum tax.

If the management team of an S corporation wants to terminate its S status, the written consent of more than 50 percent of the shareholders is required, as well as a statement from the corporation to that effect. If the corporation wants to become an S corporation at a later date, there is a five-year waiting period from the last time before it can do so again, unless it obtains special permission from the IRS.

SALES AND USE TAXES

Sales taxes are imposed at the state, county, and city level—frequently by all three at once. It is also possible for a special tax to be added to the sales tax and applied to a unique region, such as for the construction of a baseball stadium or to support a regional mass transit system. The sales tax is multiplied by the price paid on goods and services on transactions occurring within the taxing area. However, the definition of goods and services that are required to be taxed will vary by state (not usually at the county or city level), and so must be researched at the local level to determine the precise basis of calculation. For example, some states do not tax food sales, on the grounds that this is a necessity whose cost should be reduced as much as possible, while other states include it in their required list of items to be taxed.

A company is required to charge sales taxes to its customers and remit the resulting receipts to the local state government, which will split out the portions due to the local county and city governments and remit these taxes on the company's behalf to those entities. If the company does not charge its customers for these taxes, it is still liable for them, and must pay the unbilled amounts to the state government, though it has the right to attempt to bill its customers after the fact for the missing sales taxes. This can be a difficult collection chore, especially if sales are primarily over the counter, where there are few transaction records that identify the customer. Also, a company is obligated to keep abreast of all changes in sales tax rates and charge its customers for the correct amount; if it does not do so, then it is liable to the government for the difference between what it actually charged and the statutory rate. If a company overcharges its customers, the excess must also be remitted to the government.

The state in which a company is collecting sales taxes can decide how frequently it wants the company to remit taxes. If there are only modest sales, the state may decide that the cost of paperwork exceeds the value of the remittances, and will require only an annual remittance. It is more common to have quarterly or monthly remittances. The state will review the dollar amount of remittances from time to time, and adjust the required remittance frequency based on this information.

All government entities have the right to audit a company's books to see if the proper sales taxes are being charged, and so a company can be theoretically subject to three sales tax audits per year—one each from the city, county, and state revenue departments. Also, since these audits can come from any taxing jurisdiction in which a company does business, there could be literally thousands of potential audits.

The obligation to collect sales taxes is based on the concept of *nexus,* which was covered earlier in this chapter. If nexus exists, then sales taxes must be collected by the seller. If not, the recipient of purchased goods instead has an obligation to compile a list of items purchased, and remit a use tax to the appropriate authority. The use tax is in the same amount as the sales tax. The only difference is that the remitting party is the buyer instead of the seller. Use taxes are also subject to audits by all taxing jurisdictions.

If the buyer of a company's products is including them in its own products for resale to another entity, then the buyer does not have to pay a sales tax to the seller. Instead, the buyer will charge a sales tax to the buyer of *its* final product. This approach is used under the theory that a sales tax should be charged only one time on the sale of a product. However, it can be a difficult chore to explain the lack of sales tax billings during an audit, so sales taxes should be halted only if a buyer sends a sales tax exemption form to the company, which then should be kept on file. The sales tax exemption certificate can be named a resale certificate instead, depending on the issuing authority. It also can be issued to government entities, which are generally exempt from sales and use taxes. As a general rule, sales taxes always should be charged unless there is a sales tax exemption certificate on file—otherwise, the company will still be liable for the remittance of sales taxes in the event of an audit.

REVIEW NEXUS EVERY YEAR

The controller is in charge of sales taxes, so it can be a considerable embarrassment to be required to pay a fine for nonpayment of taxes. To avoid this problem, review nexus concerns every year to see if new company locations, deliveries, or other activities will make the company liable for sales tax collections and remittances. If there is a checklist of accounting actions to implement following an acquisition, include on it the company's registration for a sales tax license in the new location.

TRANSFER PRICING

Transfer pricing is a key tax consideration, because it can result in the permanent reduction of an organization's tax liability. The permanent reduction is caused by the recognition of income in different taxing jurisdictions that may have different tax rates.

The basic concept behind the use of transfer pricing to reduce one's overall taxes is that a company transfers its products to a division in another country at the lowest possible price if the income tax rate is lower in the other country, or at the highest possible price if the tax rate is higher. By selling to the division at a low price, the company will report a very high profit on the final sale of products in the other country, which is where that income will be taxed at a presumably lower income tax rate.

For example, Exhibit 12.1 shows a situation in which a company with a location in countries Alpha and Beta has the choice of either selling goods in Alpha or transferring them to Beta and selling them there. The company is faced with a corporate income tax rate of 40 percent in country Alpha. To permanently avoid some of this income tax, the company sells its products to another subsidiary in country Beta, where the corporate income tax rate is only 25 percent. By doing so, the company still earns a profit ($60,000) in country Alpha, but the bulk of the profit ($125,000) now appears in country Beta. The net result is a consolidated income tax rate of just 28 percent.

	Country Alpha Location	Country Beta Location
Sales to subsidiary:		
Revenue	$1,000,000	
Cost of goods sold	850,000	
Profit	$ 150,000	
Profit percentage	15%	
Sales outside of company:		
Revenue		$1,500,000
Cost of goods sold		1,000,000
Profit		$ 500,000
Profit percentage		33%
Income tax percentage	40%	25%
Income tax	$ 60,000	$ 125,000
Consolidated income tax	$ 185,000	
Consolidated income tax percentage	28%	

Exhibit 12.1 Income Tax Savings from Transfer Pricing

The IRS is well aware of this tax-avoidance strategy, and has developed tax rules that do not eliminate it but that will reduce the leeway that a controller has in altering reportable income. Under Section 482 of the IRS Code, the IRS's preferred approach for developing transfer prices is to use the market rate as its basis. However, very few products can be reliably and consistently compared to the market rate, with the exception of commodities, because there are costing differences between them. Also, in many cases, products are so specialized (especially components that are custom-designed to fit into a larger product) that there is no market rate against which they can be compared. Even if there is some basis of comparison between a product and the average market prices for similar products, the controller still has some leeway in which to alter transfer prices. The IRS will allow one to add special charges that are based on the cost of transferring the products, or extra fees, such as royalty or licensing fees that are imposed for the subsidiary's use of the parent company's patents or trademarks, or for administrative charges related to the preparation of any documentation required to move products between countries. It is also possible to slightly alter the interest rates charged to subsidiaries (though not too far from market rates) for the use of funds sent to them from the parent organization.

If there is no basis on which to create prices based on market rates, then the IRS's next most favored approach is to calculate the prices based on the *work-back method.* Under this approach, one begins at the end of the sales cycle by determining the price at which a product is sold to an outside customer, and then subtracts the subsidiary's standard markup percentage and its added cost of materials, labor, and overhead, which results in the theoretical transfer price. The work-back method can result in a wide array of transfer prices, since a number of different costs can be subtracted from the final sale price, such as standard costs, actual costs, overhead costs based on different allocation measures, and overhead costs based on cost pools that contain different types of costs.

If that approach does not work, then the IRS's third most favored approach is the *cost plus method.* As the name implies, this approach begins at the other end of the production process and compiles costs from a product's initiation point. After all costs are added before the point of transfer, one then adds a profit margin to the product, thereby arriving at a transfer cost that is acceptable by the IRS. However, once again, the costs that are included in a product are subject to the same points of variation that were noted for the work-back method. In addition, the profit margin added should be the standard margin added for any other company customer, but can be quite difficult to determine if there are a multitude of volume discounts, seasonal discounts, and so forth. Consequently, the profit margin added to a product's initial costs can be subject to a great deal of negotiation.

An overriding issue to consider, no matter what approach is used to derive transfer prices, is that taxing authorities can become highly irritated if a company continually pushes the outer limits of acceptable transfer pricing rules in order to maximize its tax savings. When this happens, a company can expect continual audits and penalties on disputed items, as well as less favorable judgments related to any taxation issues. Consequently, it makes a great deal of sense to consistently adopt pricing policies that result in reasonable tax savings, are fully justifiable to the taxing authorities of all involved countries, and that do not push the boundaries of acceptable pricing behavior.

Another transfer pricing issue that can modify a company's pricing strategy is the presence of any restrictions on cash flows out of a country in which it has a subsidiary. In these instances, it may be necessary to report the minimum possible amount of taxable income at the subsidiary, irrespective of the local tax rate. The reason is that the only way for a company to retrieve funds from the country is through the medium of an account receivable, which must be maximized by billing the subsidiary the highest possible amount for transferred goods. In this case, tax planning takes a back seat to cash flow planning.

Yet another issue that may drive a company to set pricing levels that do not result in reduced income taxes is that a subsidiary may have to report high levels of income in order to qualify for a loan from a local credit institution. This is especially important if the country in which the subsidiary is located has restrictions on the movement of cash, so that the parent company would be unable to withdraw loans that it makes to the subsidiary. As was the case for the last item, cash flow planning is likely to be more important than income tax reduction.

A final transfer pricing issue to be aware of is that the method for calculating taxable income may vary in other countries. This may falsely lead one to believe that another country has a lower tax rate. A closer examination of how taxable income is calculated might reveal that some expenses are restricted or not allowed at all, resulting in an actual tax rate that is much higher than originally expected. Consultation with a tax expert for the country in question prior to setting up any transfer pricing arrangements is the best way to avoid this problem.

UNEMPLOYMENT TAXES

Both the state and federal governments will charge a company a fixed percentage of its payroll each year for the expense of unemployment funds that are used to pay former employees who have been released from employment. The state governments administer the distribution of these funds and will compile an experience rating on each company, based on the number of employees it has laid off in the recent past. Based on this experience rating, it can require a company to submit larger or smaller amounts to the state unemployment fund in future years. This can become a considerable burden if a company has a long history of layoffs. Consequently, one should consider the use of temporary employees or outsourcing if this will give a firm the ability to retain a small number of key employees and avoid layoffs while still handling seasonal changes in work loads. Also, if a company is planning to acquire another entity, but plans to lay off a large number of the acquiree's staff once the acquisition is completed, it may make more sense to acquire the acquiree's assets and selectively hire a few of its employees, thereby retaining a pristine unemployment experience rating with the local state government.

The federal unemployment tax is imposed on a company if it has paid employees at least $1,500 in any calendar quarter, or had at least one employee for some portion of a day within at least 20 weeks of the year. In short, nearly all companies will be required to remit federal unemployment taxes. For the 2002 calendar year, the tax rate is 6.2 percent of the first $7,000 paid to each employee; this tends to concentrate most federal unemployment tax remittances into the first quarter of the calendar year. In many states, one can take a credit against the federal unemployment tax for up to 5.4 percent of taxable wages, which results in a net federal unemployment tax of only .8 percent.

If a company is shifting to a new legal entity, perhaps because of a shift from a partnership to a corporation, or from an S corporation to a C corporation, it will have to apply for a new unemployment tax identification number with the local state authorities. This is a problem if the organization being closed down had an unusually good experience rating, since the company will be assigned a poorer one until a new experience rating can be built up over time, which will result in higher unemployment taxes in the short term. To avoid this problem, one should contact the local unemployment taxation office to request that the old company's experience rating be shifted to the new one.

INDEX